GRAPHIC NOVELS as
PHILOSOPHY

GRAPHIC NOVELS as
PHILOSOPHY

edited by Jeff McLaughlin

University Press of Mississippi / Jackson

www.upress.state.ms.us

The University Press of Mississippi is a member
of the Association of American University Presses.

Copyright © 2017 by University Press of Mississippi
All rights reserved
Manufactured in the United States of America

First printing 2017

∞

Library of Congress Cataloging-in-Publication Data

Names: McLaughlin, Jeff, 1962– editor.
Title: Graphic novels as philosophy / edited by Jeff McLaughlin.
Description: Jackson : University Press of Mississippi, [2017] |
    Includes bibliographical references and index. |
Identifiers: LCCN 2017031118 (print) | LCCN 2017032011 (ebook)
    | ISBN 9781496813282 (epub single) | ISBN 9781496813299
    (epub institutional) | ISBN 9781496813305 (pdf single) | ISBN
    9781496813312 (pdf institutional) | ISBN 9781496813275 (hardback)
Subjects: LCSH: Graphic novels—History and criticism. | Comic
    books, strips, etc.—History and criticism. | Literature—Philoso-
    phy. | Philosophy in literature. | BISAC: LITERARY CRITICISM /
    Comics & Graphic Novels. | PHILOSOPHY / General. | SOCIAL
    SCIENCE / Popular Culture.
Classification: LCC PN6712 (ebook) | LCC PN6712 .G69 2017
    (print) | DDC 741.5/384—dc23
LC record available at https://lccn.loc.gov/2017031118

British Library Cataloging-in-Publication Data available

This one is for my brother Boomer.
Not because he has a superhero sounding nickname,
But because he's my brother.
And a super one.

Contents

3   Introduction: What Is It like to Be a Graphic Novel?
    Jeff McLaughlin

17 Philosophy in the Bargain: *A Contract with God* (1978) by Will Eisner
    Jarkko Tuusvuori

41 *Jimmy Corrigan* and the Time of Crisis
    Manuel "Mandel" Cabrera Jr.

64 Autonomy in Children: Accessing the Inaccessible Space in *Essex County Vol. 1: Tales from the Farm*
    Maria Botero

87 Love and Liberty: The Social Contract and *V for Vendetta*
    Eric Bain-Selbo

105 *Asterix*, Carnival, and the Wonder of Everyday Life
    Jeremy Barris

130 Queering Epistemology and the Odyssey of Identity in Alison Bechdel's *Fun Home*
    Ian MacRae

150 The Minor Machinery of Animal Packs: Becoming as Survival in Spiegelman's *Maus*
    Corry Shores

172 Entangled Memories and Received Histories: Reading Sacco's *Footnotes in Gaza*
David J. Leichter

189 Living in a Fictional World: Reading and Identification in *Lost Girls*
Alfonso Muñoz-Corcuera

210 Contributors

213 Index

GRAPHIC NOVELS as
PHILOSOPHY

Introduction: What Is It Like to Be a Graphic Novel?[1]

Jeff McLaughlin

Graphic novels can make the serious amusing. Philosophy can make the amusing serious. And as suggested by the title, this introductory essay is about four things: graphic novels, definitions, perception, and philosophy.

For professional philosophers, words are the way that we capture the world. We write about how the world is, or ought to be. We write about what there is and what there is not. This is both a benefit and a limitation since there are some things that we can't capture no matter how many letters and vowel sounds we combine. What does it feel like for someone—not you—to lose someone? What does it look like for someone—not you—to see a beautiful sunrise? Most importantly perhaps, what is it like to be you?

Individuals, be they philosophers or poets, can assign words that may come within a mile (or kilometer) or so of what it's truly like to be you, but we're really, simply, and completely at a loss when it comes to knowing the immediate experiences of others. It's even a greater distance if we are dealing with a translation where one language has words for things that another does not. Graphic art allows us one more opportunity to try and meet this challenge.

Sometimes there is something missing that you're unable to grasp with certainty, even though you strongly believe that whatever it is you think is out there actually *is* out there. This is because you can never escape this prison of the self to come into contact with the way things truly are "out there" beyond yourself. It's not just about inner *qualia* (that is, the stuff that a person directly experiences that others cannot, such as your own direct physical sensations of pains and pleasures); it's about the ineffable qualities of just being alive and present and aware in the world and never quite able to be directly connected with it.

Yet we can't claim to be the only ones who are privileged to potentially connect with this world. What a dog or a bat (to allude to Thomas Nagel's famous essay) sees is different from what we see, and for all of us, what we see is restricted by differing physiologies. What you see is different because your perception is driven by how you see and then how you interpret that information. This complex awareness of our own limitations in capturing (or not) what truly is, and in communicating that effectively with other people, is where art finds another one of its reasons to be. The vocabulary of art can bring understanding because of, rather than in spite of, the fact that we may not be able to verbalize what is possible.

If there is a truth out there, perhaps we can only see part of it; or perhaps there are many truths out there and the limitations of being human only allow us to see one. Art provides humans with another means of being both in and cognizant of the world. Furthermore, if the arts aren't ultimately able to bring that clarity about what connections we have with the world, then they are at least able to bring about profound connections between the artists and the viewers.

This admission of the extreme, if not insurmountable, difficulty of knowing is also one of the strengths of philosophy, for we don't ever presume that we can know things that can't be known. The great philosophers are great in part because they have not only been able to ask the right questions, but have been able to articulate so well what the right answers might look like without necessarily assuming that they themselves have found them. But just because we may never know what there truly is doesn't mean we give up. We're stubborn in that way. For if we can't reach the "ultimate truth," we can at least eliminate those things that it isn't and develop new fields of inquiry. That is, we might not knowingly move closer to the Truth (with a capital "T"), but we can nevertheless move away from falsehoods by amending or rejecting previous beliefs.

Each one of us, regardless of our abilities or number of degrees, tries to make sense out of many things, including our place and purpose, and we do so by seeking out the impressions and expressions of others to try and move closer to the truth (or farther away from what is false)—or perhaps just move closer to each other. Accordingly, when we talk about "interpretation" in the context of analyzing creative works, interpretation takes on a new level of complexity since we are not just talking about understanding what it is that we are looking at, listening to, or reading, but ultimately about interpreting what the artist sees. Graphic novels may be like the dog and the bat in that our appreciating that there are other, not necessarily better, ways to see. But if one is able to see (and appreciate) the world from many different perspectives, then perhaps one can have a more complete pragmatic picture of it, or at least a more philosophically kaleidoscopic one.

The blending of words and images (which is what I take to be essential elements of what makes a comic book a comic book and of course a graphic novel a comic book as well) can convey something different, something useful, something, dare I say it, more significant than the individual parts, since they provide us with another way to see how things may be. Accordingly, the graphic novel can be seen as being in a cyclical relationship with philosophy; that is, it can help us get a good grasp of philosophical ideas, and in turn, philosophy can help us appreciate and understand the comic art form.

Here's a simple example of what I am discussing and how we can connect well with an idea in a non-verbal manner, one that occurred as I was working on this introduction. Dr. Annie St. John-Stark, a history colleague of mine here at Thompson Rivers University, invited me, another historian, and two English professors to judge her students' term projects. She had asked her students to form small groups and gave them the task of reporting back on various lessons regarding a particular English king and his break with the Holy Roman Church. They were not asked just to write notes; rather, they had to convey this information through a graphic novel. She didn't care about how polished they looked but about whether the students could say something more with a picture and words than just with words (i.e., an essay). If they could reveal more, then it would be evidence that they had learned more. She hoped that by this project, they could show that they "got it" on a deeper level, namely, they appreciated the historical event more than just by memorizing the facts of the matter.

Most of the students' work simply replicated what you might see in television cartoons—full figures with a bit of background and a character saying something in a speech balloon. Then in the next panel the characters would have moved and would say something different and so on—typical and expected—and there was nothing wrong with that. But the judges were all drawn independently (no pun intended) to a particular panel in one submission. It was an extreme close up of the pope. His face filled the space, his eyes were wide, his mouth was curled, teeth sharpened; and above him was a speech balloon that read, "Blasphemy!!" Here we immediately appreciated the intent of the artist. The passion, the anger, and the threatening look in his expression—the pope was really mad! This was not your standard run-of-the-mill disagreement! He was personally, deeply affected. We were impressed.

The other students had merely reported the event, but in this panel we got it, and we understood it because the artist got it first. The artist had clearly connected with the class material. They hadn't just repeated what was said in class; they conveyed the great significance of the historical event.

But what was also extremely exciting for us as educators was that this panel didn't just reveal something about the pope. Instead we could see into the individual who created the panel. It was more than just a figure drawing. Significant thought went into it how the artist could convey a message of identification between the viewer and the pope. Thus there were three relationships being promoted: artist and subject, subject and viewer, viewer and artist. All three elements were participating, interwoven to help convey something as simple and as complex as an emotional reaction to an event.

The nature of comic art is such that it specifically invites the reader/viewer to participate in another's experience—sometimes even non-verbally. In doing so, it shortens the distance that necessarily exists between the perceptions of two individuals. Simply put: I am not you; you are not me; and so we often struggle to make each other appreciate who we are or what is important to us. These things can be conveyed through words, but we often look to see what a person does when we make judgments about them or attempt to learn from them. This is because action has an immediacy to it: I *see* you doing X rather than just hearing you tell me you like to do X. Yet when I see you doing X, I am only interpreting what you are doing and drawing from my own perceptions, and so my judgment is limited and may in fact be in error. I see you standing there, tears stream down your face. I interpret this using my own experience and generalizations from witnessing others doing the same thing. But my assumption that you're upset may still be quite off the mark. Yes, most of the time crying represents sadness, but it could also be that you are overcome by pure joy.

Lev Kuleshov, in showing the power of film editing, used something like this phenomenon to illicit different feelings from his movie going audience. He showed the image of an expressionless person and alternated it with other images (a bowl of soup, a person in a coffin, and so on) and the viewer interpreted the emotions of the person differently, even though the facial expression never changed. So while I might project a meaning onto your act, simply because I have an accurate picture of you doesn't eliminate the fact that—assuming you also have adequate personal insight—I still require your honest words to have a chance at grasping the act's true meaning. Accordingly, if I can have something that is more than an image, more than an action, and more than words, ideally I should have a better understanding of you or of what you are trying to tell me. This is carried out in graphic novels when words and images are combined into one. You are telling me and showing me in unison and allowing me some control while directing me using various artistic customs. This, I believe, is one way that graphic novels are useful, by allowing the viewer/reader to understand philosophy better, to grasp it more clearly and accurately, even if neither they nor the artist/writer can articulate it perfectly well.

Remember, even though a handful of people might at this time (2017) see comics and graphic novels as simply providing cheap fodder for billion-dollar film franchises, comics and graphic have their own language. Of course various art forms share techniques or have cross over elements. For example, a comic panel can look like a snapshot, and a frozen movie moment. But like paintings, comics will use shadowing, thin lines, thick lines, even blurring to create the desired effect. But while a film goes on, a comic reader can pause and take her time in immersing herself in the panels. Importantly however, she must also give voice to the speech of the characters as well as the written sound effects, and by doing so she is no longer a passive viewer, but an active participant. She has to work with the creators in ways she does not with the filmmaker. She now has a vested interest in being active in how it all unfolds, because without her it goes nowhere—whereas the film merrily moves along without her permission or control.

How well you are able to express yourself and capture the nature of the actual world is of course full of hurdles. We lie to ourselves, and we are sometimes ignorant of our own intentions. So I may have to back down from the previous claim and state that when I take meaning from the words in descriptions and dialogue and combine it with the immediacy of the images, although I might not be any closer to the real nature of the world, I can at least be a bit closer to the creators' perception of it. This "telling and showing" in combination is a powerful way of doing things that exploits the significance of both processes—the visual certainty combined with the allowed pause and personalization of text. Here then is one reason for the various contributions in *Graphic Novels as Philosophy*. There are many different ways in which artistic intention and artistic forms attempt to do this. And this is another reason the title of this work is "Graphic Novels *as* Philosophy." It is a purposeful way of connecting with others and relating to, appreciating, and understanding the concepts and ideas (and perhaps *ideals*) that human beings wish to share by a specific method that combines text and images.

If we had images without having the words, we could lose some of the benefits of novels; for example, the ability to accurately understand rather than to merely assume what is going on, for example, inside the mind of the protagonist. (Indeed, when silent movies became complicated there was a necessity for intertitles to assist the audience in understanding the visuals). Of course one cannot deny the intention of the artist who desires the viewer or reader make up his or her own mind about such matters and thus provides room for interpretation (sometimes by use of ambiguity or vagueness). There the viewer has to interpret and imagine what might be going on and even more so, ask why the artist is showing this particular scene and not some other. But the point is that the epistemological benefit (as opposed to empathetic or emotional benefits which may also be present) is that the viewer sees immediately how tall the tall man is, and how old the old buildings look.

Think also of the sorts of descriptions that you find in a typical novel. The author's words often provide room for the reader's imagination to control how they interpret what the author intends. Without the help of film, how tall is the "tall man?" What do the "old buildings" really look like? In the end, it is ultimately up to the reader to make the decision, no matter how much detail is written down (for example, the shade of yellow that I see in my imagination might be quite brighter than the one that the author envisioned and describes). In other words, with a book the reader does a lot of the heavy lifting. And because the reader does this, he or she often gets more absorbed into that fictional world—because they are helping to create it. One has to work at it and project the words (and worlds) onto the screen of one's mind. This explains why sometimes when those words are transferred from our mind to the actual screen by someone else, as is the case with movie adaptations, fans of the book might gnash their teeth in lamentation. But such is not always a justified criticism: a film cannot just replicate a book, and a graphic novel cannot just replicate either, because they are all different kinds of works and thus different kinds of experiences.

The blending of text and image gives graphic novels another way "in" regarding matters of philosophical import. I don't mean to imply that every graphic novel or comic book is philosophical, just as not every novel or film is philosophical. Some (most?) are just meant to be entertainments and that is why we seek them out in the first place. (Indeed it's often best to leave the lectures in the lecture hall!) But the fact that a writer and an artist (who may be one and the same person) purposely chose to tell the tale using the art of comics and not some other delivery method adds to my view that it is a philosophy: It is a way. It is a school of thought that states that this approach can be better or more accurate than other approaches in creating a useful and insightful means to explore, explicate, and analyze things that are (deemed) worthy of anyone's attention.

This is a bold claim. Yet nothing about any work of art aimed at any audience (or age group) precludes its being analyzed and / or perceived in ways that were not intended by its creators although obviously however some analyses may be quite off the mark. The way of the graphic novelist isn't always a better way than others but the essays herein provide the reader of when it arguably is. The construction of the image and even the construction of the letters of the words (the size and shape of the font) is the application of a technique intended to carry the narrative and the message. This in turn leads to the reader actively participating and thereby have a better chance of connecting, appreciating and understanding. It is a philosophical approach that attempts to bridge the gap between what the reader may know (or not know) and what the reader has experienced (or not) from what others (the writer/artist) know and experience and wish to share. It can provide an awareness that each method of delivery cannot efficiently achieve alone because it requires readers to not just absorb the ideas but to contribute to them as well. For example, in one of the pieces in this book, you'll see how a philosopher discovered that the panels in *Essex County* don't just replicate a philosophical argument, but they actually give evidence to a philosophical argument that could not have existed otherwise. In another essay, you'll read about how Chris Ware's manipulation of the medium demonstrates an important sense of what time is, and in doing so reveals how graphic novels provide us with a better way. In a third, you'll gain an appreciation of how silly humour is not just about being funny but about getting at the truth of the matter by dwelling in the opposite. In a fourth, you'll understand better why *Maus* is a profound work on the Holocaust because of, and not in spite of, the fact that the characters are cartoon animals rather than human. In general each essay here, each contributor, each graphic novel writer and artist are all doing the same thing: trying to tell you how it is—at least from their point of view using the most appropriate avenues for their talents.

■ ■ ■

As you may have noticed already, the graphic novels discussed in this book are well known and/ or created by well-known writers and artists. This is intentional. Critical mass has been reached regarding the acceptance of graphic novels in the public realm in North America so it is important to look at what are considered some of the best of the best to see if they ought to be valued for more than "mere entertainments" as comics were once thought of. Accordingly, although you may have already read (about) these works before, we're looking at them in a new way.

In this context, it is interestingly to remember that we speak of the Golden Age of Comics and the Golden Age of Television. They speak also of the

Golden Age of Radio. Shall we speak of the Golden Age of Graphic Novels too? And if so, are we in it? Or more accurately since we have nothing to contrast it with, will we say we were in it?

With the other forms of entertainment, television, radio and the like, the glowing predicates that have been applied to each one of them is drawn from the fact that after the appearance or creation of the particular form there was an explosion of new things to choose from. Quality didn't matter so much as the sheer amount of new material being created to meet demand and so there was bound to be a lot of good stuff being made with so much "stuff" available. And with all that good stuff to act as an example, creative people will naturally become even more inspired and follow suit—creating a newer wave of exciting materials as well as push the all the boundaries. Still, we have to be cognizant of the fact that we sometimes look back at the bright and shiny beginnings of different entertainments with a certain sense of nostalgia. As such this romanticism may colour the accuracy of how good they really were. Nevertheless, the fact is that any new form of entertainment gives people another opportunity to express themselves. And the world is never quite the same again.

If it will be determined that there is a "golden age of graphic novels," the works discussed by the contributors here highlight the real possibility that we are in it (i.e., the year 2017). One of the difficulties of establishing whether there is, or will be an age—let alone a "golden age," is knowing what exactly a graphic novel is.

Graphic novels are the artifacts of a subclass of comics and cartooning. I often just refer to them as "fat and more expensive comic books" because they are typically just that.[2] This is not a glib statement, nor is a personal observation by one legendary comic book artist that they are "comics without advertising."[3] Yet I suspect both of these characterizations are something that critics will challenge. But consider the question about what "exactly" they are. We all know that comic books are not all "ha-ha" comical, nor do they look like books as much as they look like magazines, and yet we are stuck with the terminology. Some people may refer to them as "pamphlets," but if you asked someone to go into a room and grab "a pamphlet" I don't think they would head straight for the stack of comic books first. That's because when one asks for a denotative definition of "pamphlet," something like *Action Comics* would not be used as the quintessential or obvious example. And since it wouldn't, then the reportive definition also would not rely on the term "pamphlet" either. Like the umbrella term "comic books," graphic novels aren't always graphic in the different senses of the term (although *Lost Girls* is a perfect example of one such one discussed in this book), and they clearly aren't all novels in the sense of being fictional, as shown by Joe Sacco's journalistic *Footnotes from Gaza*, or as a long single piece with a beginning, middle, and an end, as in the short stories in *A Contract with God* by Eisner. And aside from presentation formats, should we consider *Maus* a graphic novel even though it was serialized in *Raw* first and thus is a reprint? Moreover most people consider *Watchmen* a graphic novel; however, it was originally a maxi-series (and thus was included for analysis in *Comics as Philosophy*).[4]

Perhaps it is best to recognize that aside from the basic essential elements that make graphic novels comics—be it the Harvey definition of blending word and text (2007) or the McCloud definition of sequential art (1994)—the Wittgensteinean concept of family resemblance is a satisfactory pragmatic way to deal with the issue (no pun intended). This is not to admit defeat in any sense but to admit that not all things can be put into nice neat boxes. Wittgenstein writes:

> Consider for example the proceedings that we call "games" I mean board-games, card-games, ball-games, Olympic games, and so on. What is common to them all?—Don't say: "There must be something common, or they would not be called 'games'"—but look and see whether there is anything common to all.—For if you look at them you will not see something that is common to all, but similarities, relationships, and a whole series of them at that. To repeat: don't think, but look!
>
> Look for example at board-games, with their multifarious relationships. Now pass to card-games; here you find many correspondences with the first group, but many common features drop out, and others appear. When we pass next to ball-games, much that is common is retained, but much is lost.—Are they all 'amusing'? Compare chess with noughts and crosses. Or is there always winning and losing, or competition between players? Think of patience. In ball games there is winning and losing; but when a child throws his ball at the wall and catches it again, this feature has disappeared. Look at the parts played by skill and luck; and at the difference between skill in chess and skill in tennis.
>
> Think now of games like ring-a-ring-a-roses; here is the element of amusement, but how many other characteristic features have disappeared! (*Philosophical Investigations* 1953)

Thus, according to Wittgenstein, one way language works is that we pick out objects in the world that we call by the same name and note that object A shares some elements of B and B shares some elements of C but that A and C do not share the same elements. Simply defining a "game" as something that has winners and losers really doesn't help one grasp what makes a game a game. It gives us some idea, but not enough. Or consider a car. Would it still be a car if it had three wheels or six instead of four? And what makes a convertible the same as a station wagon; a four door equally a car as a two door, and so on?

Trade paperbacks and graphic novels are both comic books, but TPB and GN shouldn't be confused with each other, even though they are members of the same family. If we don't *think* about them, and instead *look* at them, we can see them for what they are. And for everyday purposes of communication; of understanding words and the objects that we are wanting to refer to, this works.

To ask if there is or will be a Golden Age of graphic novels, we claimed that to know the answer we first needed to know what a graphic novel is. Family resemblance might not be the simplest answer but it allows for people to able to take artistic license with the medium and play with it. No definition is going satisfy everyone and as such lexical definitions are short and sweet but not complete. Consider a comic book like Andy Runton's delightful *Owly* that has illustrations but no words (even the verbalizations are replaced by drawings of the actual object and not the words we use for them). We don't want to dismiss these so why not simply refer to them as "wordless comics" just as there are silent films.[5] *Maus* and *Watchmen* therefore might be reasonably called graphic novels for most people but clearly they are not "original graphic novels." It is, and will have to be messy with apparent hard cases that are exceptions to the general rule. These hard cases are what allow people to explore the medium beyond the rigid parameters set by others. By having blurred edges we allow creators to move beyond and challenge the rigid confines of what is allowed. Is this not part of what we expect from them? And so, perhaps we will have to paraphrase Justice Stewart's approach to defining pornography and state: "I know it when I see it." (Jacobellis v. Ohio, 1964) and move along.

Appropriately enough (for Eisner's work is considered the first in terms of popularizing the field), our first essay is "Philosophy in the Bargain: *A Contract with God* by Will Eisner" by Jarkko S. Tuusvuori, an independent scholar with a PHD in theoretical philosophy (University of Helsinki). In this essay, Tuusvuori examines Will Eisner's (1917–2005) classic and important work *A Contract with God* (1978) and uses it extremely effectively to touch on a myriad of such key elements as Contractualism, Philosophy of Religion and Ethics. In his view, *A Contract with God* is a distinctly philosophical book marking the new awareness of comics as a form of art and medium for serious reflection. Eisner is examining age old questions of moral right and wrong within a theological context. Are our conceptions of right and wrong only possible and only justified by a certain type of agreement or arrangement made with a deity? Tuusvuori in his analysis shows how grasping the underlying philosophical debate helps the reader gain a greater appreciation of Eisner's masterpiece.

Next up is "Queering the Canon: The Practice of Philosophy in Alison Bechdel's *Fun Home*" by Ian J. MacRae who is an associate professor in English and the Society, Culture & Environment at Wilfrid Laurier University Brantford. MacRae's own "hands on" and boots on the ground' experience with visual representation contributes to his insightful examination of how Bechdel's work peels back her own story and tackles some of the big questions that we have asked in matters of hermeneutics, phenomenology and metaphysics. MacRae also discusses how Bechdel's work provides the reader with an important avenue into queer philosophy and the related questions that are rightly receiving greater social and academic reflection.

Maria Botero from Sam Houston State University provides us not only with a perfect example of how philosophical interpretations of graphic novels can make the graphic novel even more interesting but how a work such as Jeff Lemire's *Essex County Vol 1: Tales from the Farm* can actually shape and inform our philosophical understanding by the literal illustration of the argument that cannot be equally captured by words alone. In this particular case, the question is whether it is right to extend autonomy to children in order to allow them to make important decisions.

Next we move from the autonomy of an individual to the autonomy of a nation. War is by definition a destructive force and yet entering into it is sometimes due to love of one's own country. Typically it is an external force that one is fighting against but it can also be an internal one. Eric Bain-Selbo from Western Kentucky University shows how *V for Vendetta* helps us understand this *prima facie* conundrum that seeks to use various forms of force to promote the values of peace and security in one's own society via social contract theory.

While the serious theme of *V for Vendetta* is presented with an appropriate level of solemnity, one can also be both philosophical and funny. Humour can be used as a mask that can ease people into deeper discussions about complicated topics. Simply put, life is complicated; but no one wants to be preached to, especially in a graphic novel. In "Asterix and the Wonder of Everyday Life," Philosophy professor Jeremy Barris (who also contributed to *Comics as Philosophy*) shows how silly stories can help us escape the ordinary (which is often why we seek them out) and in doing so, they can bring those very things that we take as commonplace into sharper focus and ultimately make us appreciate them even more.

Mandel Cabrera from Yonsei University tackles Chris Ware's *Jimmy Corrigan: the Smartest Kid on Earth*; or, rather he shows how Jimmy Corrigan tackles the phenomenological notion of time where at a specific moment we look back at (our personal) history and reexamine it for all its flaws and failures. Such a time can be comforting or frightening, but it is always necessarily enlightening. This work shows us how graphic novels are perfectly suited to speed up or slow down our experiences of time and duration and thus provide us with additional reason to prefer this method of explanation over others. Cabrera writes: The one graphic novel that even people who are not familiar with the field could probably name is Art Spiegelman's *Maus*. It is biographical; it is about war and politics; it is about fathers and sons; it is about how to respectfully delve into an immense topic that is the Holocaust. Spiegelman achieves this by adopting the stereotypical characters that are so closely associated with the childish nature of comic books and cartoons: cute/funny talking animals. Corry Shores from Ankara University shows us in a new way how that choice is deceptively simple. Shores quickly moves past the well-known argument regarding the use of mice and cats as a metaphorical depiction of the dehumanization of the Jews and the inhuman behavior of the Nazis. Instead, he explores and applies the more complex concept of what is known as "becoming animal," which is positive mode of social and personal transformation used for the sake of survival.

One of the wonderful things about graphic novels is the fact that their creators take on tough topics (since an entire comic book series on tough topics might be too exhausting for all involved). In doing so, they both reaffirm the positive adult connotations of "graphic novel" (as opposed to the wrongly dismissive "comic book") and at the same time reaffirm the inappropriateness of labelling everything as a "novel." Writers and artists of good graphic novels that purposely force a reader to become aware of and reflect upon how the world has been shaped should also provide the tools necessary to deal with the challenge. This does not mean to necessarily provide the right answers but to provide an environment for a direct or indirect discussion of what those right answers might be. To do so otherwise is a disservice to both the reader and the topic. It is not caring when you expose a person to real horrors without providing some means of comfort, safety and security. David J. Leichter from Marian University deftly argues for how Joe Sacco's *Footnotes in Gaza* is not just a visual depiction of the difficulties of memory and of a historical event but an opportunity to engage the reader in a purposeful reflection about who, what and why that can lead to personal, political and social amelioration.

The last in this collection of essays with another work by acclaimed writer Alan Moore. Working with his artist-partner Melinda Gebbie the two fashioned a highly controversial work using classic children's literary figures in explicit pornographic ways thereby truly putting the "graphic" in graphic novel. With this project, Moore seeks to bring fictional pornography into the mainstream, and in attempting to do so, makes the reader feel uncomfortable in having to face his own views and values (not to mention being curious as to why such a noted writer would go down this rabbit hole). In "Living in a Fictional World: Reading and Identification in *Lost Girls*," Alfonso Muñoz, who was a postdoctoral research fellow at the National Autonomous University of Mexico at the time of his contribution on *Lost Girls*, tackles the central topic of character identification in fictional works. The statement: "I just like the protagonist" is a clear enough claim to make when offering your evaluation why you enjoy what you are reading but when we unpack it, it unfolds to reveal many new and intricate designs.

We finish with *Lost Girls* because philosophy sometimes forces us to examine the difficult, and when we look, what once appeared simple and straightforward may not truly be. What we find may not be pleasant, and it may be difficult or troubling, but nevertheless it remains insightful because it helps us understand more about what it is to be a graphic novel, and what it is a graphic novelist can provide.

With that in mind, I hope you judge this collection helpful and rewarding in ways that are both expected and not. In working with the contributors in order to try and shape their views I have read their pieces many times over. Looking at these essays (ideally alongside with the original source materials), you will come to learn that they not only deserve a first reading, but a second. Accordingly, I am pleased to have worked with the great team at the University Press of Mississippi to share these with you as a sequel of sorts to *Comics as Philosophy*.

Notes

1. The title is an allusion (that should become clearer when you read on) to the classic 1974 philosophical piece by Thomas Nagel, "What Is It Like to Be a Bat?" *Philosophical Review* 83 (4): 435–50.

2. The main reason I do this is because as we all know, at one time, comic books were derided for being childish materials that no one past childhood should waste their time with. "Graphic novels" of course sounds far more "serious" and thus more acceptable.

3. As this was a personal discussion, I don't want to name the individual in question, but even if it weren't someone whose name you know, it remains an insightful observation!

4. This leads to an interesting question as to whether it was a mistake to include *Watchmen* there and exclude it here, or whether it would be permissible to have it in both.

Regardless of one's answer on this, since I did include it in the former, I didn't want to have another piece on it in the "sequel."

5. I find it intriguing that we call the original movies "silent films," but when they were first created, they were just "films." Then when sound was introduced, there were "films" and "talking films" (or "talkies"). Now the roles have reversed and talking films lost their prefix when they became the mainstream and "films" gained a prefix when they went out of fashion.

Bibliography

Harvey, R. C. "Describing and Discarding 'Comics' as an Impotent Act of Philosophical Rigor." In *Comics as Philosophy*, edited by J. McLaughlin. Jackson: University Press of Mississippi, 2005.

McCloud, Scott. *Understanding Comics: The Invisible Art*. New York: Harper Perennial, 1994.

McLaughlin, J., ed. *Comics as Philosophy*. Jackson: University Press of Mississippi, 2005.

Nagel, Thomas. "What Is It Like to Be a Bat?" *Philosophical Review* 83 (4) 1974.

Wittgenstein, Ludwig. *Philosophical Investigations*. Translated by G. E. M. Anscombe. Oxford: Basil Blackwell, 1963.

Philosophy in the Bargain:
A Contract with God (1978) by Will Eisner

Jarkko Tuusvuori

> "Will came up with a whole philosophy of comics that applied to almost every detail of them, the drawing, the writing, and, most importantly, the storytelling, the kind that occurs between the drawing and the writing."
> —Alan Moore[1]

Will Eisner (1917–2005) was the first to attempt a consummate morality with cartoonists' art and craft. At least no one had attained similar results respected by major authors, eminent critics, and avid readers of both comics and literature. Eisner's *A Contract with God and Other Tenement Stories* (1978) reshaped its medium as suitable for mature reflection upon life, so much that the received term "comic book"—not to mention "funnies"—did not seem anymore an appropriate designation (Eisner 2004). "Graphic novel" was popularized as a relatively new category of artistic composition.

Eisner's stated aims cannot be neglected in investigating the genre. In a 1988 interview, he said that after his much-appreciated crime stories with the eponymous character *The Spirit* (1940–1952) and another (partly overlapping) long stint as the creator of instructional comics for government and corporate clients, he embraced "things I feel strongly about." Discussing mortality, sexuality, and spirituality in *Contract*, Eisner drew from the fact that "we make philosophical statements based on our experiences" (Schwartz 2011, 105).

Yet relying excessively on the author's self-interpretations, one loses sight of possibilities not recommended or even considered by him. Decades after the first edition, Eisner told about his daughter's death preceding *Contract*.

While biographically decisive, the tragedy shouldn't turn inquiry into a conviction of a "viciously personal" book "based on his own anger and pain" (Callahan 2013). Nor should the "personal connection" transform his work on the main character of the title story into "a self-reflection of Eisner himself" (White 2014). What the writer-artist was going through in creating his work is one thing, and hardly anything entirely clear to him either. Another thing, the one that counts, is the end result, whose dimensions far exceed the author's intentions. *Contract* deserves to be read in its full complexity.

To be sure, it is nice that Eisner found it philosophical. An interpretation that is not biographical but philosophical must, nevertheless, surpass authorial viewpoint and attend to what is at stake in the tenement stories. Eisner's re-conception of graphic novel with important aesthetic and conceptual gains therein is fruitfully approached from the perspective of social contract theories, contractualist ethics and the history of negotiations with, and about, God.

Theme

Contract is set in the 1930s New York. The title story features Frimme the treasurer for a Jewish congregation in the Bronx. The pious man lives in a rented apartment on fictional Dropsie Avenue. As his adopted daughter and only family member dies of a fatal disease, he becomes angry at God who he takes to have one-sidedly denounced their treaty of co-operation. As a boy in the practically lawless and fiercely anti-Semitic Russia of the Tsars, Frimme had indeed scribbled on a piece of slate a charter that specified mutual obligations for him and his creator. He took it to America where he was sent as the handpicked survivor of his persecuted community. Little is revealed about his life before the family tragedy, just that Frimme received the child as an infant abandoned on his doorstep and understood this as "part of the pact."

Enraged, he throws the stone out the window to annul the accord. No more niceties from Frimme: misusing congregational assets as his own, he embarks upon a landlord career, ruthlessly accumulates personal wealth and exploits his struggling tenants. Eventually, as a real estate mogul, Frimme faces the elders of his community. He admits his fraud and negotiates a deal: in exchange for a new contract between Frimme and God, this time made out expertly by the scripture scholars, he donates to the congregation his first acquisition and former home, the tenement. However, reading with pleasure the new document he dies of a stroke. In the epilogue, a new kid on the block finds the tablet and signs the contract in his own name. Like the young Frimme before him, people see the equally kind Shloime liable to be rewarded by the Lord.

This reads like a straightforward morality story. Selfless actions merit human thankfulness and even divine commendation. By contrast, selfish conduct leads to punishment. The tale is made more engaging by its clever use of the agreements theme adding layers to what would otherwise be cut-and-dried. It attaches to ethically problematic situations a level pertaining to the meanings, motivations and disruptions of being moral.

While God's foundational role seems to make *Contract* into a piece of devotional literature, it compares to René Descartes' (1596–1650) *Meditations* starting with a description of God as the guarantor of the reliability of human faculties. By seeking to measure the latitude for human doubt, the philosopher sounds the scope of providence. Using this method, Descartes concludes that the very act of doubting and, hence, thinking is indubitable (Descartes 2010, I–III). Frimme is a man of action. Nonetheless, his attitude converges the stance of the meditator: he has put his trust in the divine benevolence sheltering him. Be it malice aforethought or reckless negligence on God's part, from the divine failure to protect the human partner Frimme infers mutual indifference.

Fyodor Dostoevsky's (1821–1881) *The Brothers Karamazov* (1880) asked, if God's absence entails that "everything is permitted" and "one can do anything?" (Dostoevsky 1990, 589). Frimme doesn't enjoy absolute permissibility. He merely infers the futility of a virtuous life. *Contract* stresses his determination over his feelings of grief. Frimme quits expecting to see immanent grace in the world. He cheats, extorts and prospers, until he is ready for a comeback in his religious community. Compared to the way he had lived, Frimme comes close to the ultimate terms of "everything" and "anything." He shaves off his beard despite biblical prohibition and Hasidic tradition and enters in a relationship with a gentile girlfriend. In secular eyes, his metamorphosis from a caring man into a pernicious upstart seems a more extreme makeover.

It is said that "Eisner relies on stereotyped images of Jews" and draws "problematically" from "the typical anti-Semitic image of the Jewish capitalist, with its thick lips and jowls, to make his point" (Dauber 2008, 33).[2] More exactly, *Contract* illustrates and magnifies racist prejudices. The slumlord character subsists somewhere between the standards of a greedy usurer and an unscrupulous lawyer, and "contract" itself suggests the old debate about legalism. These emphases reveal *Contract*'s preoccupation as not a nuanced character study but an exhortation to ponder on world-views, social stances, and rules of deportment. What looks like questionable simplification has to do with a take on communal life marked by conventions (see Ahmed 2016, chapter 1).

One thing about *Contract*'s aesthetics is of great magnitude. It's the use of sepia brown ink. Says Eisner, "It developed an intimacy between me and the reader, as if we were talking in hushed tones" (Miller 2010). Two key points need to be added. Firstly, it realizes the union of "the drawing" and "the writing" and produces an organic whole needed to secure the genre of graphic novel. Secondly, it coalesces personal reminiscing with the more general task of recollecting, reconstructing and reappraising. Suffice to say about the first point that Eisner's sepia lines evoke an art historic continuum from, say, Rembrandt's sketches, while it also stresses the need to word anything pictured, to converse about all that gets told. And it reminds us about how handwriting is always also drawing.

When it comes to sepia as the color of nostalgia, Eisner's commentators have barely said more than that it can "evoke the times past he was depicting" and "transport the reader back to early twentieth-century New York" (Levitz 2015, 134 and 138). Elsewhere, it is told about how "sepia-toned and faded photographs of ancestors" represent typical "implicit Jewish objects" to be found in many Jewish homes along with "explicit" ones (from sacred texts to Kosher wines) all assuring that "family matters, love matters, marking life cycles matters, keeping connections matters, and 'increasing and multiplying' matters" (Ochs 2007, 102–108). A few years before *Contract*, an American Jewish immigrant author wrote that "sepia-tinted photographs" stood for "something solid and respectable" (Ulanovskaya 1989, 882). This testifies to the subversive force of the tenement stories exuding anguish and infamy. On a more universal note, it was *Godfather II* (1974) that established sepia toning as the privileged narrative tool for reliving memories as part of present-day experience.[3] As Coppola's film grew from a Sicilian-New Yorker gangster drama to a study of, among other things, urbanization and clientelism, *Contract* rehearses recognizably Jewish themes all the while addressing more general social issues. The same can be said about the sepia-drenched photographic works *Old Country* (1974) and *New Country* (1976) that foreshadowed much of its efficacy.[4]

Accordingly, *Contract*'s emphasis is not on the developmental or the biographical. It is on ways and standards of representation, thinking and acting. The other tenement stories, too, concentrate on what is wrong and right. They portray the life of a community by focusing on morally intriguing situations. The title story makes all of them move on an axis of crime and punishment with social opportunities and pressures at play. *Contract* is about human interaction and the putatively transcendent norms regulating it.

Genre

Arnold Drake (1924–2007) made it sound easy. According to his testimony of 2007, he and co-writer Leslie Waller (1923–2007) surmised, back in 1949,

"Why not [build] a bridge between comic books and book-books, stories illustrated as comics but with more mature plots, characters and dialogue?" (Drake 2007, 129).

Enter graphic novels. During World War II, GIs were accustomed to comic books as a new form of reading. It was the best way to kill time and counter the fear and frustration coming with the territory. Long-form cartoons offered relaxation with concentration. The U.S. government even published instructive ones designed for the military personnel. Drake and Waller were not educators but reformers of pulp fiction and comics both thriving with *film noir* hugely popular from the early 1940s to the late 1950s. Joining forces with the illustrator Matt Baker (1921–1959) and the inker Ray Osrin (1928–2001), they created a 125-page "picture novel," *It Rhymes with Lust* (1950). St. John Publications in New York soon put out *The Case of the Winking Buddha* (1950), an "all-picture story." Lacking sales halted the series. But the market was there. Comics achieved the status of an "independent commodity" in the form of books emerging with WWII. The distinct product appeared already in 1933, but only six years later there was a demand for millions of copies (Gordon 1998, chapter 6). Commonly regarded as the first graphic novel *avant la lettre*, *It Rhymes with Lust* readjusted to unusual purposes something that was scarcely ten years of age.

Sure enough, tales told solely in pictures were older than that. Lynd Ward (1905–1985) had done *God's Man* (1929), echoing his Belgian colleague Frans Masereel (1889–1972) who had published, from 1918 onwards, wordless books with tales told solely by engravings. If these accomplishments immediately presage modern graphic novels, their prehistoric career could be traced back to cave paintings, Egyptian murals, Greek vases, or the "Mayan friezes" mentioned in Eisner's (2000 [1985], 27) reconstruction of the evolution of "sequential art" (compare to Hescher 2016, 87, on Eisner's "practical sequentiality"). Other combinations of pictures and words embellish Roman pediments, the Bayeux tapestry, and medieval illustrated bibles. Roots aside, the real history can hardly begin long before *It Rhymes with Lust*.

Eisner never seemed to acknowledge its position. Obviously, he saw his own work in crime comics as a forerunner. By 1950, Eisner had been busy for a decade with a sixteen-page, tabloid-size *Spirit* appearing as an appendix in many American Sunday newspapers' "comics sections." It was made, particularly during Eisner's service in the army from 1942 to 1945, by a studio team. *The Spirit* is now considered a seminal experiment in comic book form and an interesting hybrid of hardboiled detectives, humorous *film noir*, urban realism and superhero elements. (Andelman 2005)

But *Contract* approached "book books" (See Schmitz-Emans 2015, 388, and Baetens 2011). Eisner wanted to explore "the potential of the medium" yet "prove" that it "can produce a work in the standard classical structure of a pure novel" (Schwartz 1988, 105). He insisted on not making another comic book. In 1980, Eisner disclosed that he "didn't claim to have invented graphic novels" and praised woodcut volumes of the 30s. He was glad about how the key concept appearing in the cover of *Contract*'s paperback edition "has found acceptance" (Luciano 2011 [1988], 93).[5] Up until recently, he was widely credited for launching it. Yet "graphic novel" was used in the popular culturist Jerry Bail's (1933–2006) newly established amateur comic press association's magazine *CAPA-ALPHA* already in November 1964. The writer Richard Kyle (b. 1929) utilized it also in the 1966 spring issue of *Fantasy Illustrated* (1964–67) that even changed its name into *Graphic Story Magazine* (1967) to honor Kyle's column "Graphic Story Review." He considered the term "comic book" inapt for "genuinely creative efforts" seen or "bound to come" in the field. The old parlance would keep the medium unacceptable for "the literary world." Kyle hoped that the suggested new terms "illustories" and "picto-fiction" be replaced by his "graphic novel" (Groensteen 2006, 75; Schelly 2010, 116–119).[6]

In hindsight, this reads like a commission for *Contract*. Kyle's forum was marginal, but it's doubtful that his proposals didn't disseminate. Randy Duncan has given the most accurate, albeit brief, account of the early developments. If not from Kyle, Eisner must have heard the term "graphic novel" from Jack Katz (b. 1927), who spoke also of "graphic prose" in connection with his *The First Kingdom* (1974–86). In 1976, there appeared five publications marketed as "graphic novels." First off, Byron Preiss's (1953–2005) short-lived *Fiction Illustrated* contained *Schlomo Raven* (with Tom Sutton [1937–2002]) and *Starfawn* (with Stephen Fabian [b. 1930]), both with the tag line "America's first adult graphic novel revue" on their back covers. In the same series, Jim Steranko's (b. 1938) *Chandler: Red Tide* had the concept of "graphic novel" mentioned in the author's introduction, and that of "visual novel" in the cover. Further, George Metzger's (b. 1939) *Beyond Time and Again* shouted "graphic novel" from its title page. Finally, the artist Richard Corben's (b. 1940) version of an old Robert E. Howard (1906–1936) story, *Bloodstar*, proclaimed, halfway justifiably, "a new revolutionary concept—a graphic novel, which combines all the imagination and visual power of comic strip art with the richness of the traditional novel" (Duncan 2013, 143–150).[7]

The case of the writer-illustrator Steranko may be the most rewarding in exploring the way the conceptual and aesthetic elements of graphic novels were cooking at the time. Known for his ambitious *History of Comics* (1970–1972), Steranko even had a "graphic narrative" show in 1977 in an exhibition at Winnipeg Art Gallery. The cultural prestige of comics and their potentially thoughtful content strengthened ideas about relevant works.[8]

Duncan contends that *Contract* merits no more misplaced awe. It wasn't the first of its kind; the concept had already been developed, and it wasn't a novel at all. This last point Duncan makes twice: first with no hesitation ("not a novel but four short stories") and then less strictly ("not even truly a graphic novel") (Duncan). In turn, Green (2010) questions Eisner's work "as a proper novel" but opines that the same central character in each story—"a tenement in Bronx"—is enough "to make a case" for its being a graphic novel.[9] The building's leading role is confirmed by Royal (2011), who defines *Contract* as "neither a novel nor a collection of disparate stories" but a "graphic cycle" in the manner of the "short-story cycle" prevalent in contemporary Jewish American literature and popular among ethnic American writers.

While the perception of the centrality of the milieu is laudable, the genre question appears redundant. Varieties of form in the past few centuries make skepticism about *Contract*'s status as a novel futile. Let the cases of, say, Schlegel's *Lucinde* (1799), Lewis's *Tarr* (1918), Sarraute's *Portrait of a Man Unknown* (1948), Tolgarczuk's *House of Day, House of Night* (1998), and Kehlmann's *Fame* (2009) make it easier to call Eisner's book a novel. It makes good sense that an early graphic novel, new and hybrid, was something of a borderline case instead of anything conventional.[10]

Duncan (2013) does not dispute *Contract*'s claim to a special position in the history of long-form comic art. What set it apart were a new "sensibility" and "attitude" in the stories that "aspired to be literature," plus a different "look." In terms of content, it did justice to the first-generation American Jewish experience in the ghettoes of New York. As regards to form, "Eisner used rigid panel borders sparingly and for particular effect, set narration free from caption boxes and made it an organic part of the page." *Contract* could be sold in "mainstream bookstores" and "occupy a different cultural space" from the one housing its predecessors.

New claims have been made about *Milt Gross' New York* (1939) as a "lost graphic novel" and a "precursor to the format" (Heller 2015). Milt Gross (1895–1953) first came up with a lampooning of Longfellow's *The Song of Hiawatha* (1855) called *Hiawatta witt no Odder Poems* (1926). Then came *He Done Her Wrong* (1930), a parody of Ward's *God's Man*. The subtitle announces *The Great American Novel and Not a Word in It—No Music, Too*. It makes the work, despite all the irony, into an experiment with the novel form. In his forgotten *New York* with original dialogue and narration Gross was not anymore parodying anybody or anything except himself and his own style of telling a story. This self-parody stands out as his best shot at a genre finding its recognized form in 1950, its new name in 1964, and its new seriousness in 1978. As the first feature-length talkies only appeared in the latter half of the 20s, the work of Gross—a onetime collaborator of Chaplin—stands at the crossroads of interrelated developments.[11]

Worth mentioning also is the American editorial cartoonist Bill Mauldin (1921–2003). His wartime work that appeared initially in the soldiers' newspaper *Stars and Stripes* and finally in the volume *Up Front* (1945) earned him the respect of frontline servicemen. Grim depiction of the exhausting lot of the foot soldier and the questionable higher meaning of fighting was instrumental in lifting comics to a new level of realism. Mauldin united traits of editorial cartoon and political caricature to a more narrative touch with recurrent characters Willie and Joe. He was able to introduce moral questions (and even the deliberately misspelled term "perfessional ethics") into his down-to-earth illustrations (Mauldin 2000 [1945]; Jaissle 2014).

Contract arose from numerous sources, yet it can be said to fuse what *It Rhymes with Lust* achieved in narrative intensity with what Mauldin attained in situational poignancy. There are similarities between *It Rhymes with Lust* and *Contract* in using boldface for emphasis and extensive text boxes (albeit without outline in Eisner) for the narrator's parts. *Contract* comes close to *Up Front* in the forlorn and the miserable: a fatalistic sense of loneliness comes through from both Mauldin's gallows (or trenches) humor and Eisner's humanistic hyperbole. Single pages from *Contract* resemble *God's Man*, as do its themes of agreement, success, and disillusionment, its fable-like properties, unhappy ending, and religious dimensions. *He Done Her Wrong* resonates both in the comical elements (despite its earnestness, *Contract* borders on the zany, from its title onward) and the meta-poetic structures (consider Gross's subtitle and *Contract*'s genre specifications and foreword) of Eisner's work. *Contract*'s take on New York is like a mirthless, or quasi-solemn, version of Gross's carefree anthem to their common hometown.

No doubt, Eisner's graphic novel also reworks his own earlier productions. In Tom Kaczynski's (b. 1973) words, *Contract* sheds "the youthful exuberance" inhabiting *The Spirit*. Whereas it had nine to fourteen or even more panels per page "filled with frenetic action" and myriad details, *Contract* is happy to offer one to four with often static constellations that can be figured out in one glance. The graphic novel is "drained both of color and density"; its "visual complexity" comes from irregularity or absence of gutters and "decompressed narrative," eliciting "some grander logic" of the ever-changing urban life. As "the real protagonist" is "the street itself," architecture assumes the role of the panel borders (Kaczynski 2010).[12]

Peeters (2007 [1998]) spoke of Eisner's "virtual frame" or the "absence of precise boundaries between the images." Others accentuate "extensive shading" and "splash pages." Crosshatching technique and visible pencil lines endow "an unfinished quality to the work" reflecting "the transitional lives of the characters." The theme of "social mobility" is elaborated against the inescapable presence of the "dirty and dark" tenement. While *Contract* did not invent a new concept, it "helped lay the foundation for the rise of the genre of graphic novel." It showed "that adult themes could be addressed in graphic medium" (Reingold 2014; see also Petersen 2011, 149–150).

The Philosophical

Judged by the storyline, Eisner's work ought to be called "Two Contracts with God." Yet neither of the documents are even partially quoted, or their paragraphs shown. Likewise, no deity is visualized but only referenced. The reader must think them through on the basis of what does make its way on the pages, since *Contract with God* downplays "contract" and "God" and emphasizes living "with" (ideas of) them. The story is not so much about two particular pacts as it is about what it means to make, comply with, believe in, and live up to them.

Frimme misreads morals in terms of a deal between a human being and a superhuman deity. Ethics is better comprehended with inter-human agreements. Frimme has a knack for business and closing deals. Since his possessions include rented apartments, he is a party in many agreements of lease and hence familiar with asymmetrical concurrences. It may not be so foolish on his part to see himself contracting with God. What started as childish gullibility lives on as the adult Frimme's yearning to be someone to be reckoned with. Yet what *Contract* puts forth are not so much a (fictional) person's religious beliefs but common experiences of reacting to the unfairness of fate.

While Frimme seemingly takes his revenge on God, he actually takes revenge upon his fellow men. In the flashback sequence, we see his concept of God evolving in his contacts with people who thank him for his helpfulness. He came to think of God as someone to reward him all the good he did. When this thought expired along with his daughter, Frimme ostensibly attacked his God but really repaid it all on other people. If mortals had instilled in him a fallacious view of God, it was against them that he could feel he had a reason to retaliate in the ways of a fraudster and profiteer. Although we don't know what the early contract stipulates, it is likely something along these lines: Frimme continues to love his neighbor and so forth, thus obligating God to show him all kinds of gratitude. The equally unknown text of the later contract presumably specifies more exactly the unalterable duties of God, should Frimme fulfill his part in producing good behavior.

What makes *Contract* philosophically astute is how it fosters concentration on what is not depicted on its pages. Instead of reviewing the terms of the contracts, we are summoned to think over the act of entering into, and repudiating, an agreement with, of all parties, God, and the meaning of contracts. The reader is not so much encouraged to empathize with Frimme as to ponder why in the world we usually do the right thing and what makes us capable or incapable of doing it. Any wise discussion of the book is bound to consult philosophy for tools in making sense of its import. This will lead the readers to momentarily put the book down and reflect on their own situations and responses to them.

The Contractual

Talking about contracting with God involves a contradiction in terms similar to speaking about God's dying. It is as odd to invoke the decease of an eternal power as it is to dream of a treaty with it. If the crux of the Nietzschean notion of "the death of God" is the contradictoriness of such an event, the paradox inherent in "a contract with God" is likewise not accidental but pertinent. Cases of mortals negotiating an agreement with their immortal master have been diverse. Many modern theologians, from, say, Barnes to Barclay and Novak, have denied the possibility of a contractual bond between God and humans and defended a non-contractual religious covenant.[13] Others, from Orlinsky and Barnhart to Hirsch, Schultz, and Laytner, have had no such trouble with the contractual.[14] In *Contract*, the word carries connotations of business bargaining, but primarily it signals the most common concept to cover all cases.

Interpreters of Eisner who find his story "devoid of Jewish learning and insight" are acting in haste.[15] When the learned fathers assigned by Frimme to realize his new contract consider viewing "all religion [as] a contract between man and God" and decide to "provide him with a guiding document, so that he might live in harmony with God," this could well be backed by writings of the pro-contractual authors just mentioned. Saying that Frimme is wrong won't do; he adheres to many religious authors.[16] Relevant to his story is the way Puritans saw themselves as God's partners bestowed with a whole new continent as their property.[17] After the first and before the second contract, Frimme becomes God's competitor.

Most importantly, the issue is by no means exclusively theological. The notion of a contract with God crops up in a number of literary works featuring both existential moralities and satires by authors of all persuasions.[18] Here two seem paramount. Theodore Dreiser (1871–1945) had earned the Nobel Prize in 1930 with his melodrama framed by God's needed but doubtful intervention in human miseries (Dreiser 1925, chapters 1 and 37). Almost unknown is his short story "The Tithe of the Lord" (1938), which begins with the agonized protagonist Benziger having an idea of "a bargain with the Lord." He ponders on "such a contract": would God act "in behalf of" a sinner?

> He was going to make a deal with God, or whoever it was that ran the world, just as he would make a deal with anyone in the business world. If God would help him to get over this despair so that he could get work and get on his feet again, he would, from then on until his death, devote ten per cent of everything he should gain to helping those who needed help worse than he did. Furthermore, he would ... get married, and be helpful—and faithful—to one woman.[19]

Benziger is a precedent to Frimme's mumbling about "making a new life" seconds before his death. Dreiser paints a constellation where the outlandish but not quite unusual idea of making a deal with God pops into a secular modern mind when in grief. Actually, in 1736, a French jewel trader had "contracted a partnership with God." His inheritors were appalled, as this meant giving his handsome estate to charity. Reporters of the incident asked whether this was any different from biblical agreements between God and Noah, Abraham, or Jesus (Gayot de Pitaval 1736, 288–347). A similar case of a liquor retailer was brought to light in 1866. Experts agreed that he was eccentric, but not crazy: his peculiar contract was like the promises people commonly make in times of danger, except that they rarely write them down and even more rarely follow through with them (Chatelain 1866).[20] This is precisely where *Contract* hits. Its style might feel "schmaltzy" (Lambert 2009); it may look less than subtle, to the point of "cornball histrionics" and "over-the-top" burlesque (Schjeldahl 2005). But its authenticity is contracted from materials both typical and quotidian.

"I had made a compact with a God who was a tougher bargainer than the devil!" wrote Waldo David Frank (1889–1967). His tone of voice is simultaneously earnest and jocose as he recounts how his "covenant" was "fully worked out" at the age of fifteen:

> I was going to be an author. And authors had rewards. They made money (see Kipling). They made disciples (see Tolstoy). They won world fame (see Hardy, Meredith, and Shaw). I looked with hunger on these prizes. Well, *I was going to give them up*. Their loss would be my payment in the bargain. And what would God give in return? ... He would simply and solely *keep open* for me while I lived

the course of a *search* for truth,... which was that *God is Present.* ... What I compacted with God was to give up all the guerdons, not for the highest or deepest success but for the chance, while my life lived, to go on trying.

Frank didn't tell his classmates about "this lopsided contract." He often forgot about the "treaty" and yearned for success, while "God went on exacting payment on his side of the bargain" (Frank 1973, 45). This is another description of a relationship with God that a modern human being entertains living in a secularized world. To me, it might well be the best point of reference for *Contract*. It is in keeping with Frimme's deep-rooted experience of contracting with God and chimes well with how Eisner claimed experiential truth to his take on the life in the New York tenements.[21]

Historical cases of pacts with God illustrate *Contract* as an inter-textual nexus. This doesn't deny the originality of Eisner's achievement, but rather defines the form of its ingenuity. We shouldn't praise him for inventing either the concept or the medium of graphic novel, but for a successful transformation of them into an aesthetic term and artistic genre henceforth associated with Eisner. We shouldn't salute him for coining the notion of a contract with God, but for re-appropriating it anew so that it cannot anymore do without a reference to him.

How many owner-tenant or employee-employer contracts are based on commensurate parties? How proportionate is the bargaining power of a desperate dweller to the proprietor? The poor are likely to be taken advantage of because of the imbalance of power between the haves and the have-nots. As *Contract* zeroes in on inequalities like these, it portrays a mismatch of power between Frimme and God only as much as it discusses the confines of unjust forms of life in general.

It is said that the action takes place between the panels of a comic book. What is not shown is what readers provide to it (McCloud 1994, especially 86–88). In this graphic novel, we are not admonished to fixate on Frimme but to look for the reasons for striving for goodness. *Contract* welcomes the idea of our having a contract with society.

The Social

Thomas Hobbes (1588–1679) defines contract as "mutual transferring of right." If the thing on which the right bears is delivered later, the contract is a pact or covenant implying trust in keeping promises. Non-mutual transfer is gift: paradise was given by God's "free grace." Hobbes separates the societal from "the condition of meer Nature," where, at best, even "covenants entered into by fear" create obligation, and at worse, everybody wars with everybody. Combat ends and justice begins as people perform the covenants they make and institute a commonwealth. Then "a multitude of men do agree, and covenant, every one with every one, that to whatsoever man, or assembly of men, shall be given by the major part the right to present the person of them all." No matter if one voted for or against this "representative," everybody will "authorize all the actions and judgements of that man, or assembly of men, in the same manner as if they were his own, to the end to live peaceably amongst themselves, and be protected against other men." Rights derive from this. Some of them are conferred to the sovereign "by the consent of the people assembled" (Hobbes 1651, chapters IV and XIV).

This is how the basics of modern state and society were first formulated. John Locke (1632–1704) came up with a refined theory matching the new idea that the monarch should no longer rule without parliamentary consent. He reminded how King James I had spoken about the danger of tyranny and its prevention by a "paction made to his people," harking back "to that paction which God made with Noah after the deluge." In Locke's view, the state of nature ends only in a "compact" where everybody agrees "together mutually to enter into one community, and make one body politic." One side accepts "a limited power," the other obedience. Such an "original compact" is where one "with others incorporates into one society" (Locke 2004 [1689]).

Jean-Jacques Rousseau (1712–1778) made these ideas into a theory of "social contract." Underlining "popular consent," he wrote about a "multitude ... united in one body," so that "it is impossible to offend against one of the members without attacking the body." The contracting parties were "equally obliged" by "duty and interest" to mutual assistance. For Rousseau, building a society meant eradicating inequality. Social contract "substitutes, for such physical inequality as nature may have set up between men, an equality that is moral and legitimate, and that men, who may be unequal in strength or intelligence, become every one equal by convention and legal right" (Rousseau 1913 [1762], book I, chapters 7 and 9).

The young Frimme knew himself as the less mighty of the contractual parties. The old Frimme viewed himself as God's equal. He was first ready to give away some of his liberties for extra stability, until he took it as his goal to achieve the status from which to dictate the terms. Frimme's two raw deals do not allude to the old covenant (Moses) and new covenant (Jesus) in their respective biblical senses.[22] Instead, evoking Locke, the very first contract in the *Old Testament* is hinted at when Frimme walks home in the pouring rain. The narrator knows that he sees the tenement like "Noah's ark" about to drift away with the flood. God promised the faithful Noah that his family would rule the sufficiently stable earth as long as it lasts (Gen. 8–9).

It was the beginning of Frimme's rise to power, too. The mock-biblical tone aside, the ark comparison indicates that he won't care anymore: after loss, the deluge. As a boy, Frimme was an embodiment of attentive assistance. As a suffering adult, he grows numb. As he returned from the funeral of his daughter to her dying place, the tenement looked like the end of the world as he had known it. It was good for nothing but returning the injury. What is pivotal for interpretation is that this is one of the tenement stories. One needs to address Frimme's roles as a tenant and a landlord. The title story intimates that the others read as events guided by inter-human agreements. The stage is set for a study of a sense of belonging, group cohesiveness, inclusion and exclusion, the sacrosanct and the violable. This makes social contract philosophies good companions for Eisner's graphic novel.

Nowadays, there are Hobbesian contractarianisms developed mainly by David Gauthier and contractualisms stemming from Rousseau and mostly worked out by T. S. Scanlon. Contractarianists emphasize self-interest as the driver behind agreements that make up our moral, social, and political thought and action (Gauthier 1986 and 1990). Contractualists underline equality and mutual respect (Scanlon 1982). Both stress consent and obligation-creating agreements behind legitimate political power, as well as authority of moral norms. The distinction dates back from the early 1980s, while the individual conceptual histories are older. Contractarianism was used already in the 1960s (Rankin 1964, 106). Contractualism, in turn, is over a hundred years old.[23] Yet it was only in the late 70s when "the contract perspective" began to really find its way into ethics (Veatch 1977, 76). Hence it is not likely that Eisner knew anything about it while authoring *Contract*.[24]

It is Scanlon's goal to canvass the "motivational basis" of agreeing with others: people want to justify themselves to each other (Scanlon 1998, 5–6). Any sort of "self-interested bargaining" is "foreign to my account," he says. Scanlon's theory depicts us "not merely . . . seeking some kind of advantage but also . . . moved by the aim of finding principles that others, similarly motivated, could not reasonably reject." Contractualism does not depend on a myth of an original contract. It underscores a kind of concord renewed whenever a moral agent wishes to justify her actions to others, even if in private meditation. In Scanlon, the word "concrete" staves off an impression that the analysis would move on a high level of abstraction with universal principles. Accordingly, he traces the meaning of "being moral" to the experiences of an agent in situations where, say, somebody "counts on me" or "needs my help."[25]

Frimme's "being moral" originally derived from his helping others and only secondarily from his pact with God. Later, he faces extinction, causes destruction, and feels no remorse, until he wants to set things right again. The decision is not borne out of guilt but ambition. Frimme is oblivious to the demands of mutual recognition in his human relationships, while he is busy having God recognize his willingness to negotiate. The young Frimme made his contract with God where no social order was in effect. He was ready to abdicate some of his personal rights in exchange for protection of other rights. Because of anti-Semitism and the lot of being a poor immigrant, he wasn't cut out to trust others. Settling in the new world, he conceivably needed his contract with God for a reason that guides people to interpersonal agreements: to counter the unknown, to mitigate danger, to create propitious ties that would bind come rain or shine.

Contractualism comes often with a "counterfactual" setting. It gives "an account of rightness and wrongness in terms of the moral principles which individuals would accept or could not reasonably reject if they were in certain hypothetical counterfactual circumstances." This makes it interesting in the light of experiments of literary fiction. An "actualist" brand of contractualism says that "whether some act is right or wrong must always be determined by an actual implicit agreement within a group that includes at least both the agent who is doing the act and the people who are evaluating it."[26] With his two actual explicit contracts with God and a host of actual leases with his tenants, Frimme in fact has an implicit agreement of fairness with others. As vulnerable as he was as a parent, he doesn't realize his commitments.

Frimme grew into believing in an almighty force that had in store for him a good life in exchange for his being there for others. The death of his daughter was like a flash of deism teaching that God had transcended out of the world and had either no say or no interest in protecting his happiness. A die-hard theist, if no longer a true believer, Frimme thinks he could get better safeguards if he gained enough authority. Unable to share his grief with the ones close to him, Frimme isolates himself from his neighbors, betrays his community and starts exploiting his former inmates. He becomes a believer in his own capabilities in correcting the contractual faults, whatever these may be: readers only know Frimme's conviction that he will escape suffering with better text in black and white. His distance from a group in which he could sustain a sense of moral and rational acceptability leads him astray. His increasingly self-serving opinions and beliefs ruin his capacity to communicate.

He is as lost in transgression as the opportunistic protagonist of the most effectively drawn tenement story, the "Street Singer," who cannot settle into his home or city. Hardened by the death of his loved one and too obdurate to take heed of others, Frimme won't accept a shadow of a breach. He might have been on good—and then not so good—terms with God but is deprived of vital peer support and peer criticism. Eisner captures this best in the picture where people visit him after the funeral, "offering Hersh the usual words of comfort which he accepted in stony silence." Unable to make his own the usual or unusual joint practices into the source of mutual strengthening, Frimme is left alone with his silent tablets of stone. More philosophically, he fails to fathom his real partners in a treaty called communal life.[27]

Epilogue

"They are true stories. Only the telling and the portrayals have converted them to fiction." The drawn preface complicates *Contract*'s interpretation. Its Bronx is as fictional as Dropsie Avenue. One is to be wary of any account of what happens there. Accounts of the borough and the tenement move from the sphere of the real or directly experienced toward the unreal or indirectly experienced. The two sentences plus Eisner's signature under them make the five stories self-conscious, aware of their refined status as results of artistic molding.

In his preface to the 2004 edition, the author described them as "drawn from the endless flow of happenings characteristic of city life." In order for there to be stories, there have to be happenings. But in order for us to perceive happenings, we have to have something like stories to conceive of them by. "Some are true, some could be true," Eisner added now. Readers find they agree just enough with what they know about the types of characters, events, sentiments, and places in the book. Out of bounds, Frimme is hardly identifiable but amply replaceable by the readers with their characteristics and conditions. This underlines the philosophical nature of Eisner's work. The real situation at hand, at a time t, in a place p, for an individual X, is worked out with the help of other situations in the past, possible situations in the future, and conceivable situations in theory and imagination. Resources for this elaboration are drawn from X's history of situations and capacity to conceive of others similar or dissimilar to it in relevant respects. It is in this meta-ethical neighborhood that Dropsie Avenue leads right into.

Eisner refers to the reading conventions ("left to right, top to bottom") and "common cognitive disciplines" as a "very voluntary cooperation" grounding "the contract between artist and audience" (Eisner 2000 [1985], 40). *Contract* creates a space for the readers to fill in with their own experiences of, and thoughts on, life as humans. Eisner's sepia-ink power line enlivens a set of historical experiences only as much as it makes us attentive of conventions guiding, and conceptions permeating, our own experience. In its dexterous combination of pictures and text, visual cues and verbal allusions, *Contract* enhances philosophical reflection on the social construction of reality just as much as on moral disengagement. As its take on life varies from the casual to the pompous, it manages, largely because of the famous Eisnerian "weighty" line (see Feiffer 2003 [1963]), to sustain a sense of the real while occupying the reader's judgment and prompting questions about its own truthfulness. In this, Eisner's *A Contract with God* keeps its contractual promise with us to both entertain and enlighten.

Notes

1. See Andelman 2005, 355.

2. Dauber goes on to discuss (34–36) Eisner's later *Fagin the Jew* (2003), loaded with criticism of "a classic stereotypical Jew."

3. It was followed by, for example, *Once Upon a Time in America* (1984), *Radio Days* (1987), *Mr. Saturday Night* (1992) and *Sunshine* (1999), all of which have a strong Jewish dimension to them.

4. They were authored by the Warsaw-born New York journalist Abraham Shulman (1919–1999), with fine critical essays on, for instance, the political aspects of Hasidism and Jews' "relation to God." See especially Shulman, *The New Country* (New York: Scribner, 1976).

5. Compare to Kaplan 2008, 153, on how Eisner read Ward in 1938 and "toyed with the idea of developing a serious work in comics form."

6. Kyle's examples of ambitious works were the Captain Storm story "Killer Hunt" (1964), drawings by Joe Kubert (1926–2012), and a picto-fiction series from the 1950s. In 1972, the magazine *Graphis* used the term *roman graphique*, but it appears already in the historian John Grand-Carteret's (1850–1927) *Les moeurs et la caricature en France* (Paris: Librairie Illustrée, 1888), 503–504, in reference to Albert Robida (1848–1926) and his "couplings of written and graphic thinking." Moreover, both English painter William Hogarth's (1697–1764) works of sequential art and American author James Fenimore Cooper's (1789–1851) illustrated *Lionel Lincoln* (1825) were referred to in the early-nineteenth-century Anglo-American press as "graphic novels." The Italian expression *romanzo a fumetti* was in use from the 1950s onwards.

7. Steranko's work is, in fact, an illustrated novel, while Metzger's book is a collection of magazine stories. Still, the three others deny Eisner most of the pioneer's glory. To Duncan (2013), not only *It Rhymes with Lust* but also the Japanese *Four Immigrants Manga* (1931) "have much better claim" to being the first graphic novel than *Contract*. Duncan adds that a number of candidates were also released in 1978, but he doesn't name names. Compare to Kane 2012: "When combined with the fact that none of these volumes has ever been

reprinted ..., and that the stories, except for *Chandler*, are only of cursory interest, it is not surprising that they have been forgotten." Kane lists as *Contract*'s contemporaries *Sabre: Slow Fade of an Endangered Species* (1978) by Don McGregor (b. 1945) and Paul Gulacy (b. 1953); *The Silver Surfer* (1978) by Stan Lee (b. 1922) and Jack Kirby (1917–1994); *Comanche Moon* (1979) by Jack Jackson (1941–2006); and *Tantrum* (1979) by Jules Feiffer (b. 1929). In addition, two French items were published in the U.S. in 1977 as "graphic albums." By the early 1980s, largely due to Eisner, "graphic novel" had become a commonplace denomination for a variety of comic books.

8. Compare to Hesse-Quack 1970, 62–71, on how comics deserve closer study because of their critical cultural potential. See also Kaukoranta and Kemppinen 1970, especially pages 11 and 15, on how they matured similarly to the way novel had become "middle class culture in the 18th-century England." Specifically, Eisner's *Spirit* is cited as an example of energetic results achieved without the "form of legend," as in *Phantom* or *Tarzan*. Yet Carrier (2000, 123) still had to opt for rehabilitation: "This book has tried to show why a slight-seeming art is of great philosophical interest." See also Lopes 2009, especially page 179, on Eisner's role in "winning respect for this art form" of comic books.

9. The title of the Finnish edition means "A House in the Bronx"; Eisner, *Talo Bronxissa* (1978), translated by Annikki Malin (Helsinki: Jalava, 1982).

10. Compare to Kane 2012: "While some detractors claim that *Contract* is actually a collection of short stories, and not a novel *per se*, the use of multiple stories with an underlying connective theme is not without precedent, and is the basis for books such as *Winesburg, Ohio* (1919) by Sherwood Anderson (1876–1941), and *The Wild Palms* (1939) by William Faulkner (1897–1962)."

11. See Kaplan 2008, 46. Compare to Beronä 2008 and Yoe 2010. See also Buhle 2004, 108, on how Eisner introduced "a cinematic reach into comics and thereby [transformed] the field, during the 1940s."

12. Kaczynski points out that in the sequel to the 1978 book, *A Life Force* (1985), *The Spirit*'s exuberance recovers with more story, more panels, and more characters.

13. Barnes 1962, 1282–1283. Compare to Barclay 1976 [1955], 91, on how men "cannot *bargain with God*" or "argue about the terms of the covenant," but "only accept or reject the offer that God makes." And see Novak 2005, "The Covenant," in which every Jew is said to have "a covenantal identity," and where using "contract" and "covenant" interchangeably is deemed "a serious mistake" and "great conceptual confusion."

14. See Orlinsky 1960 [1954], 21–22, on the early Hebrews' broadening the scope of contracts to religious and moral thinking, whereas the more magically oriented Mesopotamian peoples had only economic use for "contractual relationships." The basis of Orlinsky's (one of William F. Albright's [1891–1971] students) theory has been challenged, as the historicity of patriarchs are difficult to prove. Here Orlinsky is consulted as an interesting interpreter of the Torah. Compare to Barnhart 1975, 88: "God is hardly the unmoved, changeless Necessary Being that Thomas' cosmological argument projects." Compare also to Hirsch 1837, 94: "Each Sabbath ... you renew your contract [*Vertrag*] with God and dedicate yourself to serving God, who, in turn, bestows to you renewed light of spirit, warmth of mind, blessing

of strength." See also Schultz 1971, 32, on "a contractual agreement" between Israel and God. And see, finally, Laytner 2004 [1999], xiii–xiv: "The Jewish relationship with God has, almost from the very beginning, been expressed in terms of a mutually beneficial contract."

15. See Klingenstein 2007, 81–87, where it is contrasted with more "brilliant" literary workings on the theme of "the justice of God and the suffering of the righteous" (such as Elie Wiesel's *Night* [1958]), accused of being "completely antithetical to Jewish thought, which is community-oriented," and blamed for revolving "around a single idea." To Klingenstein, Frimme's character lacks Job's "inner heft and substance" and becomes "near-imbecilic," so that "this is not a recognizable Jewish story." Compare to Tabachnick 2014, 119, on how Eisner's story "seems to show that even the religiously observant have no contract with God." Enlarging this to accommodate *The Contract with God Trilogy*, he imputes to the "left-leaning" Eisner "a completely secular view," according to which "religion *per se* is of no particular worth to humanity and even breeds delusions that God cares about individuals." It is only "the prejudice that the Jews face" and his own socialization to "Jews as an ethnic group" that keep Eisner attached to Judaism, although he has "little use for ideas of God."

16. Compare to Dauber 2008: "Eisner references larger theological issues." However, the only example Dauber gives is Ukrainian Hasidic rabbi Levi Yitzchok of Berditchev (1740–1809), who is said to have exclaimed to the Lord in the middle of a prayer, "I want to propose a deal. We have many sins and misdeeds, and you an abundance of . . . atonement. . . . So you must balance the deal by giving us life, and children, and food besides!"

17. See Mosier 1952, 11–12, on how Puritans insisted on a "contract, signed by the high contracting parties, God and the sinner, and sealed by the blood of Christ." Man the loyal servant was "granted a probational grace on condition that he perform honestly and faithfully the articles of the contract." Quoting Thomas Shepard (1605–1649), who came to America to preach piousness linked with ownership, Mosier sees "the collective guilt of feudal times" transforming with the rising capitalism into "a more personal bond and contract involving individual crime and punishment." Compare to Sheldon 2014, 10, on Puritans' thinking "they had made a covenant, or contract, with God, like the people of ancient Israel." The standpoint was federal or covenant theology. It was also a theology of success: Puritans promised "to obey His Laws, in return for which God would bless them with peace, happiness, and prosperity."

18. See Malègue 1965 [1940], 125, addressing his father's mourning and embitterment after his child's death; compare to Dallago 1924, 524. On a humorous case, see Pinski 1914.

19. Dreiser 1938. See also Griffin 1985, 123–127, on how the old Dreiser handled not only the possibility of "a transcendent benevolent force" but, more generally, "themes that are essentially philosophical, moral and religious."

20. Compare to Liggett 1928, chapter XXXIX, on how the character Jake's "contract with God" is merely a petition at the toughest spots of his adventures: "God will get us through."

21. See Yronwade 2011 [1978], 71–72: "I feel you have to have lived in a tenement at about that period—or even today—to understand."

22. Compare to Russell 2014, chapter 5: "Dying without God can seem like a *raw deal*. With God, death is part of a deal. With God dying is part of a glorious deal."

23. See de Greef 1909, 86–87, on "contractualism" as "basis of the system of political federations and confederations," present and future. The word denoted a "special and superior form of social adaptation."

24. For a conceivable exception, see Sorokin 2010 [1937–40], 445–463, on historical varieties of familistic, contractual, and compulsory types of social interchange. From the late eighteenth to the early twentieth century, to Sorokin, compulsory relationships decreased, making contractualism "the most typical mark of the ... Western society of the nineteenth century." Yet from the Great War onward, compulsory relationships have been on the rise.

25. Scanlon 1998, 5–6 and155–156. See also pages 132 and 341. Contractualism tends to oppose the idea of a universalizing and principled moral philosophy as the climax of ethics, and insists on the perspective of an individual agent who cannot "envisage the reactions of every actual person" but "can consider representative cases." Ibid., 171.

26. See Suikkanen 2014, 114–115, explaining the fallacy as follows: "Placing X in the hypothetical circumstances C changes the nature of X in such a way that whether X is G in those circumstances will be irrelevant for whether X is F in the actual circumstances."

27. On *semblables*, see Rousseau 1913 [1755]. Compare to Pekelis 1950, 63: "Rather *a deal with God* than with the neighbors, who had been bad neighbors to him or to whom he had been a bad neighbor."

Bibliography

Ahmed, Maaheen. *Openness of Comics: Generating Meaning within Flexible Structures*. Jackson: University Press of Mississippi, 2016.

Andelman, Bob. *Will Eisner: A Spirited Life*. Milwaukee: M Press, 2005.

Baetens, Jan. "Graphic Novels." In Leonard Cassuto et al. (eds.), *The Cambridge History of the American Novel*. Cambridge: Cambridge University Press, 2011. 1137–1153.

Barclay, William. *The Letter to the Hebrews*. Louisville: WJLP, 1976.

Barnes, Albert. *Notes on the New Testament*. Grand Rapids: Kregel, 1962.

Barnhart, Joe E. *Religion and the Challenge of Philosophy*. Lanham: Rowman & Littlefield, 1975.

Buhle, Paul. *From the Lower East Side to Hollywood: Jews in American Culture*. London: Verso, 2004.

Callahan, Timothy. "The Anatomy of Expression: Will Eisner and *A Contract with God*." *Comics Alliance*. April 3, 2013.

Carrier, David. *The Art of Comics*. University Park: Pennsylvania State University Press, 2000.

Chatelain, M. "Contrat de société avec Dieu." *Annales médico-psychologiques*. No. 8, 1866, 66–74.

Constandinides, Costas. *From Film Adaptation to Post-Celluloid Adaptation. Rethinking the Transition of Popular Narratives and Characters across Old and New Media*. New York: Continuum, 2010.

Couch, N. C. Christopher, and Stephen Weiner. *The Will Eisner Companion*. New York: DC Comics, 2004.

Dallago, Carl. *Der große Unwissende*. Innsbruck: Brenner, 1924.
Dauber, Jeremy. "Comic Books, Tragic Stories: Will Eisner's American Jewish History." In *The Jewish Graphic Novel* 2008, 22–42.
de Greef, Guillaume. *Précis de sociologie*. Paris: Alcan, 1909.
Descartes, René. *Meditations on the First Philosophy*. Translated by Donald A. Cress. Fourth edition. Indianapolis: Hackett, 2010 [1641].
Dostoevsky, Fyodor. *The Brothers Karamazov*. Translated by Richard Pevear and Larissa Volokhonsky. San Francisco: North Point Press, 1990 [1880].
Drake, Arnold. "Afterword: The Graphic Novel—And How It Grew." In Arnold Drake, Leslie Waller, Matt Baker, and Ray Osrin, *It Rhymes with Lust*. Milwaukee: Dark Horse, 2007 [1950].129–133.
Dreiser, Theodore. *An American Tragedy*. New York: Boni & Liveright, 1925.
———. "The Tithe of the Lord." *Esquire*. Vol. 10, 1938, 36–37, 150, 155–158.
Duncan, Randy. "A Contract with God." In Randy Duncan and Matthew J. Smith (eds.), *Icons of the American Comic Book: From Captain America to Wonder Woman*. Santa Barbara: ABC-CLIO, 2013. 143–150.
Eisner, Will, *A Contract with God and Other Tenement Stories* (1978). New York: Norton, 2004.
———. *Theory of Comics and Sequential Arts*. Nineteenth printing. Tamarac: Poorhouse, 2000 [1985].
Feiffer, Jules. *The Great Comic Book Heroes*. Seattle: Fantagraphics, 2003 [1963].
Frank, Waldo David. *Memoirs*. Edited by Alan Trachtenberg. Amherst: University of Massachusetts Press, 1973.
Gauthier, David. *Morals By Agreement*. Oxford: Oxford University Press, 1986.
———. *Moral Dealing: Contract, Ethics, and Reason*. Ithaca: Cornell University Press, 1990.
Gayot de Pitaval, François (ed.). *Causes célèbres et intéressantes avec les jugemens qui les ont decidées*. Volume 4. Paris: Legras, 1736. 288–347.
Gordon, Ian, *Comic Strips and Consumer Culture, 1890–1945*. Washington, DC: Smithsonian Institute, 1998.
Green, Diana. "A Building, a Soldier, a Conspiracy: Stylistic and Narrative Evolutions in Three Key Eisner Graphic Novels." *Will Eisner Week* 2010.
Griffin, Joseph. *The Small Canvas. An Introduction to Dreiser's Short Stories*. Rutherford: Farleigh Dickinson University Press, 1985.
Groensteen, Thierry. *Un objet culturel non identifié*. Angoulême: L'An 2, 2006.
Gross, Milt. *Milt Gross' New York*. New York: Yoe Books, 2015 [1938].
Heller, Steven. "Rediscovering a Lost Predecessor to the Graphic Novel." *The Atlantic*, April 2, 2015.
Hescher, Achim. *Reading Graphic Novels: Genre and Narration*. Berlin: de Gruyter, 2016.
Hesse-Quack, Otto. "Die soziale und soziologische Bedeutsamkeit der Comic Strips." In Hans D. Zimmermann (ed.), *Vom Geist der Superhelden*. Berlin: Mann, 1970. 62–71.
Hirsch, Samson Raphael. *Horev, oder Versuche über Jissroél*. Volume 2. Altona: Hammerich, 1837.
Hobbes, Thomas. *Leviathan, or the Matter, Forme, & Power of a Common-Wealth Ecclesiastical and Civill*. London: Crooke, 1651.

Jaissle, Bill. "*Up Front*: How Bill Mauldin's Cartoons Captured the Truth of WWII." *Sequart. org*. December 18, 2014.

Kaczynski, Tom. "Notes on Will Eisner's *The Contract with God* Trilogy." *Will Eisner Week*. March 3, 2010.

Kane, Brian. "Graphic Novels Are Not Literature." *GraphicTextbooks.blogspot.fi*. September 9, 2012.

Kaplan, Arie. *From Krakow to Krypton. Jews and Comic Books*. Philadelphia: The Jewish Publication Society, 2008.

Kaukoranta, Heikki, and Jukka Kemppinen, *Sarjakuvat*. Helsinki: Otava, 1970.

Klingenstein, Susanne. "The Long Roots of Will Eisner's Quarrel with God." *Studies in American Jewish Literature* 26 (2007): 81–88.

Lambert, Josh. "*A Contract with God and Other Tenement Stories* by Will Eisner." In Josh Lambert, *American Jewish Fiction*. Philadelphia: The Jewish Publication Society, 2009. 111–112.

Laytner, Anson. *Arguing with God. A Jewish Tradition*. Lanham: Rowman & Littlefield, 2004.

Levitz, Paul. *Will Eisner: The Champion of the Graphic Novel*. New York: Abrams, 2015.

Liggett, Walter W. *The River Riders*. New York: Macauley, 1928.

Locke, John. *Two Treatises of Government*. New York: Barnes & Noble, 2004 [1689].

Lopes, Paul. *Demanding Respect. The Evolution of the American Comic Book*. Philadelphia: Temple University Press, 2009.

Luciano, Dale. "Will Eisner." In *Conversations*, 2011 [1980]. 87–102.

McCloud, Scott. *Understanding Comics. The Invisible Art*. New York: HarperCollins, 1994.

Malègue, Joseph. *Sous la meule de Dieu*. Paris: Chalet, 1965 [1945].

Mauldin, Bill. *Up Front*. New York: Norton, 2000 [1945].

Miller, Frank. "The *Walk Through* the Rain: *Will Eisner Interview*." In Ben Schwartz (ed.), *The Best American Comics Criticism*. Seattle: Fantagraphics, 2010.

Mosier, Richard David. *American Temper*. Berkeley: University of California Press, 1952.

Novak, David. *The Jewish Social Contract: An Essay in Political Theology*. Princeton: Princeton University Press, 2005.

Ochs, Vanessa L. *Inventing Jewish Ritual*. Philadelphia: The Jewish Publication Society, 2007.

Orlinsky, Harry M. *Ancient Israel*. Second edition. Ithaca: Cornell University Press, 1960 [1954].

Peeters, Benoît. "Four Conceptions of the Page." Translated by Jesse Cohen. *ImageText* 3 (3): 2007 [1988].

Pekelis, Alexander Haim. *Law and Social Action. Selected Essays*. New York: Cornell University Press, 1950.

Petersen, Robert S. *Comics, Manga, and Graphic Novel: A History of Graphic Narratives*. Santa Barbara: Praeger, 2011.

Pinski, David, "Doch einmal geweint." In Artur Landsberger (ed.), *Das Ghettobuch. Die schönsten Geschichten aus dem Ghetto*. München: Müller, 1914. 363–368.

Rankin, H. D. *Plato and the Individual*. London: Routledge, 2013 [1964].

Reingold, Matt. "*A Contract with God*." In M. Keith Booker (ed.), *Comics through Time: A History of Icons, Idols, and Ideas*. Santa Barbara: ABC-CLIO, 2014. 533–534.

Rousseau, Jean-Jacques. *Discourse on the Origin and Basis of Inequality of Among Men.* Translated by G. D. H. Cole. London: Dent 1913 [1755].
———. *Social Contract.* Translated by G. D. H. Cole. London: Dent, 1913.
Royal, Derek Parker. "Sequential Sketches of Ethnic Identity: Will Eisner's *A Contract with God* as Graphic Cycle." *College Literature* 28 (3): 2011, 150–167.
Russell, J. A. *The Power of the Word.* Bloomington: Author House, 2014.
Scanlon, T. S. "Contractualism and Utilitarianism." In Amartya Sen & Bernard Williams (eds.), *Utilitarianism and Beyond.* Cambridge: Cambridge University Press, 1982. 103–128.
———. *What We Owe to Each Other.* Cambridge, MA: Harvard University Press, 1998.
Schelly, Bill. *Founders of Comic Fandom.* Jefferson: McFarland, 2010.
Schjeldahl, Peter. "Words and Pictures: Graphic Novels Come of Age." *New Yorker.* October 17, 2005.
Schmitz-Emans, Monika. "Graphic Narratives as World Literature." In Daniel Stein and Jan-Noël Thon (eds.), *From Comic Strips to Graphic Novels: Contributions to the Theory and History of Graphic Narrative.* Berlin: de Gruyter 2015. 385–406.
Schultz, Samuel J. *Deuteronomy: The Gospel of Love.* Chicago: The Moody Bible Institute, 1971.
Schwartz, Ben. "Mastering the Form: An Interview with Will Eisner." In M. Thomas Inge (ed.), Will Eisner, *Conversations.* Jackson: The University Press of Mississippi. 103–107.
Sheldon, Garrett Ward. "The Philosophical Trinity of Jefferson's Political Theory." In M. Andrew Holowchak (ed.), *Thomas Jefferson and Philosophy.* Lanham: Lexington Books, 2014. 1–14.
Sorokin, Pitirim. *Social and Cultural Dynamics. A Study of Change in Major Systems of Art, Truth, Ethics, Law, and Social Relationships.* New Brunswick: Transaction, 2010 [1941].
Spiegelman, Art. "The Woodcuts of Lynd Ward." *Paris Review.* October 13, 2010.
Suikkanen, Jussi. "Contractualism and the Conditional Fallacy." In Mark Timmons (ed.), *Oxford Studies in Normative Ethics. Vol. 4.* Oxford: Oxford University Press, 2014. 113–137.
Tabachnick, Stephen E. *The Quest for Jewish Belief and Identity in the Graphic Novel.* Tuscaloosa: The University of Alabama Press, 2014.
Ulanovskaya, Bella. "Journey to Kashgar" [1973]. Translated by Catriona Kelly. In Maxim D. Schrayer (ed.), *An Anthology of Jewish Russian Literature: Two Centuries of Dual Identity in Prose and Poetry I–II.* London: Routledge, 2015. 879–896.
Veatch, Robert M. *Case Studies in Medical Ethics.* Cambridge, MA: Harvard University Press, 1977.
Weiner, Stephen. *Faster Than a Speeding Bullet: The Rise of the Graphic Novel.* Second edition. New York: NBM, 2012.
White, Desmond. "Making Love the Will Eisner Way: Intercourse Discourse in *A Contract with God.*" *Sequart Organization.* March 8, 2014.
Yoe, Craig (ed.). *The Complete Milt Gross Comic Books and Life Story.* New York: IDW/Yoe Books, 2010.
Yronwade, Cat. "Will Eisner Interview" (1978). In *Conversations* 2011, 47–78; 71–72.

Further Reading

Fagin the Jew (2003), art and text by Will Eisner.

The Plot. The Secret Story of the Protocols of the Elders of Zion (2005), art and text by Will Eisner.

El Eternauta (1957), art by Francisco Solano López and text by Héctor Germán Oesterheld. An important early graphic novel (albeit first published in a serial form) by the great Argentine writer and collaborator of, for example, Hugo Pratt.

La rivolta dei racchi (1967), art and text by Guido Buzzelli. Classic illustory of societal inequality.

Alois Nebel (2003–2005; 2006), art by Jaromír 99 and text by Jaroslav Rudiš. A Czech book including some of the best contemporary European picto-fiction with powerful scenes and a weird sense of humor reminiscent of, among others, Eisner.

Jimmy Corrigan and the Time of Crisis[1]

Manuel "Mandel" Cabrera Jr.

Philosophical questions are often born of crisis. That is, they tend to arise when the people engaged in an endeavor like science or art face the possibility, not so much that their endeavor won't succeed, but that they don't really understand what success would consist in. For example, in science, we can find ourselves struggling to articulate what our subject matter really is—e.g. as mathematicians, what numbers are; or as physicists, whether we're to study substantial forms or natural laws.[2] Or, we can feel confused as to what modes of investigation, inference, and explanation are apt for understanding that subject matter (e.g. "What makes for a good proof?" or "Are empirical inductions valid?"). Likewise, in art we can struggle to grasp the nature of artworks (e.g. "What makes a collection of sounds music?"); or, to understand what methods, forms, and critical frameworks are appropriate to them.

These are crises of self-understanding. However, they each concern our understanding of something we're *doing*—some collective, embodied set of practices. Thus, to address them, we can't simply turn inward and introspect. Rather, we must inquire into our practices themselves, as well as the things with which we deal when engaging in them. And in many domains, doing so often involves a mixture of self-discovery and self-invention: discoveries about our practices and their objects, but also re-inventions of those practices themselves in light of such discoveries.

In the domain of art in particular, critics of course undertake this labor. They attempt, for example, to formulate satisfactory accounts of what painting or poetry are, or to figure out which critical approaches to such works are most illuminating. However, many artists think that confronting such questions is part of the process of artmaking itself. On this view, art is always art about art, at least when it's at its best. That is, an artist should, through her artworks themselves, and not just through theoretical discourse about them, pose questions about or even take a stand on the nature of those artworks as well as of the artistic activity that produced them. When she does so, she treats artmaking as an activity in perpetual crisis—one that's perpetually struggling to understand itself. And this is cause for celebration rather than anxiety, because part of what makes art vibrant rather than stagnant is the artist's commitment to exposing herself to a fundamental sense of uncertainty about what she's doing—never taking for granted that it's a settled question what the nature of her own medium or genre, or of art in general, really is.

Yet the onset of such a consciousness can be precipitated by a sense of crisis that seems threatening rather than tantalizing. There's perhaps no better example of this than what's happened in the last century among artists working in popular genres like science fiction, fantasy, and horror; and in popular media like comics. Such artists have often been routinely dismissed as creating mere entertainment rather than genuine art. And while they've sometimes resigned themselves to or even embraced this accusation, sometimes in response they've tried to resist it by rallying around new labels. New labels for a genre or medium can describe it in ways that jettison popular misconceptions about it, express its distinctive character and promise, as well as overcome its ghettoization by integrating it into the history of the arts. And in doing so, such labels can serve as vehicles for reflective engagement in both criticism and artmaking itself, helping us understand and make works of art in new ways.

For example, whereas the term "fantasy" has often carried the suggestion that the genre is merely an avenue for escapism, J. R. R. Tolkien's term "mythopoeia" casts it as a literary form that taps into one of the original wellsprings of literature: the practice of crafting and recounting myths. Indeed, as Tolkien understood the genre, it does so more directly than any other literary form, since the mythopoeic writer's principal creation isn't a text, but rather an entire world. Likewise, many have used Robert Heinlein's term "speculative fiction" to suggest that various forms of imaginative fiction are unified by a common methodology: speculation about ways the world could be that are fundamentally different from our own. This methodology is restricted neither to its application to any particular subject matter (as suggested by "science fiction"), nor to its production of any particular psychological effect (as suggested by "fantasy" and "horror"). Thus, the term reveals how strikingly broad the possibilities for imaginative fiction really are.

Now, it might seem hyperbolic to say that these critical stances and the artistic production that has marched under their banners can be called philosophical. However, they're at the very least proto-philosophical. What we have here in each case is an attempt to articulate the nature of some activity and its objects. Of course, such attempts don't always take discursive forms we'd recognize to be philosophy as such. This is especially evident when they take the form of artmaking itself—an activity that can't plausibly be reduced to presenting and arguing for theses at all. However, they're continuous with the work of philosophers of art: they attempt to make sense of the nature of this or that artistic endeavor.

In this respect, we can recognize in popular art the same struggle for self-understanding to be found in highbrow art. But in the former case, this struggle has often been troubled by systematic insecurity and self-doubt. As illustrated by the examples from Tolkien and Heinlein, popular artists can indeed be found articulating their work in terms of lofty aesthetic ambitions. But in the face of pervasive critical derision, they can also find themselves doubting whether their art is up to the task of achieving these ambitions; or, resenting having been made to feel the need to justify themselves in first place, and becoming skeptical that their art stands in need of "elevation" just to appease a crowd of snobs who marginalize or dismiss their work.[3]

For our purposes, the most important examples of such ambivalent proto-philosophical reflection on popular art concern the medium of comics, for which Will Eisner's term "sequential art" has served as a rallying point. Eisner urged that, despite what the word "comics" might suggest, the medium is capable of much more than providing trivial amusement. Just as Tolkien did for fantasy, Eisner used his term to argue that they're the modern guise of "an ancient form of art."[4] And just as was done using the term "speculative fiction," he characterized this art formally—as one that "deals with the arrangement of pictures or images and words to narrate a story or dramatize an idea."[5] This allows us to see, he thought, that comics are no more restricted in their aesthetic potential than any of their forebears.

But if Eisner's term really expresses genuine insight about comics, how should we develop that insight? Below, I'll consider his label with a view to clarifying the distinctive forms of sequentiality in comics, which, I'll argue, concern how they present and are presented in time. However, my ultimate goal will be to look for insight on these matters in the ways artists themselves have, through their works, struggled with the nature and possibilities of the medium. In particular, I'll turn to one of the most outstanding examples of this: Chris Ware's *Jimmy Corrigan: the Smartest Kid on Earth*.

At the book's thematic center are the ways we experience and respond to time. This plays out in the story of the Corrigan men—in the ways each of them relates to his individual and familial history during key moments of crisis. However, Ware juxtaposes this main narrative with two others: one concerning the history of modern America; the other, the history of comics. In part, this simply allows him to frame the historical concerns of the main narrative. But that narrative, in turn, shapes the book's treatment of these broader historical contexts. That is, the Corrigan men's uncertainty about how to understand the past and face the future is reflected by an uncertainty of the same kind about comics—their nature, their history, and their place in modern American culture. In other words, the book articulates crises of self-understanding at both the micro level of individual characters and the macro level of artistic and national identity. Yet in the latter case, rather than crumbling in the face of this crisis, Ware rises to meet its challenge. In particular, he does so formally: by exploiting the medium's dormant possibilities to address the book's historical concerns in ways that would be impossible in other media. That is, he confronts the sense of crisis about comics precisely by showing that they're distinctively suited to conveying our relationship to time—to history, and the crises we face in relation to it.

Sequence and Time

Let's first try to understand what I've called the "dormant possibilities" of comics by considering Eisner's term more carefully.[6] Even at first blush, it's obvious how the notion of sequence applies to comics, because they're made up of arranged images. However, the same can be said of many other media: e.g. painting, sculpture, and film. Thus, we need to make the notion of sequence we use to characterize comics more precise. We can do so by taking note of the kinds of images contained in comics, as well as the various ways they're ordered.

First, the images in comics are pictorial rather than plastic. That is, they're images inscribed on some surface rather than constructed by manipulating some plastic medium.[7] This distinguishes comics from plastic arts like sculpture. Further, while various pictorial media use images to represent motion, they do so in different ways. Comics contain perceptually *static* images exclusively, while films contain perceptually *dynamic* ones: i.e. we as spectators perceive the images in comics to be motionless, whereas we perceive many film images to be moving.[8]

What, though, distinguishes sequential art from other pictorial arts that employ ordered, perceptually static images? To answer this question, let's distinguish two kinds of image ordering that serve different but related functions in comics. First, there's an ordering among images that characterizes the organization in time of the events that they represent—e.g. the order in which various events in the story occur. Second, the image ordering in a comic dictates the order in which the reader is to take in images. That is, given that I'm at a certain point in the reading process—e.g. looking at a certain image on a certain page—the image ordering mandates where to proceed next. Let's call these two kinds of ordering *narrative ordering* and the *reader ordering*, respectively.[9]

Both have to do with time, but in different ways. Narrative ordering concerns how images present time—i.e., the temporal properties of and relationships among the things and events that those images represent. Reader ordering, in contrast, concerns how images are presented *in* time—i.e. over the course of the temporally extended reading process. The two orderings are often intimately related. For example, we often find cases in which we're to look at image A first, and image B next, where B portrays events that happen after those portrayed in A. However, the two orderings can also diverge: e.g. if B begins a flashback, then even though we're to look at A first, the events that B portrays occur before the ones that A does. Thus, the two orderings are distinct. Nevertheless, what's distinctive about comics is that in them, both are constituted by arranging images in *space*—most commonly, on the surface of a page. Art Spiegelman has expressed this point elegantly by saying that "cartooning is the art of turning time back into space."[10]

Now, in a typical comic, both orderings are established in large part through a range of conventions for spatial organization that have developed over the course of the medium's history. Let's start by considering reader ordering. In its most conventional forms, it has various aspects, which we might consider from the smallest scale to the largest. First of all, within a panel or splash page, there are ordering conventions: e.g. thought and speech bubbles are typically to be read roughly from top to bottom and left to right. Panels, in turn, are conventionally organized in like manner on a page: i.e. we're to read them roughly from top to bottom and left to right. And in a multi-page comic, pages are ordered so that one begins reading it by opening the volume with the spine to the left and turning pages from there.[11]

Thus, the most common conventions for reader ordering in comics are very similar to those for prose text. Of course, I'm speaking here about comics in English and other Western languages. Interestingly, though, we find a closely analogous correspondence between comics and prose conventions in Japanese *manga*. In traditional Japanese *tategaki* writing, text is written from top to bottom in vertical columns ordered from right to left; and pages are ordered in volumes in such a way that one begins reading a volume by opening it with the spine to the right. Likewise, in *manga*, panels and elements within them are conventionally to be read from right to left and top to bottom; and pages are ordered in just the way that they are in prose volumes. It's also noteworthy that Korean comics (*manhwa*) have been much more decisively influenced by *manga* than by Western comics. Yet modern Korean prose observes the same conventions of reader ordering as in English; and correspondingly, *manhwa* do as well.

Such correspondences are, of course, no coincidence: the conventions for comics partly piggyback on those for prose, so that readers can apply their prose literacy skills in reading comics. Because of this influence, reader ordering in conventional comics is, as in prose text, largely both *determinate* and *linear*. It's determinate in the sense that in the reading process as dictated by reader ordering, given that the reader is at any particular point in the process, there are some particular "next steps" she can take. And it's linear in that, supposing that the reader is at a point A in the process, there's a unique next step B she's to take, which in turn has A as its unique previous step. In other words, given that a comic is finite, one begins reading it at *the* beginning, and then takes in the images one by one in a certain order until one reaches *the* end.

Of course, like comics, film is a pictorial art in which images are organized so as to establish "reader" orderings.[12] And indeed, comics have been just as influenced by film as by prose. However, this influence hasn't, by itself, undermined the tendency toward determinate and linear reader orderings, since conventionally, such orderings in film are also determinate and linear: one begins watching at the beginning of the film, and the images play in a particular order in linear succession until one reaches the end.

If such details seem obvious, this is perhaps because no other modes of reader ordering have occurred to many readers. One important result has been that the construction of narrative ordering in narrative comics has leaned heavily on techniques from prose and film. Specifically, because reader ordering in these latter two media is conventionally both linear and determinate, they've traditionally lent themselves to narrative orderings that are as well. First, the default narrative mode in both media is to represent events in the determinate, linear order in which events are ordered in time. Second, a host of formal techniques have developed to communicate this order when it doesn't correspond directly to reader ordering—e.g., special signals to readers when the narrative portrays events that happen at roughly the same time as ones just recounted; or when it flashes forward or back. Narrative comics have emulated prose and film techniques in both respects. Just like movies or novels, they usually tell linear stories from beginning to end; and when diverging from this, they employ flashbacks or cut back and forth between simultaneous narratives to keep us clear about the timeline.[13]

But suppose we agree that comics constitute a pictorial medium in which "time is turned into space"—that is, in which perceptually static images are spatially organized in order to produce reader orderings, and on the basis of this narrative ones. This, we should notice, doesn't by itself restrict comics to determinate and linear orderings. This fact is significant because failing to see that the medium has a nature quite different from both prose and film can blind us to possibilities for conceiving of comics on their own terms—a lacuna in understanding that has been a roadblock to sequential art's ability to distinguish itself as a medium.

But there's cause for puzzlement in what I've said so far. Perhaps reader orderings need not be determinate and linear. However, the structure of time is both. That is, at least as we ordinarily think if it, there's a *chronological* order to events. And so what would it even mean for narrative ordering—the organization of a story's events in time—to be indeterminate and non-linear? As I'll argue below, Chris Ware provides an answer in *Jimmy Corrigan*. That is, he thematizes historical consciousness—the ways in which his characters, as well as the social milieu surrounding them, make sense of things in terms of the histories in which they understand themselves to be imbedded. But a historical consciousness isn't just a chronology: as we experience, conceive of, and actively engage with it, historical time has a far richer structure. To capture this structure, Ware employs unconventional reader orderings, thereby dramatizing historical consciousness in distinctive ways. It's in this sense that he exploits dormant possibilities of comics to accomplish the work of the book—in particular, to comment upon crises of self-understanding that arise for his characters, for the culture at large, and for the creators and readers of comics.

Historical Consciousness in *Jimmy Corrigan*

To understand how Ware accomplishes this, we can begin by sketching *Jimmy Corrigan*'s treatment of history. Initially, the title's reference might seem obvious: Jimmy is the child introduced at the beginning; and the anxious, lonely man that we see he becomes. However, by the end we know that this Jimmy is in effect simply Jimmy III, whose father and grandfather are also named James Corrigan. And by interweaving the stories of their lives, the book makes it clear that its title refers not so much to any one of them as to the trajectory of their family's history—a trajectory of decay rather than progress. The book is a kind of anti-*Bildungsroman* unfolding over nearly a century, and tracing a history in which what begins as Jimmy I's desperate longing for love atrophies and rots until it becomes in Jimmy III a total incapacity, not just to seek out human connection, but even to accept it when it's offered.

In many ways, the book presents this narrative quite conventionally, shifting back and forth between the story of Jimmy III's encounter in 1991 with the father he's never met; and that of Jimmy I's early childhood in 1893 with a father who's present, yet cold and abusive.[14] Yet Ware also employs reader orderings that are indeterminate and non-linear in crucial sections. Scattered through the book, we find: a spread of tiny postcards portraying the imaginary town of Waukosha, Michigan; cut-out paper models of a zoopraxiscope,[15] a house, and Jimmy III himself; and several of the diagram-like tableaux so distinctive to Ware, which can be read using any number of starting and ending points, tracing many different paths along the way. These sections are unconventional, and can seem marginal to the main course of the narrative. However, their importance shouldn't be overlooked, because they're the means by which Ware situates the Corrigan family history in relation to the history of modern America and of comics.

Why are the latter two histories so important for understanding the book? We can begin by noting that, just as in the history of the Corrigan family, in both of them we find a trajectory of decay—from grandiose ambitions to exhausted impotence. And this isn't just a trajectory of change *through* time—from 1893 to 1991—but also one in which what changes concerns our relationship *to* time—i.e. concerns the ways in which we relate our past, present and future to one another in the historical narratives that shape our experience and action.

The book jacket introduces us to the grand stage of American history. It unfolds into a large double-sided sheet—by far, the most complex Warian tableau in the book.[16] There, Jimmy III's life is presented as a matter of world-historical importance. At the center of the inner side is an image of the Earth surrounded by a complex diagram of the Corrigan family history. Various episodes are indexed to locations on the map, and although the diagram reaches back to Colonial America and is replete with tributaries and distributaries, it ultimately converges on minutiae of Jimmy III's existence. At the center of the jacket's outer side, this existence is vastly expanded. The spherical head of Jimmy III as a child is accorded the same size and position as the Earth on the inner side; and surrounded by an array of images shot through with a web of lines interlinking aspects of his life, just as episodes in the history of his forebears are on the other side. In other words, his importance is pictorially equated to that of everything that precedes him.

However, there's a palpable ironic tension between this hyper-aggrandized vision of Jimmy III and the man it actually portrays. We see Jimmy III's pitiable character conveyed in the drawing of his face as a child—with eyes framed by the lines of discomfort and anxiety that will dominate every image we see of him from here on out. We see a sexuality dominated by unrequited fantasy, uncertainty, and anxiety. We see his relationship to a mother whose daily phone calls are the closest things in his life to authentic human connection; and to a father whose absence he imagines in terms of a superhero's anonymity. We see a typical day in his isolated life, and a comically inept lonely hearts ad by him in place of the usual book jacket blurb.

In these ways, the grandiose depiction of Jimmy III is at the same time made ridiculous and pathetic. However, this same irony is reproduced in the narrative of American history within which his family lineage is situated. Jimmy I's story unfolds against the backdrop of the final preparations for the 1893 World's Columbian Exposition, whose master narrative was one of civilizational progress. It harkened back to a great European past, but only to paint a picture of a bright American future toward which it was leading: the U.S., at the frontier of human endeavor, guiding us toward ever increasing scientific, technological, and artistic sophistication.

Once we turn to 1991, though, this vision of triumphant modernity crumbles. Waukosha—the nowhere town where Jimmy III meets his father for the first time—is made to embody this failure by a series of mock postcards depicting places of which no one would ever want a postcard: freeway stops, unremarkable restaurants, etc.—all dreary, all devoid of people.[17] Yet each image's caption describes it reverently: a discount store is a "beneficent reminder of the commercial bloodlines which bind us all together," and a tiny clinic is "a truly modern, yet nostalgic scene of Midwestern modesty and efficiency."[18] And throughout, it's made clear that the town's past has been effaced to pave the way for this bleak, modernized future.

In this way, the promise of modernity championed by the great 1893 Exposition is portrayed as one that turned out to be treacherous. At the forefront of the book's portrayal of this treachery is the history of comics as framed by the front endpapers. There, comics are accorded a privileged place in art history: "the culmination of over two thousand years of civilized endeavor, and the highest expression of man's achievement yet to appear."[19] This art began, we're told, in ancient Mesopotamia. However, its development was stalled when Homer, described as an ancient con man, began using a primitive notation system for financial record-keeping to cheat people of their money. And "thus was born 'literature,' and the means by which to fashion all manner of falsehood and perjury."[20] Only now that the long Dark Ages that Homer initiated are over have comics risen again in an 'Age of Enlightenment.' The traditional marginalization of comics is thus inverted: we're told that literature had for centuries deceived its way into our high regard, but also that comics are now winning the day.[21]

Ware situates the advent of this Age of Enlightenment squarely in the Chicago Exposition as portrayed in the book—specifically, in Eadweard Muybridge's renowned "Zoöpraxicographical Hall," where Muybridge displayed the results of his photographic studies of animal motion—most famously, a series of still photographs through which he proved that all four of a galloping horse's hooves leave the ground at once during every stride. These studies are typically understood as precursors to cinema. And indeed, Muybridge used his zoopraxiscope to simulate motion just as it's simulated in cinema: through a quick succession of still images. However, for Muybridge, the zoopraxiscope's importance lay in its ability, not to *create* illusions of motion, but rather to *expose* them for what they are. By laying out momentary photographs of a horse's gallop side-by-side in sequence, he revealed what we can't ordinarily see when the world simply moves before us. In other words, he used the technological marvel of high speed photography to "turn time back into space"—to traverse time, and overcome its deceptions.

Thus, as Ware depicts Muybridge's innovations, they're precisely instances of sequential art; and, they perfectly exemplify the hope that his imaginary history of comics holds out for the medium. That is, they reveal the world as it is, in contrast to the "pre-modern" literature that dissimulates it. And in doing so, they're simply one manifestation of the Exposition's vision: they present a paradisaically comprehensible future made possible by technology.

However, if we return to the front endpapers, we find this majestic conception of sequential art undermined almost as soon as it's articulated. We're told there that it "holds no hope of ever expressing anything but the meanest and most shallow of sentiments"; and that it's only been through a "dive in the general intelligence of the populace" that comics literacy is now enjoying a resurgence, allowing for new ways to exploit people: "Dumb people are eating it up. . . . They love it. Especially people who buy a lot of stuff. This could be big."[22]

What's being expressed here, albeit in a tongue-in-cheek way, is a profound ambivalence about comics—the ambivalence of the devoted artist. First, there's the conviction that the medium can hold onto lofty artistic aims. But on the heels of this conviction there follows a deep insecurity—the nagging worry that such aspirations are absurd; that comics will never be more than amusements for the barely literate. And once we turn back again to 1991 in the main body of the book, this insecurity isn't challenged but rather confirmed. In the lives of Jimmy II and Jimmy III, comics, along with other contemporary media, are merely cold comforts: superheroes are escapist fantasies, and movies only reinforce the boundaries between people through which they avoid genuine connections with one another.

Again, what we have here is a parallel movement—from 1893 to 1991; from the overblown optimism of the Exposition to its disappointing fulfilment in modern America; from Muybridge's grand revelations to the banal distractions of contemporary comics and video rental stores. And in each case, we're carried from grandiose hopes all the way to the bleak exhaustion of all hope. Because of this, the shift from 1893 to 1991 is more than a shift from one historical period to another: it is, I will suggest, a shift from one kind of viewpoint on history to another. The structure of time, in other words—the shape of history and our own place therein—looks different from these two kinds of viewpoint.

In order to understand better how Ware's formal conceits are important for his treatment of history in *Jimmy Corrigan* we need a better handle on the difference between these two structures. However, to do so, it's useful to first look at the continuity between them. Thus, another philosophical detour is in order. Specifically, we'll consider one important way in which our conception of history can shape our view of ourselves and the world, which we can understand using the concept of *kairotic time*.

Historical Consciousness and Kairotic Time[23]

Kairotic time is a way in which time can be understood to be ordered: (a) according to our practical concerns; where (b) we take this order to be determined in part by our place in history; and more specifically (c) by our sense that we're at a crisis point in history that demands decisive action of us. To understand this characterization, let's consider each part in turn.

We can begin by noting that the term derives from the Greek word *kairos*, used in ancient rhetoric and philosophy to refer to opportune or appropriate times for action. In rhetoric, for example, it was used to refer to those moments that a *rhetor* (a master of the art of rhetoric) knows how to seize in order to persuade his audience—using just the right rhetorical techniques at just the right times.[24] In other words, *kairos* was used to express the idea that a *rhetor* is perceptive concerning a certain dimension of time: he can perceive the time during which he speaks as structured according to what is and isn't appropriate in the situation. He can see, for example, that there's a time to bow his head solemnly, and a time to use grand gestures; or a time to soothe his audience with hushed tones, and a time to shock them with a jarring outburst.

This is aspect (a) of kairotic time. We often understand time as being organized according to the practical demands of the context. We see it in terms of "times to" and "times not to"—a dimension of experience aptly expressed in a famous passage from Ecclesiastes:

> There is a time for everything, and a season for every activity under the heavens: a time to be born and a time to die, a time to plant and a time to uproot, a time to kill and a time to heal.[25]

The idea, then, is that moments and periods in time strike us as calling for certain kinds of action and abstention; as opening up particular activities as appropriate and closing off others as forbidden. This way of understanding time is, in fact, pervasive—for example, when we think the weekdays are a time to work, while the Sabbath isn't; or that Mardi Gras is a time for raucous joy, while the anniversary of a mass death is a time for solemn reflection.

The *rhetor* simply has, in the domain of rhetoric, insight into a kind of temporal structure found in other domains. Other skills involve the same kind of insight in other domains. As we sometimes put it: they require a good sense of timing.[26] A skilled doctor has a good sense of timing in the domain of medicine—knowing when, for example, to administer a treatment, and when to let the symptoms take their course. Or, a skilled general has it in the domain of military strategy—e.g. knowing when it's time to attack, and when it's time to retreat. Now, the most general domain, in an important sense, is that of one's life as a whole. And here, too, the Greeks applied the notion of *kairos*. For Aristotle, for example, living well requires a kind of understanding that he called *phronêsis* ("practical wisdom"). And a practically wise person has in the most general way what the *rhetor* has in rhetoric, the skilled doctor in medicine, and the general in military strategy: an understanding of what Aristotle called *ho kairos*—the good in respect of time. In other words, she has a good sense of timing when it comes to living life in general, understanding how to feel and act at any given time.[27]

This sort of temporal understanding—a sense of timing—requires a grasp of much more than chronological order. Chronological order concerns only the placement of things on a timeline—e.g. when and for how long things happen, as well as which events take place before or after which others. In contrast, understanding *ho kairos* (to use Aristotle's term) involves grasping time in a richer way—in short, in terms of its practical significance.

Aspects (b) and (c) of kairotic time trace back to a more specific application of the notion of *kairos*—namely, in Christian theology, where the ancient Greek word comes up for discussion largely because of its use in the

New Testament.[28] For example, after the transformative experiences of his baptism and temptation in the wilderness, Jesus embarks on his work as the Christ: "Jesus went into Galilee, proclaiming the good news of God. 'The time [*kairos*] has come,' he said. 'The kingdom of God has come near. Repent and believe the good news!'"[29] "The time" here designates the right time for us to do certain things—repent and believe. However, this demand is determined by our being in a very specific context.

We can understand this context by looking at some important elements of Christian theology—especially of the millenarian sort. The notion that "the time has come" here makes sense against the background of a certain conception of history—namely, Christian providential history. According to this history, the people whom Jesus was addressing—his contemporaries, but also all of us who've come afterward—live at a crucial historical moment. The messiah, the Christ, has come; and he not only announces but also makes possible (through sacrificing his life) both the imminent arrival of God's kingdom, and the salvation that will result. Thus, unlike those who came before Christ's crucifixion, we live in the most critical period of universal history—the end times, when God's kingdom is soon on its way; and during this period, Christ's sacrifice offers us a sacred gift—the gift of grace—that we can either accept or reject.

Christian theology here manifests a more general tendency—namely, for our sense of timing to be shaped by our conception of history and our place in it. This tendency shows up at the level of individual history. For example, when I think of my wedding anniversary as a day to celebrate, it's because I understand myself to occupy a certain place in a certain history—the history of my relationship to my wife. We can also find the tendency at work at the level of collective history. For example, in the U.S., Memorial Day is designated as a day to honor those members of the U.S. armed forces who've died in the line of duty. Here, a collective sense of timing—of what we (citizens of the U.S.) are to do at a certain time—is shaped by a conception of our collective history—that of the U.S., understood as a nation whose continued prosperity is something that we enjoy, and that is made possible by brave military sacrifice.

This is aspect (b) of kairotic time: time as we understand it according to our practical concerns (i.e. using our sense of timing); but more specifically, where that sense of timing is, in turn, shaped by our historical consciousness—our understanding of history and our place therein. This dimension of experience is likewise pervasive. The relationships one has lived with; the promises one has made; the commitments one has undertaken; the national, cultural, religious, and institutional traditions one has inherited—all of these are among the things that matter a great deal to people in their understandings of how to live, including in their understandings of *ho kairos*: their senses of timing. And so, we might, as a contribution to the Aristotelian project of understanding the wise person's sense of timing, ask the question: how ought we to think of our individual and collective histories, and live in light of them? In fact, this is a fundamental question in the philosophy of history, which we might call the question of the *ethics of history*.

As Christians sees things, providential history provides an answer to this question. Because of our place in universal history, the time of any human life is to be spent laboring at a single fundamental task: that of recognizing and accepting the gift of grace so as to partake in God's imminently arriving kingdom. But as the theologian and philosopher Paul Tillich observed, elements of this view have had a monumental influence beyond the sphere of theology.[30] This influence shows up, he thought, in a consistent tendency in the Western tradition to embrace views of history and its ethics that are, in an important sense, apocalyptic.

The Christian view is apocalyptic in the sense that it tells us that the present historical moment is a time of crisis—a tipping point, when we face the imminent prospect of world-altering change, and decisive action is demanded of us. As it's sometimes put, from this viewpoint, "the end is nigh," and the present is a "kairotic moment"—a "come to Jesus moment" we must confront. And although the word "apocalypse" nowadays signifies disaster, the end that Christians have in mind has more to do with the word's etymological origins in the Greek word *apokalypsis*: a revelation that is, quite the contrary, the inspiration for all genuine hope.

Likewise—and likely due, at least in part, to Christianity's influence—apocalyptic narratives are widespread in the Western tradition. Sometimes (as in many scenarios from speculative fiction), they portray massive disasters, such as destructive natural occurrences, invasions, or plagues. However, in line with the Christian conception, sometimes the world-changing future events to which they look are invested with rapturous hopefulness—e.g. the prospect of a revolution of the proletariat, or of a gleaming ultra-modern future. And sometimes, the radical changes they anticipate aren't in the world at large, but in the life of single person—as when we talk about someone's "world falling apart." The more examples one notices, the more it can seem that the notion of world-altering, watershed moments calling for life-altering decisions is one of the central myths of Western culture—one that is propagated, not just in art, literature, and film, but in political discourse, and the ways people conceive of their own lives.

This, finally, is aspect (c) of kairotic time. When we think of time kairotically, we have a certain kind of historical consciousness, and thus a certain perspective on the ethics of history. Namely, our understanding of what we're called to do in the present is shaped by an apocalyptic conception of history. We take ourselves to be living in a time of crisis, when the world as we know it is ending; so that as a result, we face problems or tasks that are of enormous significance for the world-changing future that we're facing. If Tillich is right that this conception of time is a fundamental one in the Western tradition, then it deserves careful attention in the ethics of history. Should we understand time kairotically? If so, why, how, and in what cases? And what difference would doing so make to how we live, both individually and collectively?

Comics and Kairotic Time in *Jimmy Corrigan*

Jimmy Corrigan is concerned with questions like these. The book is a drama of apocalypse in the above sense, and at both the individual and collective levels. It dramatizes the emergence of apocalyptic conceptions of history, as well as the kairotic moments they bring forth—in the lives of its characters, but also in our received understandings of modern history and the history of comics that's situated therein. And as it does so, it provokes the question of how we have and ought to respond to such moments—i.e. the question of the ethics of history as it pertains to kairotic time.

First, at the individual level, the book's two main storylines each culminate in a personal crisis. And for both Jimmy I and Jimmy III, the father is both the focal point of that crisis, and the figure who embodies the history that's led them to it.

The story of Jimmy I's increasingly alienated relationship with his father William is also the story of William's loosening bonds with his familial past. William's mother dies, and in the inheritance struggle that follows, he also loses his family home and his personal ties to the rest of his family. As a result, he falls into dire straits. He begins living in relative prosperity, but ends up in a shabby boarding house room with his son—eating canned food, bathing in a bucket, and having sex with a prostitute on the floor. In all of this, Jimmy I is helplessly carried along. As the principal target of William's resentment, he's pulled ever deeper into isolation and despair; until at last, William abandons him at the Exposition, and he's left to face a future that's terrifyingly untethered from the past.

Jimmy III's moment of crisis similarly disconnects him from a past dominated by the specter of his father, and thus by that of his familial history. Though Jimmy II has been absent from Jimmy III's life, he's nevertheless been a ubiquitous presence therein by way of the figure of the Super-Man–a TV superhero who's served as his metonym in Jimmy III's mind since childhood. This figure serves as a focal point for an imaginative understanding of his own life's history through which Jimmy III has shielded himself from the outside world. That is, having taken comfort as a child in this imaginary substitute for his real father, he's lived a life in which his escapes into fantasy serve as his primary solace from—but also the primary cause of—his own loneliness. Thus, even though the sudden appearance of his real father promises to bring into Jimmy III's life the sense of connection he's wanted for so long, it also threatens to destroy this imaginary father on whom his sense of his own past and of how to cope with life depend. So, even though Jimmy III consents to meet Jimmy II, internally he rebels, fantasizing all manner of ways to exit the situation. And at the end, his father's death provides him the escape route he seeks, and he bolts from Waukosha at the first opportunity.

In this way, each storyline culminates in a kairotic moment. Each protagonist is thrust into circumstances where it seems that his world is coming to an end. The precipitating event is different in each case: for Jimmy I, it's when his father leaves his life; while for Jimmy III, it's when his father enters it. However, in both cases, the result is the same: precisely through the actions of his father, each becomes alienated from a conception of himself and his life history that's anchored in the figure of that father. That is, the reality in which he finds himself is one to which that conception simply no longer applies: for Jimmy I, because his father's abandonment severs all ties to his past; and for Jimmy III, because he discovers that his father is nothing like the superhero he fantasized him to be. Consequently, each is confronted with a radically uncertain future that puts into question his sense of timing—i.e. whether he understands how to face up to the frightening, exhilarating, potentially life-altering significance of this moment.

Much of *Jimmy Corrigan*'s appeal stems from these two stories of personal apocalypse—intimate dramas of characters losing their past and being called to face a seemingly alien future. However, the drama of these confrontations with kairotic time derives, in part, from the large-scale histories that Ware uses to frame them. And this is because these histories are themselves apocalyptic; each of them, that is, stages the same sort of confrontation.

In the Chicago Exposition's narrative of American progress, the U.S. stood at the vanguard of Western civilization—the culmination and torch-bearer of its progress. And in its majestic architecture; in its numerous exhibitions of art, music, technology, and science; in its sheer scale, the Exposition issued a patriotic rallying call: to bear witness to and bring forth the bold new future in which America fulfills its world-historical role. By doing so, the Exposition placed a demand, as it were, on the nation's sense of timing: that

Americans collectively rise up to the challenge of the times and take up their place in history.

Ware's imaginative history of comics similarly stages a kairotic moment. It tells us that we live at a turning point in art history, when the sequential art that for millennia has been suppressed by the deceptions of literature is finally being reborn. In doing so, it issues its own rallying cry: for practitioners and connoisseurs of the art to live up to the promise of this rebirth.

In the bombast with which these calls to action are expressed, it's clear that they're meant to be, at the collective level, every bit as poignant as the ones that Jimmy I and Jimmy III face at the individual level. In fact, this poignancy precisely serves to intensify the kairotic moment that each of these characters faces—namely, by way of strong associations between the two large-scale historical narratives and the two paternal figures. On the one hand, William isn't just one of the laborers building the Exposition. More specifically, he's working to construct Muybridge's Zoopraxographical Hall—the exact location where Muybridge unveiled the results of his studies of animal motion to the public, and thus the matrix of the rebirth of which Ware's speculative history of comics speaks. On the other hand, in Jimmy III's fantasized version of him, Jimmy II embodies the single most culturally prominent image from comics: the superhero. More specifically, he's a version of Superman—an instance of (and in Jimmy III's fantasies, surrounded by) the retro-futuristic imagery through which American culture has often imagined its own historical destiny. Because of these associations, William and Jimmy II acquire, in the imaginations of their sons, a kind of mythic stature—embodiments of the apocalyptic narratives against whose background the stories of Jimmy I and Jimmy III unfold.

We're then left with the question: in what does the difference between the viewpoints of 1893 and 1991 consist? In section 2, that is, I claimed that the book depicts the historical shift from the former period to the latter as the shift from grandiose hopefulness to numb exhaustion. What light, if any, can the continuity between *Jimmy Corrigan*'s individual and collective narratives—their dramatization of kairotic time—shed on this shift? What I want to suggest is that it's here that we see the ethical-historical stakes of the book. That is, the difference between hopefulness and exhaustion that it portrays is the difference between two ways of responding to kairotic moments.

The hopefulness of 1893 is encapsulated at the climax of Jimmy I's story, when his father abandons him on the roof of the Manufactures and Liberal Arts Building. This is the most tragic moment in a book chock-full of them. But at the same time, it's also the moment when Jimmy I becomes free of his life's greatest obstacle—his father's cruelty. He's left horrifyingly alone, yes, but also to look out toward the promise of the future, expressed as it is the vast Exposition grounds, which he sees in the grandest way possible—from atop the world's largest building.

The hopelessness of 1991 is likewise encapsulated at the climax of Jimmy III's story. In contrast to his grandfather, he flees the promise of the future rather than facing it. Despite his desperate longing for love and familial connection, he runs away from the new possibilities with which he's faced—away from Amy and the elderly Jimmy I in Waukosha, and away from his mother and her new fiancé. Unable to face his barren apartment, he goes to his workplace, where he meets his new co-worker Tammy. The book ends as she invites him to Thanksgiving dinner, and we're left to wonder what he'll decide.

The contrast between these two kinds of response is a contrast in the ethics of history. In noticing the contrast between Jimmy I and Jimmy III, we can't help but wonder how to evaluate each their respective ways of facing the future. The question is far from trivial. For we might ask: are the hopes that Jimmy I embraces—which, by association, aren't just his own individual hopes, but also those touted in the histories of American and of comics—worth embracing? As we've seen, the book expresses both optimism and pessimism about these hopes. Thus, while Jimmy III's flight from the promises of the past can seem cowardly and self-destructive, it can also seem like a flight from promises that were barren and deceptive all along; so that his encounter with something completely new (in the form of Tammy) holds out the real promise: that of a genuine break with the past, unhindered by historical delusions.

It's because *Jimmy Corrigan* deals with such issues that it's a drama of apocalypse—one that addresses the ethics of understanding history kairotically. And in the book's staging of this drama, Ware's formal innovations occupy a central role. That is, in order for the book to articulate the kairotic conceptions of history that form its backbone, its images must convey things about how the past, present, and future are related that go far beyond their orderings on a chronological timeline. And as we've seen, Ware accomplishes much of this in those key sections—e.g. the book jacket, the endpapers, the postcard spread, and the various papers models scattered throughout—where he transcends a preoccupation with chronology by transcending the determinate and linear reader orderings conventionally used to convey it. In doing so, he embraces a hope of his own: he doesn't directly answer the ethical-historical questions he raises, but rather demonstrates that his medium is well-suited to reflecting on them, because in its visual rhetoric, it allows us to dramatize non-chronological dimensions of our understanding of time.

Conclusion

In light of my proposed reading of *Jimmy Corrigan*, we can discern a development from Eisner to Spiegelman to Ware, in which the nature of comics is articulated with increasing precision. Eisner recognizes, in his definition, that the medium's formal distinctiveness lies in the sequential arrangement of images. In his definition, Spiegelman, in turn, hones in on what's special about such sequences: as I put it above, the fact that they order how images present and are presented in time. And finally, Ware frees Spiegelman's insight from its conventional constraints, demonstrating that comics' capacity for presenting time is richer than their historical dependence on the conventions of prose and film might lead us to believe—precisely because time itself as we experience it is richer than what can be captured in a mere chronology.

In my account of this last step in the story, I've offered a kind of philosophical reconstruction of something that took place in the art itself. In *Jimmy Corrigan*, that is, Ware doesn't contribute to this development through critical theorizing. Rather, it's through artistic innovation that he teases out what was only implicit in the definitions of Eisner and Spiegelman. In doing so, Ware offers, through the construction of the book itself, a response to the anxieties and uncertainties about comics that he expresses therein: he invigorates the medium by revealing new ways of understanding the range and significance of its aesthetic possibilities.

I began by claiming that the crises that provoke philosophical inquiry are often crises of self-understanding. However, insofar as they challenge us to reflect on the ethics of history, so are the crises around which kairotic time is structured. Thus, as I've told the story, Ware addresses the first kind of crisis by addressing the second. In this sense, he faces up to times of crisis in one sense by facing up to times of crisis in another.

Notes

1. Thanks to Tucker McKinney and Nate Zuckerman for helpful comments on a previous draft of this paper.
2. I choose these questions because they were decisive in paradigm examples of modern scientific crises. The first was an animating concern for Richard Dedekind and Gottlob Frege, and consequently for a great deal of late nineteenth and early twentieth century work by mathematicians (alongside philosophers) in the foundations of mathematics. The second was crucial to the seventeenth century transition from Aristotelian science (in which the

concept of substantial form was central) to early modern science (in which the latter concept was largely supplanted by that of natural law).

3. One representative example of the latter sentiment can be found in an exchange between Margaret Atwood and Ursula Le Guin. Despite the fact that Atwood novels like *The Handmaiden's Tale* and *Oryx and Crake* are often praised as classics of science fiction, Atwood's consistently claimed that she doesn't write science fiction, which, she contends, deals with "things that could not possibly happen" (Atwood 2012, 6). In response, Le Guin has complained that "this arbitrarily restrictive definition seems designed to protect her novels from being relegated to a genre still shunned by hidebound readers, reviewers and prize-awarders. She doesn't want the literary bigots to shove her into the literary ghetto" (Le Guin 2011).

4. Eisner, Will, *Comics & Sequential Art* (Tamarac, FL: Poorhouse Press, 1985), 5.

5. Ibid.

6. My aim won't be to offer necessary and sufficient conditions for being a comic. Instead, I'll attempt to develop Eisner's conception of sequential art by contrasting it to other media, with the understanding that he took comics to be the paradigm example of the former. I remain neutral (as Eisner does) as to what, if anything, distinguishes comics from any other forms of sequential art—a distinction that may very well be historical rather than formal.

7. A plastic medium is, roughly, a three-dimensional one—e.g., clay as used in sculpture. The distinction I've drawn between plastic and pictorial media is rough: it allows for borderline cases—e.g. images composed in relief.

8. To say straight out that images in comics *are* static, while those in film *are* dynamic, is likely to provoke the objection that film is made up of series of static images that only produce the *illusion* of movement. While I'm skeptical of the claim that filmic images don't move, I've taken a position here that avoids this issue altogether. Note also that I've committed myself to claiming that motion comics aren't sequential art. It seems to me that they constitute a *hybrid* medium: a hybrid between comics and animation (a sub-species of film).

9. One interesting case to consider here is that of abstract comics, many of which explicitly thematize and challenge received conceptions of sequentiality. Some abstract comics, for example, set out to employ images that don't represent things or events at all, and thus arguably fail to have a narrative ordering. However, such comics do contain a reader ordering. In fact, the absence of a reader ordering, it seems to me, is sufficient for an artwork's failing to be sequential art at all. For an exemplary sampling of this genre, see Molotiu 2009, as well as Molotiu's blog *Abstract Comics*: http://abstractcomics.blogspot.com.

10. Spiegelman has formulated this claim in a number of ways in the talk "What the %@&*! Happened to Comics?" that he's given in various venues, such as Spiegelman 2014. Notably, Ware has cited the claim very favorably in a number of places, such as Ware 2012 and 2015. It's from the latter that I've quoted this precise formulation.

11. For reasons of expressive simplicity, I'm ignoring the example of digital comics. Many distinct conventions have developed for the ordering of panels, depending on the reading device, the app used for reading, and the digital publisher(s). However, these differences

aren't important for our purposes, since even in conventional digital comics, reader ordering is determinate and linear.

12. I've put "reader" in scare quotes to indicate that I use the term in an extended sense that can encompass what would more aptly be called *viewer* ordering in the case of film—the order in which the viewer watches film images. I'll continue to use "reader" in this way below when talking about film.

13. In the above discussion, I must emphasize that I'm simply characterizing the most common ordering conventions used in comes. As will become clear below, I've done so in order to highlight the ways in which *Jimmy Corrigan* diverges from such conventions. However, I don't mean to suggest by any means that it's the only work in comics to do so.

14. The former date is a rough conjecture based on inconsistent evidence from the text.

15. The zoopraxiscope was an early precursor to the modern film projector. Images inscribed on a disk (in *Jimmy Corrigan*, images of a robot) were analogous to film frames, and these images were shown to the viewer in rapid succession by rotating the disk. It was invented by Eadward Muybridge, whom I discuss below.

16. Note that this refers to hardcover editions: paperback editions of the book lack a book jacket.

17. Ware 2000, 168–69.

18. Ware 2000, 169.

19. Ware 2000, front pastedown.

20. Ibid.

21. Ibid.

22. Ibid.

23. The following attempt to explicate the notion by reference to its history owes a great deal to Tillich 1936, Smith 1969, Taylor 2007 (especially chapters 1 and 2), and various essays in Sipiora and Baumlin 2002.

24. For example, in the thought of Isocrates. For a discussion of the role of *kairos* in Isocrates's thought, see Phillip Sipiora's "Introduction: the Ancient Concept of *Kairos*," Sipiora and Baumlin 2002, 1–22.

25. Ecclesiastes 3:1–4, NIV. I owe the idea of using this passage to explicate *kairos* to John E. Smith: see his "Time and Qualitative Time," in Sipiora and Baumlin 2002, 46–7.

26. I owe this link between *kairos* and the colloquial notion of "timing" to Smith 1969.

27. Aristotle mentions *ho kairos* in his survey of the various senses of goodness in *Nicomachean Ethics* I.6. And the role of understanding *ho kairos* in *phronêsis* comes up in his sketch of the doctrine of the mean in II.6, where he claims that one aspect of virtue—the application of *phronêsis*—is feeling and acting at the right times. See Aristotle 2004, 7, 29–30.

28. For a survey of the use of *kairos* in the New Testament, see Phillip Sipiora's "*Kairos*: the Rhetoric of Time and Timing in the New Testament," in Sipiora and Baumlin 2002, 114–27; as well as Smith 1969.

29. Mark 1:15, NIV.

30. See Tillich 1936.

Bibliography

Aristotle. *Nicomachean Ethics (Cambridge Texts in the History of Philosophy)*. Translated and edited by Roger Crisp. New York: Cambridge University Press, 2004.

Atwood, Margaret. *In Other Worlds: SF and the Human Imagination*. New York: Anchor Books, 2011.

LeGuin, Ursula K. "The Year of the Flood by Margaret Atwood." *Guardian*, 29 August 2009, accessed January 15, 2016, http://www.theguardian.com/books/2009/aug/29/margaret-atwood-year-of-flood

Molotiu, Andre. *Abstract Comics: The Anthology*. Seattle: Fantagraphics Books, 2009.

Sipiora, Phillip, and James S. Baumlin. *Rhetoric and* Kairos: *Essays in History, Theory, and Praxis*. Albany: State University of New York Press, 2002.

Smith, John E. "Time, Times, and the 'Right Time'; 'Chronos' and 'Kairos.'" *The Monist* 53 (1969): 1–13.

Spiegelman, Art. "What the %@&*! Happened to Comics?" Lecture. Celebrity Series of Boston from Harvard College, Cambridge, MA. May 9, 2014.

Taylor, Charles. *A Secular Age*. Cambridge, MA: Harvard University Press, 2007.

Tillich, Paul. "Kairos and Logos." In *The Interpretation of History*. New York: Charles Scribner's Sons, 1936. Translated by Nicholas Alfred Rasetzki and Elsa L. Talmey. 123–75.

Ware, Chris. *Jimmy Corrigan: The Smartest Kid on Earth*. New York: Pantheon Books, 2000.

———. "Why I Love Comics." *New York Times*, October 6, 2015, accessed November 28, 2015, http://www.nytimes.com/interactive/2014/07/17/books/review/18ware.html?_r=3.

Ware, Chris, and Zadie Smith. "Building Stories: Chris Ware in Conversation with Zadie Smith." Lecture. Live from the NYPL from the New York Public Library, New York, NY. December 11, 2012.

Further Reading

Chris Ware, *Building Stories*, 2012
A work composed of fourteen volumes contained in a box, printed in a variety of formats—traditional comic books, broadsheets, a flip-book, a newspaper, etc.—and detailing the lives of the inhabitants of a single Chicago brownstone. By constructing the work in this way, and encouraging readers to read the volumes in any order they wish, Ware expands his exploration of indeterminate and non-linear reader and narrative orderings.

Jim Woodring, *Congress of the Animals*, 2011
A graphic novel featuring Woodring's most renowned character, Frank, and recounting his adventures of the titular hero in a hallucinatory world that defies description in words alone, thereby highlighting the distinctiveness of the comics medium.

Andrei Molotiu (author, editor), *Abstract Comics: the Anthology*, 2009

A collection of comics that challenge the medium's traditional representational character. By dispensing—either partly or completely—with narrative ordering, they thereby function, among other things, to underscore the special significance of reader ordering.

Richard McGuire, *Here*, 2014
On every page of this book, we find the space occupied by one and the same corner of one and the same room, shown from one and the same angle every time—but over the course of hundreds of thousands of years. By rendering the setting of his work entirely static, McGuire provokes us to reflect on the significance of narrative and reader ordering, as well as on the nature of historical time.

Nick Sousanis, *Unflattening*, 2015
Originally submitted as Sousanis's doctoral dissertation, this is a work of philosophy written in the form of a graphic novel, and which is devoted to meditating on the nature of the medium itself.

Autonomy in Children: Accessing the Inaccessible Space in *Essex County Vol. 1: Tales from the Farm*

Maria Botero

> We make ourselves in our father's sunshine
> but also in his shadow:
> what he beams down we bend away from.
> —Adam Gopnik, "The Driver's Seat"

In Jeff Lemire's *Essex County Vol. 1: Tales from the Farm*, we find the portrait of Lester, a recently orphaned ten-year-old living on his uncle's farm in southwestern Ontario. Ever since his mom died, Lester has been wearing a mask and cape and disappearing into a solitary dream world of comic books where no one else is allowed, especially not his uncle Ken who has full custody of him. Buying comics, Lester meets Jimmy Lebeuf, a former hockey star and local gas-station attendant who suffered a head injury in his first and only professional game. Through this unlikely friendship, Lester finds more than a companion for his imaginary adventures; this new relationship changes the ways in which Lester relates to others and understands himself and ultimately helps him to decide who he wants to be.

Lemire's portrait of Lester offers a depiction of a child who is able to be autonomous. Traditionally, because they are not fully developed rational agents, children are not considered autonomous. Thus, Lemire's portrait of autonomy is in opposition to traditional theories of autonomy (Kant 1785;

Rawls 1971) where autonomous agents are able to choose by themselves who they want to be and how they want to act; where autonomous agents are rational agents who are free to make decisions about the moral law and justice and to provide reasons to justify their choices, choices that are not the result of any force outside of themselves. Given that traditionally autonomy is one of the requirements for a moral agent to be held responsible for his or her actions, granting children autonomy is in defiance of tradition and forces us to understand both autonomy and children in a different light.

To understand this departure from tradition, Lemire's work can be read from the perspective of Amy Mullin's work (2007, 2014). As part of a new area of philosophy called Philosophy of Childhood, Mullin argues for granting children minimal or local autonomy. Philosophy of Childhood compromises a diversity of philosophical questions about children and about the relationship between adults and children. Within this realm Mullin argues that children's attachments to those they love can be a source of autonomy in a minimal sense. She claims that it is in the relationship with those whom the child loves that the child is able to find meaningful activities and is able to care for someone or something. Rather than merely relying on pure reason, it is in the way that the child is caring for someone or something, that allows the child to be able to exercise autonomous decisions as a moral agent. Accepting Mullin's perspective means understanding autonomy as a capacity no longer exclusive to fully rational agents but available to individuals capable of love. Moreover, it invites us to consider children as moral agents whose voices need to be included in moral and legal decisions. This is where *Essex County* comes in.

Jeff Lemire's portrait of Lester in *Essex County Vol. 1: Tales from the Farm* embodies the opposite of the traditional view of children and autonomy. Lester's actions and decisions toward his uncle and toward gas station worker Jimmy Lebeuf reveal a fully autonomous agent who is capable of self-governance when he decides how to conduct his own life in service of the people he loves and for whom he cares. Moreover, Lemire's graphic novel as an example of art, provides us with a more complex understanding of the child's mind (as opposed to purely theoretical accounts of the mind) and this understanding through art supports the argument of autonomy in children. I will argue that through the use of images as a language, Lemire is able to take our understanding of autonomy in children a step further and bridge the gap between being and adult and being a child. He provides adult readers with a qualitative insight into the mind of the autonomous child; an insight into "what it is like" to be an autonomous child in the context of their love for others.

Children's Autonomy: Why Does It Matter?

Defining autonomy is not an easy task. There are several definitions that emphasize different aspects of autonomy (see Arpaly 2002 for a review of different approaches). Following Mullin, I will focus on personal autonomy as opposed to global autonomy (Dworkin 1988). Personal autonomy focuses on the person's ability to use her desires, considerations, beliefs or characteristics to guide her behavior and thoughts. This kind of autonomy is exercised when a person confronts the choice of what to do in a specific situation, asks her/himself what s/he can do, and takes a course of action in accordance with her/his personal desires, consideration beliefs, etc. For example, someone deciding whether she should cheat in an exam and then refraining from cheating, in accordance with her personal beliefs and desires, is an example of someone who is exercising their personal autonomy. The desires, considerations, beliefs, and characteristics that guide personal autonomy do not come from an external source but are chosen by the person herself because she believes that they best define her. Continuing with this example, she would chose not to cheat on her exam because she is guided by her personal beliefs on honesty rather than by an external force such as the threat of failing the class if she cheats on an exam. Since personal autonomy refers to the way personal desires, considerations, beliefs, and characteristics guide an agent's behavior, it is necessary to distinguish it from global autonomy, a form of autonomy that must be assessed over a person's entire life and way of living. For example, global autonomy is what has guided a lawyer to conduct his lifetime of professional practice with compassion and honesty.

The concept of autonomy plays an important role in helping us define what or who a person is, understand responsibility, understand moral responsibility, and determine social policies and political theories. Thus, it is important to determine whether we can grant children autonomy since acknowledgment of their autonomy entails allowing them (or not) to have a voice in difficult and important contexts such as child-custody cases or cases of terminal illness. For example, if it were recognized that children have autonomy, then judges, rather than attempting to determine the best interests of a child without the child's input, should start including the child's preferences in their deliberations. Supporters of voluntary euthanasia typically argue in favor of mercy killing on the grounds that the person making the decision of terminating his/her life is an autonomous person (Brock 1992). Despite many people denying autonomy in children, in 2014 the parliament in Belgium passed a measure that as of 2015 grants, with written consent of the parents, the choice of euthanasia to children who are terminally ill, close to death, experiencing "constant and unbearable suffering" and able to demonstrate they understand the consequences of such a choice (Bilefsky). Thus, because of cases such as the ones just described, it is clearly important to consider whether we should grant autonomy to children and allow them to make important life-altering decisions.

Denial of Autonomy in Children

Authors who provide theories of morality and justice that deny autonomy to children describe children as lacking well-developed cognitive capacities such as those found in fully able adult humans. This view of children is found in some conceptions of justice and society; for example, Rawls (1971) argues that society is composed of members who are rational. For that reason he argues that children, because "their powers are undeveloped and they cannot rationally advance their interests" (249) should be subjected to paternalism, that is, adults making decisions on the behalf of children. Rawls states "Those who care for others must choose for them in the light of what they will want whatever else they want once they reach maturity" (207–208).

It is possible to find a similar perspective in morality, such as in historical approaches to autonomy as being a property of *rational* agents (Kant 1785), and subsequently, not of children. For Kant, humans have practical reason, that is, the ability to use reason to choose their own actions, and this, in turn, presupposes that humans are able to understand themselves as free. From this, they can be held morally accountable. However, for Kant, children are not fully rational agents that possess this kind of freedom from external forces that influence their will and the ability to use the law to guide their decisions. Contemporary approaches such as that of Wilkes (1988) maintain that we should limit the term "persons" to those who are rational agents, are able to use language, and have complex forms of consciousness. Only persons in this stipulated sense can be moral objects and moral agents. In this view, children, because of their undeveloped conscious abilities, are not persons and therefore are not moral agents. Baker (2000) offers a similar position arguing that children are not self-conscious since they have not yet acquired the linguistic capability that allows them to adopt and refer to the first person perspective, "to conceive oneself as oneself" (68). Others have argued that children are not autonomous because they are unable to care stably about anything (Oshana 2005) or because they lack critical reflection (Levison 1999). It is in the context of these standard arguments that Amy Mullin presents us with a radical new idea: children as autonomous agents, more specifically as agents who have a basic form of personal autonomy.

Love as a Form of Autonomy in Children

According to Amy Mullin, most who deny autonomy in children adopt the view that children cannot be autonomous agents for two reasons. First, they lack volitional stability; that is, they do not have a series of stable desires that guides all their choices; instead, they have random desires or beliefs that guide their decisions in various and inconsistent ways. Second, they argue that children are incapable of critical self-reflection, that is, they are incapable of reflecting on their own desires or beliefs and incapable of being aware of how their desires and beliefs guide their choices. Consequently, they are incapable of reflecting whether those choices reflect who they think they are or reflect their own sense of self. Consider, for example, how children's preferences for one type of food, a specific toy, or a friend at school may change constantly and randomly, without clear explanations for the changes[1].

Mullin agrees partially with traditional approaches to autonomy and argues that to have self-governance (to be able to guide your life in accordance with your beliefs and desires) a person must have a *volitional self*, that is, a part of the self that is stable and consistent and is able to govern her actions in accord with what she values and wants to accomplish. However, for Mullin, this kind of volition does not have to be something that a person is directly aware of and does not have to be guided by reason. Mullin argues that *volitional stability* (the stability of the desires and behaviors that an autonomous agent uses when guiding his/her life) can be provided by intimate relationships rather than self-conceptions, and, in this way, she believes that volitional stability rather than critical self-reflection is the key to autonomy.

To demonstrate this idea, Mullin first emphasizes that to understand autonomy it is necessary to understand the goals people have in terms of self-governance. In other words, to understand autonomy, it is necessary to understand how an autonomous agent chooses a goal that matters so much to her that she is willing to use it as a guide to conduct her life. However, Mullin argues that abstract-rational reasons seem insufficient for understanding what agents choose as guides. I concur. Consider the following example: Amy loves animals and has several pets. She cares for them carefully since she firmly believes they can feel pain. Amy is also a food-blogger and specializes in the type of food she loves most: cheeseburgers. One day, she watches a documentary on food that depicts factory-farming practices and shows the cruel ways in which animals that will be used for consumption are raised and killed. This same documentary also shows how small children die of starvation in some developing countries. After watching this documentary, Amy decides to stop eating meat. To understand her behavior, we may explain how she agrees with the principle of equality, where the needs of sentient creatures should be equally considered; however, her agreeing with this principle is not enough. Rather, it is necessary that we understand how Amy's goal of quitting meat is based in something that really matters for her and how her care for animals and their welfare will guide who she wants to be from that moment on. Based on the principle of equality, she may agree that children should be helped, but since this is not something that matters as much for her, it does not guide her to conduct her life in a different way, such as donating to children's charities.

To understand what matters to an individual, Mullin is, first, following Frankfurt's (1999) argument on love. Even though Frankfurt does not believe children have autonomy, he provides a definition of love that is quite useful for Mullin's purpose. Frankfurt defines love as caring about things, ideals and persons; love, in other words is *volitional* as it guides and motivates the agent's conduct and preferences.

Second, Mullin argues that the love children experience as a way of guiding their lives does not necessarily have to be a guide in a conscious/rational way. In this way, Mullin does not agree with the idea that children can only become autonomous agents once they develop rational selves capable of rational forms of self-reflection.[2] She argues that children are autonomous agents as soon as they are capable of a basic form of self-conception rooted in what they love.

Moreover, for Mullin, when an autonomous agent loves another person, that agent is able to care for the other person and is willing to give up momentary satisfaction to help or avoid hurting them. Children are able to act in accordance with love (such as caring for the well-being of a loved one), and avoid outcomes that are in conflict with this love. In other words, stable volitional commitments are developed in children through the love for their caregivers. This way, through love, the child gains a basic form of autonomy where s/he can use his/her desires to guide his/her decisions. For example, the love that a child has for his adoptive mother will provide him with a series of stable desires and beliefs that guides his choices conducting his life, from small choices, such as who he would like to be comforted by when he is afraid or who he wants to feed him or tuck him at night, to more significant choices such as who he would like to live with. Loving something or someone is what gives the child stable commitments that can be used to guide his/her life. And since they do have this ability, various decisions that they make based upon love can and should be respected.[3]

In other words, Mullin argues two things: she argues that volitional commitments (the ability to commit to decisions based on what matters to the self) are necessary for autonomy, and she argues that it is possible to grant children a basic form of personal autonomy because, through their intimate relationships, children are able to exercise that autonomy by choosing and engaging in activities that are meaningful for them.

Autonomy and Dependency

Traditionally it has been argued that an autonomous agent is able to live a good life without the need for others (Arpaly 2002). Therefore, children who are dependent on their parents or caregivers cannot be autonomous. According to Mullin, dependency, rather than being a limitation, actually helps autonomous behaviors. She believes that the person whom an autonomous agent loves (and therefore who helps the autonomous agent create goals that guide his or her life) can also provide what is needed by the child: both sustenance and an affective relationship. This way, it is through the relationship with their caregivers that children are able to express what matters for them and to shape how they relate to others. Mullin views the relationship between children and their parents as a source of autonomy because this relationship is important for children, and as such it becomes a source of self-managing activity for them. This is because it helps them create a volitional self, that is, a self that is stable and consistent and is able to govern actions in accord with what the agent values and wants to accomplish. For that reason, children's dependency can support rather than diminish the role love can play in autonomy.

I agree with Mullin on this last point. I believe that it is the love for others that becomes a source of autonomous decisions by children. For example, imagine a child who gets a lot of pleasure from an annoying or dangerous activity. Imagine that this child also loves her grandfather. If the grandfather, as opposed to an uncle she doesn't care for, asks her to stop this behavior because it is affecting him in a negative way, the love the child feels for her grandfather becomes the source of a self-legislating decision and activity; that is, it guides her into deciding to stop that behavior. It is also possible to imagine how the love that the child feels for her grandfather is stable and accordingly will lead to many other decisions in the child's life that will involve her grandfather's welfare.

It may be argued that children have little control over their lives since adults usually dictate most of children's everyday lives—their daily schedules, what they are allowed to do—and that makes it is difficult to find an area where children are allowed enough freedom to exercise their autonomous decisions. However, I still believe that Mullin is right and that it is possible and necessary to both look for those areas where the child has the opportunity to choose how to guide her own life (an opportunity given by the parent or taken by force by the child), and to understand how a child's stable relationships, where she cares for someone or something, lead to stable decisions and actions in her life.

Mullin concludes her argument by stating that three of the capacities that aid children to develop autonomy through caring relations are: emotional skills, imaginative skills, and self-confidence. Emotional skills—learning how to shape emotional responses rather than just experiencing the emotion—will aid an autonomous agent because they help her use her emotions to reflect the current volitional commitments. Imaginative skills—imagining different roles—aid the autonomous agent by providing a method of trying different ways of relating to others so that the agent may decide what she wants and doesn't want. Finally, self-confidence—the agent's belief that she is capable of bringing forth a desirable outcome—allows the agent to exercise her autonomy through guiding her behavior based on her own goals. These capacities are on display front and center in Jeff Lemire's *Essex County Vol. 1: Tales from the Farm*, to which we now turn.

Essex County Vol. 1: Tales from the Farm: Art and Children's Autonomy

Jeff Lemire's *Essex County Vol. 1: Tales from the Farm* (TftF) is a form of art that allows us to understand children as autonomous agents. Lemire literally illustrates several of Mullin's concepts of local autonomy in children. Through this medium we can see (directly perhaps) a child express his autonomy through the love he has towards objects and people that surround him.[4] As well, through the artwork, Lemire manages to go beyond Mullin's concepts, providing us with a more complex approach to a child's notion of self that is fundamental for a satisfactory theory of autonomy. As an artist Lemire bridges the gap between being and adult and being a child and provides adult readers with a description of the child's mind that is closer to solving what is known as "the hard problem"; that is, Lemire provides us with a qualitative insight of "what it is like" to be an autonomous child.

Mullin, Lemire and the Autonomous Child

Following Mullin's ideas, in TftF, Lemire depicts the different relationships that Lester, a ten-year-old boy, has with the ones he cares about: his uncle Ken and the gas station attendant Jimmy Lebeuf; Through this difference, Lemire illustrates how children as autonomous agents are capable of creating stable volitional patterns (desires and behaviors that are stable through the child's life) and are capable of guiding their behavior and their choices, based on the different ways in which they love others.

Hockey as an Object of Love and Uncle Ken

The reader of TftF is able to perceive how, in his relationship with his uncle Ken, Lester is able to express what matters for him and how this shapes the manner in which Lester will relate to others. To demonstrate that Lester develops as an autonomous agent, I will focus on how his relationship with his uncle Ken unfolds through an object that Lester loves: hockey.

In TftF Lemir uses hockey as a form of positive associations, perhaps love, as he explains in the following excerpt: "*Essex County* was my perspective on Canada as a naive 20-whatever year old who loved the classic old-age feel of hockey and nostalgic things that we positively associate with Canada" (Lu). Lemire's love for hockey is embodied in Lester's love for hockey, and as such it can be interpreted as a clear example of how children are able to care in a stable way about some things and use this care as a guide to their actions. Lester's love for hockey is a used throughout the book to demonstrate how Lester is capable of using his unchanging love for hockey as a stable commitment through which he can exercise his choice of interacting and loving (or not) the people who surround him.

After his mother's death, Lester creates a *volitional stable self*: a notion of himself as a solitary and imaginary superhero. He behaves in accordance with this self-conception when he distances himself from his uncle. For example, the first hint of Lester's relationship with his uncle Ken is that Lester chooses not to watch the hockey game with him but instead goes downstairs and watches it by himself on a smaller TV while wearing his superhero mask (14–16).[5] Through the depiction of this interaction the reader is able to perceive that Lester does not want to be close to his uncle Ken and chooses instead to be a solitary imaginary superhero. However, after experiencing several changes in his life, Lester decides he does not want to be a lonely imaginary hero anymore and decides to accept his uncle's love. Lemire shows us this change in Lester's new self-conception and how it guides his actions through three sequential moments at the end of the story: it starts when Lester and Uncle Ken are working together, making plans to watch the hockey game on TV (89–90). Then, Lester remembers how, after his mother's death, Uncle Ken picked him up to come live with him and as way of getting closer to him, invited him to a hockey game (106–109). Finally the reader observes Lester's superhero costume hanging from a tree and Lester walking away from the tree (110).

Lemire uses this final sequence as a form of *encapsulation*. Let me pause for a moment here to explain this concept. This term is coined by Duncan and Smith (2009) to explain the artist's choice of what will be presented in the panels, in which panels it will be presented, how many panels will be used to present the action, and the size and layout of the panels. The order and layout of the panels can influence the meaning of these panels that goes beyond the meaning of each individual panel. Encapsulation is distinctive to comics and is one of the essential decisions that the artist has to make in his work. To convey to the reader the change that has occurred for Lester, Lemire introduces Lester's memory of his history with his Uncle Ken in the middle of a sequence of events (i.e., the memory of how after his mother's death, Uncle Ken picked him up to come live with him and as way of getting closer to him, invited him to a hockey game). This form of encapsulation allows the reader to understand how this memory works as a guide for Lester's current and future life. Lester's decision to recall this particular memory shows the reader how Lester has finally accepted his uncle's love and this acceptance explains why Lester is ready to abandon his fantasy world where he is a superhero and embrace his new life with his uncle Ken.[6] Lemire's use of this sequence, as opposed to individual panels, makes TftF into a medium that mimics the way Lester's mind works.

This way, from the beginning of the story to the end, we see Lester's love for his uncle guiding his choice of being with him, of sharing (or not) with him the objects of love (hockey). Through encapsulation the reader can observe how Lester's love for hockey has played a fundamental role in his relationship with his uncle either in present time or in the way Lester's memories work as a guide for his current and future life. In other words, through hockey—an object that Lester loves—Lester develops his autonomy. As readers we have access to Lester's mind and see how though the interaction of the relationships with his uncle Ken and with hockey, Lester changes as an autonomous agent.

Moreover, following Mullin's argument of how autonomous agents can still be dependent on another, we can see through Lemire's work that the dependency that Lester has on his uncle Ken allows for the development of Lester's autonomy. As argued, at first glance it seems inconsistent to argue for an agent being both autonomous and dependent; however, it is through the love found in the relationship between Lester and his uncle Ken that Lester can express his interests and commitments. In Mullin's approach love means caring for the person independently of what that person provides for us.

In making this point, Mullin argues for dependency in a general sense. I suggest that we go beyond this general and traditional sense of dependency and instead adopt a more particular definition that differentiates between two kinds of dependency: physical dependency (i.e., food, shelter) and psychological dependency (i.e., need for care, love). I believe this particular definition allows us to understand better how dependency and autonomy are compatible: even though all children are dependent upon adults for material needs, they have some form of autonomous control over the psychological/affective needs. Lemire's work reveals how these two senses of dependency and autonomy can be compatible. What Lemire shows us is that, even though Lester is completely dependent on uncle Ken for every physical needs—food, shelter, money for comics (for example see pages 14–15, 17–18, and 29)—Lester is able reject the affection that his uncle provides him (for example on pages 16, and 39), exercising his own choices in this relationship and it is in this sense that Lester, even though is dependent in a material sense, still is an autonomous agent because he maintains independence in his psychological needs. In other words, if we divide dependency into physical and psychological dependency we can understand how, just as in the case of the relationship with Uncle Ken, children like Lester can develop who they want to be and are able to guide their behavior in ways that reflect their choices.

If we accept this idea, it would follow that the children's input as autonomous agents should be taken into account when making important decisions about their lives; for example, in custody cases. Accepting that children can have personal autonomy means that not only the child's physical needs should be consider but also their psychological needs in reference to how meaningful they are for the child.

Imagination and Relationships, Uncle Ken and Jimmy

The other important character in Lester's life is Jimmy Lebeuf, a former hockey player who had been drafted by the Toronto Maple Leafs and after an injury came back to his hometown. The appearance of Jimmy in Lester's life is one of the crucial moments of the story because it provides Lester with the opportunity to deal with being separated and abandoned from those he loves and who should love him (towards the end of the story both the reader and Lester realizes that Jimmy is his father), and this in turn allows Lester to redefine who he is and how he wants to act.

All of this information is conveyed to the reader through Lemire's artwork. The reader is able to see that the way Lester engages in a relationship with Jimmy guides many of Lester's decisions throughout the story. This helps the reader understand how Lester is an autonomous individual who is capable of having a self, based on what matters to him, that governs his own activities. To understand this, let's look at the relationship that exists between Lester and Jimmy mediated by Lester's imaginative capacities. Imagination is crucial for Mullin's concept of autonomy, as argued earlier she briefly claims that when children imagine different roles they are capable of trying different ways of relating to others and deciding what they want and don't want.

For example, consider the different roles that children adopt during pretend play: through the role of police, a firefighter, the mom, the dad, or the "bad guy" who runs away from the police, the child tests different ways to relate to others. During this kind of pretend play, children can begin to decipher in a rudimentary way who they want to be, in particular, who they want to be in relation to others. In Lemire's work we can understand this idea in two ways. First, how he depicts the difference between memory, present time and imagination. Second, when we observe the different ways in which Lester's imagination plays different roles in contrasting his relationships with Jimmy and Uncle Ken.

To argue the first point I will focus on how Lemire's carefully chooses different kinds of lines and colors to convey Lester's mental states in particular how Lester, as an autonomous child, uses his imagination to exercise his decisions. Lemire depicts memories in a series of grayish, diluted-black-ink thin lines; these lines, like memories are more like the suggestion of a line than a real one. Meanwhile he draws present time in black ink. He uses heavy and thick strokes that suggest landscapes and buildings and a mix of thin and thick black lines and heavily shadow areas to convey emotions in the characters' faces (see for example page 47).[7] What is really interesting about his choices of color and strokes for depicting Lester's mental states is that Lemire does not use any different color of ink or type of stroke to depict the difference between imagination and reality. This choice of *not* conveying a difference between what is real and imaginary for Lester conveys Mullin's idea of imagination as a capacity necessary in autonomous agents. Lester's imagined existence and Lester's reality are both realities for him as an autonomous agent. Lester uses his imagination to try different ways of relating to others, deciding what he wants and doesn't want and from there he is able to formulate a plan of action. As it will be expanded later, this is particularly obvious in the last imaginary play of the story where Lester acknowledges that Jimmy is his father and comes to terms with death, the death of his mother, the absence of his father, and then his choice of loving his uncle Ken.

To illustrate the second point on the role of imagination and different relationships let's focus on an example. Even though Uncle Ken takes care of Lester, Uncle Ken never enters the realm of imagination for Lester. First, Uncle Ken doesn't understand why Lester wants to collect so many comic books (18). Meanwhile, the first time Jimmy appears in the story, he discusses comic books with Lester and gives him one as a gift (19–20). Later, Lester shares with Jimmy a comic book he has drawn titled "Heroes and Villains" (57–65).[8] It is in the difference between the ways Lester engages with Uncle Ken and with Jimmy that it is possible to observe once more how Lester is capable of a *volitional self*, that is, a self that is stable and consistent and is able to govern different actions in accordance with what Lester values and wants to accomplish.

This contrast is even more noticeable through Lester's use of the superhero costume. After interrupting Lester's imaginary flight (11–14), Uncle Ken asks him to take the costume off, and Lester complies. He moves his mask from covering his eyes to the top of his head. Later (15–16), when Lester refuses to watch the hockey game with his uncle Ken, the mask goes over his eyes again. Every time that Lester talks with his uncle the mask goes up, and every time Lester refuses to share time with his uncle, upon wanting to be alone, he brings the mask down again. Meanwhile, the second time Lester meets Jimmy (37–38), he tells him he is a superhero who combats aliens and Jimmy's response is to build a lookout for Lester to fight the aliens (56).

Lemire depicts the difference between the way Lester relates to Uncle Ken and Jimmy not as dialogue but as visual (and visible) behaviors, and through these behaviors, Lemire demonstrates that Lester is an autonomous agent able to engage in different ways, with people he cares for regardless of how dependent he is upon them for care. Lester is able to act in accordance with love when he refuses to go with his uncle for a burger or watch a game, when he runs away from the farm to be with Jimmy, and when he invites Jimmy to join his fantasy. Throughout the story Lester exhibits stable volitional commitments that are developed through love of those he cares for.

Drawings: A Mode through Which Readers Can Perceive How Autonomy Unfolds through Relationships

In one of the most interesting parts of the story, Lemire uses *encapsulation* to show the reader, through the interaction of a series of panels, the moment Lester decides to wear a costume and the moment when he decides to take off the costume. This choice of sequence in the panels also reflects Lester's notion of self. In previous panels (83), the reader has seen that Lester had not worn a superhero costume before his mother's death but now the reader is able to notice that Lester starts wearing a superhero costume after his mother, at the moment of her death, calls him a hero. The reader has also seen schoolmates tease Lester for wearing a superhero costume (26), and in every panel that depicts Lester's imagination, the reader can see him flying alone (10–12). This indirect way (for it is never shown directly in one panel or described in dialogue) mimics, in a beautiful way, the working of Lester's mind, and indicates that the relationship with his mother influences his current commitment to being a superhero. These panels also show the reader the kind of relationship (i.e. lack of relationship) Lester has with other children. Through images, Lemire illustrates the consequences of Lester's autonomous decision to become an imaginary hero; Lester becomes the object of ridicule and feels rejection and loneliness.

Another example where Lemire use of encapsulation to show how children can understand the world and use this knowledge in their autonomous decision is how Lemire shows the reader how Lester understand that Jimmy is his father. Throughout the story it is suggested that Jimmy is Lester's father but there is never an explicit statement of his paternity.[9] This entails that at no point of the story someone tells Lester that Jimmy is his father however, the reader has a clear sense through Lemire drawings (not dialogue), that Lester understands that Jimmy is his father.

Moreover the reader experiences with Lester the moment he acknowledges this truth, without critical self-reflection but rather imagination, and how this has an impact in his notion of self that will guide his autonomous decisions. In the last part of TftF (86–88), Lemire presents the reader with Lester's memory of his mom's funeral, and the reader is able to see Lester noticing Jimmy crying. After this memory there is a series of panels (91–105) depicting Lester going back to the woods past the hideout Jimmy built for him and stopping at the creek where he met Jimmy for the first time. Lester imagines Jimmy waiting for him in his Toronto Maple Leafs uniform (Jimmy's superhero uniform), ready to combat the aliens. Lester then imagines that the aliens mortally wound Jimmy. After that, Jimmy encourages Lester not to run from his problems anymore by hiding behind the superhero mask: "No ... No more running. It's time to face things Lester. I'm a goner kid ... You gotta do this." To which Lester responds: "But I can't do it alone" and Jimmy answers "Sure you can pal ... Yer the hero" (2007, 97–98). After this dialogue Lester flies and destroys the aliens. He returns to Jimmy (102–105), Jimmy gives Lester a hockey card that depicts his brief time with the Leafs and together they look at the sunset. They repeat together, "Red sky at night, sailor's delight,"[10] and Lester puts Jimmy on a raft. While Jimmy is floating away on the river, Jimmy's cigarette smoke echoes the nasogastric feeding tube of Lester's mother when she was in the hospital. They wave goodbye.

The book ends with a significant final memory (106–109): Uncle Ken picking Lester up and taking him to his farm and they're talking about hockey. After that memory (109–110), in another use of encapsulation, Lemire takes the reader to present time, showing Lester taking his superhero mask off. The superhero mask, which has played such an important role in conveying Lester's use of imagination and escape, hangs from the tree, and Lester walks back to the farm.

Lester's perspective is expressed through encapsulation, through a selection of images that are closer to the way a child understands the world. In a hauntingly beautiful way, Lemire illustrates that even though sometimes children are protected by their caregivers by withholding certain information, children perceive the information anyway, in their own way, and this unique form of understanding helps them define who they are and the choices they make. Lemire manages to depict how this understanding can take place without using complex concepts such being conscious of a certain knowledge that can be readily accessed by conscious introspection. He illustrates how through his imagination the child is able to rehearse how he want to interacts with others and the significance that this has for his own life. Through the depiction of different people that are gone from Lester's life (the mother and the father), by calling him a hero, the reader is able to understand how Lester defines himself through the figure of the hero, the superhero, and how that self-image guides his actions. Thus, through encapsulation Lemire shows us how memory and imagination work in a child's mind to help him make an autonomous decision about his life. That is, through encapsulation Lemire is helping us see what is like for a child to experience these mental states and use them to make a decision such as accepting the loss of his mother and his father and face the reality of his new life with his uncle.

Children's Mind as the Hard Problem

As argued in previous sections, when we adopt an approach to autonomy of children such as the one proposed by Mullin, we need to focus on children's ability to love. When a child as an autonomous agent, loves another person, s/he is able to care for that person and is willing to give up momentary satisfaction to help those she loves or to avoid hurting them; if the child loves someone, she is capable of caring for the welfare of those she loves. Mullin defines love as caring about things, ideals and persons and argues that this is a volitional nature that motivates the children's conduct and preferences. This volitional nature does not have to be conscious or guided by reason. However, according to Mullin (2007) it is difficult to find empirical support for these claims because causality is difficult to establish and also because some of the concepts in psychological research do not map those concepts used in philosophical discussion. However, this limitation, rather than being an empirical limitation, is because of Mullin's narrow definition of self-consciousness. By using Jeff Lemire's work as an example, the graphic novel, allows us to understand in more complex ways the mind of the child as an autonomous agent. We can literally see what the child sees rather than be limited by a theoretical description. This is what makes the art form of the graphic novel ripe with philosophical potential.

Consciousness, Children, and Autonomy

In her approach, Mullin does not want to attribute self-consciousness to children, understood as complex forms of self-conception that are readily accessed by conscious introspection and can be used to discover what matters to the autonomous agent. For example, traditionally it has been argued that because I am a self-conscious agent I know that (for example) I am willing to pay my taxes because I *think of myself* as a member of society and *I am aware that I believe* that everyone who is part of society should pay for projects that benefit everyone like highways or schools. It is clear that a child would not have the concepts or the language to emulate this kind of self-reflection. This denial of complex forms of self-consciousness to children is a view shared with several authors (Carruthers 1996; Dennett 1976; Wilkes 1988). They argue that the ability to attain self-consciousness is only achieved when a human has developed the ability to conceive him- or herself as an agent and has the linguistic and conceptual capability to refer to him- or herself.

As described earlier, Mullin is able to argue for an autonomous agent without this complex form of self-conception.[11] She argues that it is not necessary for an autonomous agent to be able to access what she cares for in this complex way and to support it. She provides examples of non-conscious reflection types of experiences that allow us to understand what matters to the agent, such as the experience of dissatisfaction, depression or regret at not achieving a goal. In this way she believes that unconscious thought processes, imaginative activity, and emotional responses will help an autonomous agent reveal what matters for him/her. However, Mullin doesn't elaborate on exactly what those unconscious experiences are. I believe that her argument can be clarified if she adopts a broader perspective of consciousness. A broader understanding of consciousness, without these complex forms of self-conception, would provide us with a clearer picture of how autonomous agents can find and use what matters to them as a guide to conduct their lives.

In researching consciousness, several authors (Nagel 1974; Searle 1992) have maintained that to have an experience means that there is a qualitative aspect to that experience, where there is a subjective "feel" to the experiencer, a quality of "what it is like." Usually these authors evoke a bodily sensation such as pain: there is something like the pain of hitting your toe against furniture, and there is something like feeling a toothache. This qualitative feeling is also true for perceptual experiences, experiences of desire, feeling and even thinking. There is something qualitatively distinctive in seeing our loved ones. There is something qualitatively distinctive in remembering our loved ones. And finally, there is something qualitatively distinctive in desiring and imagining being with a loved one.

This problem is known as "the problem of qualia," and it has given rise to one of the most famous distinctions in philosophy of mind: the hard problem and easy problem (Chalmers, 1995). According to Chalmers there are two general kinds of problem when studying consciousness. The first kind is known as the easy problem, and it refers to any question regarding consciousness that can be solved through the methodologies used in cognitive science or neurophysiological accounts of the mind, such as the ability to discriminate, categorize, and react to environmental stimuli or understanding the focus of attention. These kinds of problems are considered easy not because they are trivial but because we have the tools to solve them currently or in the near future. Meanwhile the hard problem describes all the questions about the qualitative aspects of consciousness, such as qualia, that cannot be solved through the methodologies used in cognitive science or neurophysiological accounts of the mind.

I believe that there is something "what it is like" for a child who loves someone, who cares deeply about things and people in exercising their personal autonomy. Loving and caring for others in different ways is a form of consciousness, a first person qualitative perspective that exhibits children as autonomous individuals. I believe that the difficulty of finding empirical support to Mullin's argument stems from the fact that it is a qualitative problem. In other words, to fully understand Mullin's argument we need to incorporate a broader notion of consciousness that includes qualia and to introduce the distinction between the hard and easy problems to be able to provide an account of what it is like for a child to experience a relationship with others as a localized autonomous agent.

However, introducing this distinction also opens a problem that is distinctive to the hard problem: how do we provide an account of the children's qualia if the methodologies from the cognitive sciences and neurophysiological approaches are not useful for these kind of problems? Moreover, as philosophers we are adults, and it is difficult (if not impossible) to understand what it is like (and what it was like) to be child. I believe that this gap between the adult experience and the qualitative experience can begin to be bridged through art, more specifically through Jeff Lemire's TftF in where he creates a portrait of what it is like to be a ten-year-old who experiences love and cares for others in different qualitative ways. It is through the medium of graphic depiction that we can have access to this qualitative stance.

Lemire's Depiction of the Qualitative State of an Autonomous Child

Professional philosophers who attempt to understand children's autonomy are not children any more but were children at some point. When trying to understand children as autonomous agents, philosophers attempt to think and feel from another's point of view, and this form of thinking cannot be done exclusively through rational thought because children haven't yet developed these complex rational concepts. The gap between an adult and a child is an ever greater gap than the one between one human and other humans; the mind of a child is particularly inaccessible because of their use of language. Children don't have some of the concepts that humans as adults take for granted.

In an interview Lemire argues that for an artist the ideas expressed through art are part of this qualitative experience of being conscious of who one is at a particular time in life. He argues,

> Each book marks the place you were in when you did it, and it's really hard to go back and be the same person you were. You mentioned holding onto that core idea and not losing it, but when you finish something it goes away and you get another core idea. It's really hard to go back and find that original idea, especially when that idea inspired your first book. I was in a very different place compared to where I am now, so it'd be very difficult to do more *Essex County* that would fit with what I was doing before (Lu).

When writing TftF, Lemire was closer to being a child than a parent, he even includes a comic he drew at the age of nine and portrays it as being done by Lester (see endnote 8). As a result, Lemire expresses in TftF a particular qualitative feeling of him as a child. He describes in an interview how

> on a basic creative level, I have always enjoyed writing from a child's perspective. It comes very naturally and I seem to have a knack for it. I think I'm interested to look back in a few years and compare the stuff I wrote before I was a father to the

stuff I wrote after and see if the early works were about being a child while the later ones are about being a parent.... I think *Essex County* was about me fictionalizing and dramatizing my childhood. It's where I grew up. On the other hand, *Sweet Tooth* and *Descender* are much more about my fears for my son and me wanting to protect him and his perspective about the world. (Lu)

Words in a graphic novel are usually presented through speech or thought balloons. However, in TftF there are no thought balloons, all the reader sees are speech balloons. At first glance this will mean that we have no insight into the characters minds. However, on every page it becomes obvious what the characters are experiencing. It has been argued by Carrier (2001) that the speech balloon bridges the gap between word and image, that is, the speech balloon is not just a description of the image, rather, because the speech balloon is placed in the image, it becomes a hybrid between the word and the image and this can convey another layer of meaning for the reader. Lemire uses speech balloons in this way throughout his work, yet, I would like to argue that in Lemire's work the main meaning is *not* given through dialogue expressed in the speech balloons but is given in the images.

Lemire (Titan Books) argues, "I try not to over-write. I try and only say what needs to be said and let the images tell the rest. In my experiences, people rarely say what's on their mind. I let the setting and imagery fill in the blanks." In TftF what Lemire chooses to *encapsulate* through his images are vivid expressions of the mental and emotional life of the character. For example, in pages 50–55 there is a winter scene where Uncle Ken is putting the chickens that Lester has fed throughout the summer and fall in his truck to be sold in the market. He has just told Lester a story about his father. In smaller square panels Lemire uses dialogue boxes where it is explained that Lester doesn't want the chickens killed. We watch Lester cry. But is not through the dialogue in these panels that the reader gathers a real insight into the emotional life of Lester. The insight is gathered through three rectangular panels (54–55), two panels at the beginning of the page, and one at the end of the opposite page. The first of the three panels is a close-up of Lester's masked eyes followed by a panel that is entirely occupied by a close-up of a caged chicken's eyes. The scene ends with a rectangular panel that shows Lester's boots partially buried in snow. The snow is still falling. Groensteen (2013) argues that graphic novels which do not depend on speech or thought bubbles convey meaning through the way the story is presented as a narration. Working with this idea then, in the narration, presented through a carefully selected sequence of panels, Lemire allows the reader into the inner life of these characters, a subjective experience grasped by an outside observer. Lemire manages to show the reader or rather, more significantly, makes the reader experience Lester's qualitative state. The reader experiences what it is like to be Lester in those rectangular panels.

One of the most emotional and significant moments in the novel is a series of panels over two pages (82–83). It starts with the empty chicken coop and footprints in the snow. In rectangular panels with a diagonal line (instead of a straight line) the reader comes closer to the chicken coop's door and then inside the building to find Lester curled on the floor. Following Duncan and Smith (2009), changing the shape of a frame, is part of the act of composition that helps Lemire convey the meaning of the change that is taking place in Lester as an autonomous agent.

However, it is not only through the use images in the individual panels that Lemire manages to convey meaning. Instead he is using one of the most powerful tools that artist have to convey meaning in graphic novels: using images to construct a narrative. As Carrier (2000) argues, "Two images already constitute a narrative, for their meaning is inscribed in the succession." (51). In other words, through images, Lemire is mimicking the narrative of Lester's mind. To continue with the example, after those panels in a series of square panels, the reader sees a close-up of Lester's masked eyes wide open (83), then a memory, in a water down-grayish ink stroke, the mother in her hospital bed. Again the reader's perspective in the next panel is moved to take a close look at the mother. A single line, sometimes a trace in black, sometimes just a suggestion in diluted grey ink, depicts the mother's nasogastric feeding tube, and this line evokes her fragility and imminent death. In this memory she asks Lester, to come close and in the next panel the reader comes close to Lester and then the reader's perspective changes to show Lester's mother closer, and she calls him her hero. The final panel shows the reader an even closer portrait of Lester's masked eyes wide open. Lemire brings the reader closer where there is hardly any distance left between the reader, Lester, and his mother. Bringing the reader closer means that Lemire has drawn a bridge for the readers, to walk from our adulthood to Lester's childhood.

Conclusion

Both adults and children are humans, but they are located at different ends of the spectrum, each with distinct cognitive capacities; Lemire's graphic novel works as a point of contact. A graphic novel is a world in itself, not a study, not a description. In Lemire's hands the graphic novel becomes a zone for thinking an inaccessible place: the child's mind from the adult perspective.

Lemire as an artist negotiates the optical physical surfaces and calls us to consider and negotiate the space between the adult and the child. He uses these surfaces as a language to bridge the gap between the child and the adult and help us understand children as autonomous agents. This is an important contribution since it will allow us to understand how children can demonstrate autonomy in some of the ways in which they conduct their lives and how this may be reason enough to grant them a stronger voice when significant decisions that would affect their lives are made on their behalf.

Notes

1. It may be argued that a child can have a favorite toy or a best friend early on. As it will be argued later, cases like those are what Mullin may call love and the basis for personal autonomous choices.

2. She is arguing against authors such as Haji and Cuypers (2005), who deny that love can be a source of autonomy in children because an agent needs to be able to grasp the concept of love to be able to use love to guide her behavior as an autonomous agent. As a response to this criticism Mullin argues against defining self-governance as an abstract goal that is followed only because it is considered true, right or well-reasoned (as the case of Amy the cheeseburger lover). She also opposes the need for highly developed critical skills in an autonomous agent. Following Arpaly (2002) she argues that autonomous agents are capable of following reasons without engaging in critical reflection. Actions that respond to what agents believe in and care for can reflect reasons in a non-critical-reflective way. She argues that the experience of dissatisfaction, depression, or regret at not achieving a goal is an example of a non-conscious reflection-type of experience that allows agents to understand what matters and to use this love to create a notion of self that is stable and will guide his/her decision and actions in life.

3. It is important to remember that Mullin is focusing on personal autonomy rather than granting children global autonomy, a form of autonomy that must be assessed over a person's entire life and way of living (Dworkin 1988).

4. Mullin is describing autonomy in children much younger than Lester. By children she refers to three and eight years whereas Lester is ten years old. In this sense her concept of "self-consciousness" is not as cognitive complex as the self-consciousness exhibited by Lester. However, I believe that the main concepts still apply.

5. The first edition of TftF (2007), as an individual story, lacks page numbers. To be able to cite page numbers, I will be using the *Collected Essex County*, second edition (2010); however, I do not intend to refer to the entire *Essex County* collection. Some of the arguments made in TftF may not be extrapolated to the other stories in *Essex County*.

6. It is interesting to notice that when Lester abandons the costume in the tree and decides he doesn't need it anymore (110), he is exercising one of the characteristics Mullin describes as necessary for an autonomous agent: self-confidence to bring about the outcome they care about.

7. As it will be expanded in more detail later, Lemire's use of lines and colors allows observers to have different perceptions when characters of TftF experience a memory or present time, these differences in perceptual experience grants observers a form of perceptual access to the character's mind.

8. To depict this comic book, Lemire copies a comic book he drew when he was nine years old. I will show the relevance of this fact in the next section.

9. The closest is a dialogue on pages 74–77 between Uncle Ken and Jimmy that makes the reader suspect that Jimmy is the father.

10. Lester learns this line the first time uncle Ken gives him any information about his father.

11. Mullin even argues that critical self-reflection sometimes may even be a detriment to accessing what matters to us since sometimes these self-conceptions are wrong.

Bibliography

Arpaly, Nomy. *Unprincipled Virtue. An Inquiry Into Moral Agency*. Cary: Oxford University Press, 2002.

Bilefsky, Dan. "Belgium Close to Allowing Euthanasia for Ill Minors." *New York Times*, February. 13, 2014 http://www.nytimes.com/2014/02/14/world/europe/belgium-close-to-enacting-sick-child-euthanasia-law.html?_r=0

Duncan, Randy, and Matthew J. Smith. *The Power of Comics: History, Form and Culture*. New York: Continuum, 2009.

Carrier, David. *The Aesthetics of Comics*. University Park: Pennsylvania State University Press, 2000.

Carruthers, Peter. "Language, Thought, and Consciousness: An Essay in Philosophical Psychology." *Philosophical Psychology* 11 (1998): 91–95.

Chalmers, David J. "Facing Up to the Problem of Consciousness." *Journal of Consciousness Studies* 2 (1995): 200–219.

Dennett, Daniel. "Conditions of Personhood." In Amelie Oksenberg Rorty (ed.), *The Identities of Persons*. Berkeley: University of California Press, 1976. 175–96.

Dworkin, Gerald. *The Theory and Practice of Autonomy*. Cambridge; New York: Cambridge University Press, 1988.

Frankfurt, Harry G. *Necessity, Volition, and Love*. New York: Cambridge University Press, 1999.

Groensteen, Thierry. *Comics and Narration*. Jackson: University Press of Mississippi, 2013.

Haji, Ishtiyaque, and Stefaan E. Cuypers. "Moral Responsibility, Love, and Authenticity." *Journal of Social Philosophy* 36.1 (2005): 106–126.

Kant, Immanuel. *Groundwork for the Metaphysics of Morals*. Translated by Allen W. Wood and J. B. Schneewind. New Haven, CT: Yale University Press, 2002.

Lemire, Jeff. *Essex County Vol. 1: Tales from the Farm*. Atlanta: Top Shelf Productions, 2007.

Lemire, Jeff. *Collected Essex County*. Atlanta/Portland: Top Shelf Productions, 2010. Second printing.

Levinson, Meira. *The Demands of Liberal Education*. Oxford: OUP Oxford, 1999.
Lu Alexander. "Jeff Lemire on the Past, Present, and Future of his Comics Career." June 23, 2016. http://www.comicsbeat.com/interview-jeff-lemire-on-the-past-present-and-future-of-his-comics-career/
Mullin, Amy. "Children, Autonomy, and Care." *Journal of Social Philosophy* 38.4 (2007): 536–553.
Mullin, A. "Children, Paternalism and the Development of Autonomy." *Ethical Theory and Moral Practice* 17.3 (2014): 413–426.
Nagel, Thomas. "What Is It Like to Be a Bat?" *Philosophical Review* 1974: 435–450.
Oshana, Marina. "Autonomy and Self-Identity." In *Autonomy and the Challenge to Liberalism*. Edited by J. Christman and J. Anderson. Cambridge: Cambridge University Press (2005): 77–97.
Rawls, John. *A Theory of Justice*. Cambridge, MA: Belknap Press, 1999.
Searle, John R. *The Rediscovery of the Mind*. Cambridge, MA: MIT Press, 1992.
Titan Books. *Interview with Jeff Lemire*. July 30, 2010 http://titanbooks.com/blog/interview-jeff-lemire/
Wilkes, Kathleen V. *Real People: Personal Identity without Thought Experiments*. New York: Oxford University Press, 1988.

Further Reading

For a different take on childhood by Jeff Lemire, see *Sweet Tooth*, Top Shelf. (2010).

For an alternative way of using images to convey meaning on the topic of childhood, see Chris Ware, *Jimmy Corrigan: The Smartest Kid on Earth*, Pantheon Books (2000).

For the perspective of an adult attempting to understand her childhood through her relation with her mother, see Alison Bechdel, *Are You My Mother?* Houghton Mifflin Harcourt (2013).

Not related, but really cool: Seth, *Clyde Fans*, Drawn & Quarterly (2014).

Love and Liberty:
The Social Contract and *V for Vendetta*

Eric Bain-Selbo

Social contract theory is one of the most dominant ways in which political philosophy is done. At least one important objective of the contract is to use the power and force of the collective to achieve a level of security for individuals and their property. The trade-off for this security is the loss of some degree of individual freedom. The graphic novel *V for Vendetta* (Alan Moore and David Lloyd, with Steve Whitaker and Siobhan Dodds) puts this trade-off into stark relief. The society portrayed in the novel (late twentieth century England) is a tightly controlled police state. Individual liberty is greatly curtailed by a regime that is racist, homophobic, and xenophobic. Yet the citizens have a relatively high level of security from threats both within and without the country (even if some of the threats are created or exaggerated by the regime for political purposes). For V, the protagonist of the novel, the trade-off is unacceptable. His terrorist acts are designed to topple the regime and spur the population to reclaim the freedom that they long since had relinquished. For him, the order and security of the regime is not worth the oppression and injustice required to maintain it.

But *V for Vendetta* is not simply about a cost/benefit analysis of a particular social contract. It is about love—the love that V has for liberty and his fellow citizens and the love that the leader of the regime (Adam Susan) has for his country. The graphic novel raises important questions about the role of emotions in the political order. Drawing upon Martha Nussbaum's recent work, *Political Emotions: Why Love Matters for Justice*, this essay will explore how love in a political context leads us to a more subtle and nuanced understanding of the social contract—with *V for Vendetta* providing an illustrative example. For within the graphic novel there is love of country and love of freedom; as well as the love for specific people, and how those love relationships can have political dimensions. Finally, there's love that we must have for our fellow citizens.

In short, this essay explores social contract theory through the graphic novel *V for Vendetta*, and uses Nussbaum's work on political emotions as a way of extending our insight into both social contract theory and *V for Vendetta*.

Social Contract Theory: A Brief Introduction

The idea of a social contract undoubtedly pre-dates the use of the term. Human beings for millennia have pooled their resources and forsaken some of their freedom in order to form collectives to live more secure lives. However, it was only about five-hundred years ago that specific theorists started to work through the central elements of social contracts.

Almost all early social contract theorists began with a notion of the state of nature. The state of nature is the condition in which humans lived or would live (theorists sometimes understood it as a historical reality, others simply as a thought experiment) if not for their agreeing to live together under a social contract (again, the moment of agreement is perhaps a historical reality for some, for others simply a way of engaging in political philosophy). For someone like Thomas Hobbes (1588–1679), the state of nature was a living hell—assuming you could keep yourself alive. He famously described it as a state of war, and "such a warre, as is of every man, against every man" (185). In such a state, life tended to be "solitary, poore, nasty, brutish, and short" (186). Though the state of nature allowed humans to be free of any control by a government, such freedom was hardly worth it. In *Leviathan*, Hobbes makes the case for why people would forsake the freedom of the state of nature for the security under a powerful Sovereign (the Leviathan himself). While the Sovereign's power (e.g., the king) was derived from the people, it was wielded by a single person and his army in order to maintain order and provide security for the people. In other words, in theory the Sovereign was dependent on the people for his power, but in practice the Sovereign could be experienced as a very distant and uncontrolled force that kept you in constant fear (thus preventing you from doing something stupid, like stealing a loaf of bread from the baker).

While Hobbes can be viewed as the beginning of the social contract theory tradition in the Western world, Jean-Jacques Rousseau (1712–1778) may be the most recognized such theorist. Rousseau famously begins the first chapter of *The Social Contract* with the line "Man is born free, and yet we see him everywhere in chains" (5). It is a line that, as we will see, would resonate with V.

Rousseau hardly had the same extremely negative view of the state of nature that Hobbes had. Perhaps it just was a matter of a different time and place. But Rousseau still viewed the advantages of living in a society to be greater than the freedoms (albeit precarious) of the state of nature. In fact, moving from the state of nature to the civil state was not a diminishing of our freedom, but an enhancement or extension of our freedom. "Man loses by the social contract his *natural* liberty, and an unlimited right to all which tempts him, and which he can obtain; in return he acquires *civil* liberty, and proprietorship of all he possesses" (19). While we cannot just take anything we like, at least within the social contract we can be secure in the possession of those things that we peacefully and legally have acquired.

Rousseau also viewed the sovereign a bit differently than Hobbes did. While Hobbes's Leviathan was a distant figure who was very detached from the people (all the better to administer punishment and maintain order), Rousseau emphasized how the sovereign's power was grounded in the will of the people. He wrote about the "general will" and how it was the real source of the government and its laws. Whereas Hobbes stresses the relinquishing of our freedoms to the Leviathan in order to preserve our lives and property, Rousseau views the sovereign as an *expression* of our freedom as a people. We *are* the sovereign. We do not relinquish our freedom when we put ourselves under the rule of the sovereign (either as a king or a representative body). We, in fact, act freely when we do so together and in an uncoerced way. To relinquish our freedom to a sovereign against our will is not only a political failing, but a moral one as well. As Rousseau writes (again, another line that could be embraced by V): "To renounce our liberty is to renounce our quality of man, and with it all the rights and duties of humanity" (10).

One of the problems with traditional social contract theory is the power of the majority. It is nice to imagine everyone coming to an agreement and having the sovereign represent our agreement or our general will. But we know that consensus is unlikely. Thus, does not social contract theory rely about the principle of majority rule? And when we rely on that principle, what prevents harm being done to minority populations?

In the twentieth century, John Rawls took up the task of reviving social contract theory against what he saw as the predominance of utilitarianism in political philosophy and public policy.[1] The tyranny of the majority is a particular problem for utilitarianism. In its simplest form, utilitarianism argues that "the greatest happiness of the greatest number" should be the rule or principle that guides our actions. But what if achieving this aim results in the violation or oppression of a minority—even a very small minority? Minorities might be at a particular risk if utilitarianism is at the heart of a society's politics and public policy. Rawls recognizes this danger, and works out a theory that protects the rights of everyone—whether they are in the majority or the minority.

Rawls has something like a state of nature in his theory, though he calls it the "original position" (OP). The OP definitely is *not* a historical moment in time. Rather, it is a heuristic device used to reveal or lay out the fundamental conditions or characteristics of our moral thinking. The purpose is to get us to the moral point of view. Once there, the parties in the OP can reason about the principles of justice that they would choose for their society.

Critical to the OP is what Rawls calls the "veil of ignorance." Behind the veil of ignorance, the parties in the OP do not know certain critical facts about themselves. They do not know what their intrinsic abilities or handicaps are (in other words, they do not know how they did in the "natural lottery") and they do not know anything about their social standing (into what kind of family they are born, how wealthy their family or community is, etc.). The point for Rawls is to eliminate all those contingencies about us that are morally irrelevant. For example, how tall you are or smart or fortunate in family background should have no bearing on what we conclude is morally right or wrong.

With the OP laid out, Rawls proceeds to demonstrate how the parties would reason their way to principles of justice. It is beyond the scope of this essay to give a full account of that reasoning process, but let me present the principles and some of the rationale for them and their ordering.

The first principle of justice is, "Each person is to have an equal right to the most extensive total system of equal basic liberties compatible with a similar system of liberty for all" (266). In other words, there are fundamental liberties that every citizen must have in an equal amount. The second principle is a bit longer:

> Social and economic inequalities are to be arranged so that they are both:
> (a) to the greatest benefit of the least advantaged, consistent with the just savings principle, and
> (b) attached to offices and positions open to all under conditions of fair equality of opportunity. (266)

There is more to this principle than we need to explore here, but the point is that social and economic resources should be distributed equally. When they are not distributed equally, any inequalities must be to the "greatest benefit of the least advantaged." Rawls calls this the "difference principle."

The reasoning here is pretty straightforward. Behind the veil of ignorance, the parties are going to want to guarantee themselves (once the veil is removed) the same rights and liberties that everyone else has. Because we do not know what kind of person we are going to be after the veil is removed (our particular skills and capacities, the wealth and power of our families, even our aversion—or lack thereof—to risk), we will choose in the OP an equality of rights and liberties to protect us no matter what the particulars are of our future selves. The parties in the OP also realize that social and economic resources may not be distributed equally. But if so, that unequal distribution must be part of a system that ultimately serves the least advantaged (for example, we may want to provide larger incomes to physicians in order to increase the prospects for good health care for all citizens). Each party in the OP will agree to the difference principle because outside the OP, after the veil of ignorance is lifted, they might be the "least advantaged."

It is important to note (especially for this essay), that the principles are lexically or serially ordered. In other words, the first principle takes precedence over the second. We cannot trade (except under the most extreme circumstances) some of our basic liberties just to increase social or economic benefits. Again, the parties in the OP always will want to preserve their basic liberties.

The securing of social and economic benefits—and the very security or preservation of them—is a basic reason for entering the social contract. This reason holds for Hobbes, Rousseau, Rawls, and many other social contract theorists. What we see with Rawls, however, is an argument that preserving or securing those benefits cannot justify the relinquishing of our basic rights and liberties. This fundamental tension between rights and liberties, on the one hand, and the preservation and security of social and economic benefits, on the other, is at the heart of the political philosophy of *V for Vendetta*.

Political Emotions (Especially Love)

It may not be quite right to characterize Martha Nussbaum as a social contract theorist, though certainly she shares fundamental commitments with someone like John Rawls. In fact, she acknowledges that what she is doing is a supplement to or even a completion of Rawls's theory of justice. She notes that in *A Theory of Justice* Rawls provides an account of how the emotional life of those in a "well-ordered society" would develop and flourish. She also notes how Rawls later had doubts about this part of his work and, in *Political Liberalism*, left "a space for a needed account of a 'reasonable moral psychology'" (9). She then adds: "In effect, the present book [her book] aims to fill that space, with reference to an account of a decent society that differs from Rawls's in philosophical detail, but not in underlying spirit—although its focus is on societies aspiring to justice, rather than on the achieved well-ordered society" (9).

Social contract theorists rightfully are criticized for promoting a very naked conception of the person entering the social contract. The parties are portrayed as only pursuing their self-interest with very little affection or sympathy for one another. Rawls perhaps compounds the problem by stripping the parties in the OP of any idea about their personal identity and future commitments. All they are able to consider are the basic rules to govern the society in which they will have a personal identity and various commitments. These parties then would seem to have an emotionally-vacuous moral life. Nussbaum, however, recognizes the critical role that emotions do and must play in political life. She thus provides us with necessary insights to help us gain clarity about what *V for Vendetta* can teach us.

Covering incredible ground historically and geographically, Nussbaum argues that love (among other emotions) is critical to justice and a society that works to the benefit of all citizens.[2] "Love ... is what gives respect for humanity its life, making it more than a shell," Nussbaum argues. "If love is needed even in Rawls's well-ordered society—and I believe it is—it is needed all the more urgently in real, imperfect societies that aspire to justice" (15). Through much of her work, she examines various accounts of "civil religion"—the notion that the society or nation can be the object of religious devotion, both being supported by and eliciting powerful emotions. One central European figure she covers is Auguste Comte (1798–1857). She writes

> Intellectuals from many nations [she covers many, including those from Europe and India], convinced that human progress required some type of humanistic "civil religion" to counteract the power of egoism and greed, rallied to his call for a new "spiritual power," a "religion of humanity" that could guide nations toward progress through emotions of sympathy and love. (57)

In a sense, civil religion—with its attendant emotional life—is what is needed as a supplement to Rawls. Towards the end of her work, she concludes

> If purely abstract and principle-dependent sentiments are too tepid and empty of motivating content, as we have argued, and if a deeper and more powerful altruism

has its roots in and is modeled on personal particular love, then we have to think hard about how this love can support justice, not subvert it. (Rawls left this project unelaborated, and that is how I believe my project complements his.) (386)

Nussbaum describes two tasks for emotions in a liberal society. First, the emotions are "to engender and sustain strong commitment to worthy projects that require effort and sacrifice" (3). Principles alone, regardless of how rationally compelling, are not enough to elicit that kind of commitment among citizens—at least not broadly enough. Second, "the cultivation of public emotion is to keep at bay forces that lurk in all societies and, ultimately, in all of us: tendencies to protect the fragile self by denigrating and subordinating others" (3). We feel a strong bond with our family members, friends, and some others. But in a large and complex modern society, what prevents us from harming the stranger (even if a fellow citizen) in order to advance our interests (or those of family, friends, etc.)? Again, simple principles of justice may not be enough. There has to be an emotional component to our citizenship.

Nussbaum is writing for what she calls an "aspiring society"—not the ideal well-ordered society of Rawls, but a society striving toward justice. The aspiring society has several important characteristics. While economic growth certainly is important in the aspiring society (as it is in any society), it is not the most important measure of success (as, unfortunately, it has become in many societies). Instead, the aspiring society is interested more generally in "human development," which includes "a wide range of goals, including health, education, political rights and liberties, environmental quality, and many more" (118). This wide range of goals is a consequence of the fact that "human equality," based on all human beings being of "equal worth," is at the very core of the aspiring society (119). In other words, recognizing the equal worth and equality of all citizens means recognizing a diverse range of goods or ends. Some of these we all share in common (for example, we all generally want good health), but others are more particular (for example, some of us want to be teachers, others astronauts, etc.). But an aspiring society is one that is going to provide a system of justice that allows citizens to pursue a wide range of goods or ends (within, of course, the parameters of justice).

Our commitment to such a system of justice may be supported by our rational assent to the principles that underlie the system. But as we noted, those principles are not enough. We need an emotional connection to the society as a whole and to its members. Patriotism clearly is an emotion that will help greatly, and is at the core of a country's civil religion. "Patriotism is a strong emotion taking the nation as its object," Nussbaum writes. "It is a form of love, and thus distinct from simply approval, or commitment, or embrace of principles. This love involves the feeling that the nation is *one's own*, and its rituals usually make reference to that idea" (208).

Patriotism, however, must be accompanied by compassion for our fellow citizens. Only in that way will we take seriously the aims and concerns of one another. Nussbaum describes compassion as "a painful emotion directed at the serious suffering of another creature or creatures" (142). When we identify with our fellow citizens, we feel compassion when they are unable to achieve their aims (aims within the parameters of justice, of course)—especially when they are prevented from achieving their aims by faults or even injustices in the system. We feel compassion when they are sick, hungry, or in psychological distress. We want to help them because as part of the nation they are part of us. And we want justice to be pervasive in our basic structure of society so that people can pursue their aims. "Compassion, however altruistic, can't run a fair tax system," Nussbaum observes. "So, we turn many things over to institutions and laws. Nonetheless: these institutions and laws will not sustain themselves in the absence of love directed at one's fellow citizens and the nation as a whole" (214).

One final note before turning to *V for Vendetta*. It is *not* the case that love, compassion, and the other political emotions require us to be uncritical in our approach to the basic structure of our society or the actions of our fellow citizens. "Our [aspiring] nations are committed to developing political emotions that support their cherished goals," Nussbaum writes. "But they also encourage vigorous criticism and debate. A vigilant critical culture is, indeed, a key to the stability of liberal values. Vigorous cultivation of emotion can coexist, albeit sometimes uneasily, with the protection of an open critical space" (124).

If "patriotism" is a good overarching term to describe the set of political emotions for which Nussbaum advocates, it is certainly not the naïve kind of patriotism that can lead to so many terrible injustices in the name of one's people (of course, we have to think of Nazism here, but recent history is filled with cases of patriotism gone awry—such as xenophobic attitudes and campaigns against Muslim citizens or fear-driven plans for building a massive wall between the United States and Mexico). Nussbaum's patriotism "can be inspiring, making the nation an object of love and cultivating extended compassion, while also activating rather than silencing the critical faculties" (249).

V for Vendetta

The graphic novel is set in London in the late twentieth century. London can be a dreary city with cold, soaking rain, but the London of *V for Vendetta* is even more dreary. The scenes tend to be dark and foreboding, and it is hard to find a panel with any sunshine in it.

The story of England leading up to the time of the graphic novel is the story of the origins of a strange social contract. Though the details may not be laid out clearly, we learn much of the story from Evey, a leading character in the plot. There was a terrible war involving the United States, Russia, and other countries. The war included the use of nuclear weapons, leading to catastrophic climate change. Panels show the Thames river flooding the entire city and the sky a frightening black and yellow (27). Subsequent panels show the collapse of order and descent into chaos. Evey says, "There were riots, and people with guns. Nobody knew what was going on. Everyone was waiting for the government to do something... But there wasn't any government anymore. Just lots of little gangs all trying to take over, and then in 1992 somebody finally did" (28). We then see marching troops clearly determined to restore order (28). Evey continues, "They soon got things under control. But then they started taking people away ... all the Black people and the Pakistanis. ... White people too. All the radicals and the men who, you know, like other men. The homosexuals. I don't know what they did with them all" (28). A panel showing the "Larkhill Resettlement Camp," however, reveals that anybody who was different or might pose a threat to the regime was taken out of society (29).

Out of all this chaos and destruction, a new order was established. It is an order, however, maintained by a government that uses military, police, and surveillance forces to prevent any kind of dissent or instability. The citizenry appears extremely passive, willing to abide by government control so that order can be maintained. The government stokes fear in the population as a way of maintaining the public's desire for security. Even in the opening panels we hear a radio story about a terrorist ring being uncovered, though we do not know if there really was a terrorist ring or not (all media are controlled by the government).

In social contract language, we might say the citizens have relinquished some of their basic liberties for the sake of security—even if it is only the security for the mainstream population. The social contract here is driven by a utilitarian calculus—that a secure oppression is better than chaos, that tremendous injustice against minorities is justified in order to protect the majority. This social contract is central to the implicit and explicit arguments of the protagonists in the graphic novel.

In Chapter Five of Book One, we see the leader of the country, Adam Susan, traveling in a government car through the dark streets of London, and we read his thoughts. He describes himself as a fascist, but he is unconcerned with labels. In order to preserve the country, he realizes that he must rule with a strong hand:

> One twig could be broken. A bundle would prevail. Fascism ... strength in unity./ I believe in strength. I believe in unity./ And if that strength, that unity of purpose demands a uniformity of thought, word and deed then so be it./ I will not hear talk of freedom. I will not hear talk of individual liberty. They are luxuries. I do not believe in luxuries. The war put paid to luxury. The war put paid to freedom./ The only freedom left to my people is the freedom to starve. The freedom to die. The freedom to live in a world of chaos. Should I allow them that freedom? I think not. I think not. (37–38)

In short, Susan understands that the people must forego some of their freedom so that order and their very preservation can be achieved. And when order and preservation are at stake, the marginalized—minorities—are expendable. Any level of control and oppression is justified. Consequently, the state has an elaborate system of cameras, microphones, and surveillance personnel—all designed to monitor the population to prevent any dissent and potentially a fall into chaos. The information from all these sources eventually becomes data for Fate, a computer system to which only Susan has access—helping him make decisions and control the population. Controlling the population includes the limiting of privacy and freedom, detention and execution, and even experimenting on individuals in state custody. In fact, it was at a detention camp (the very same Larkhill Resettlement Camp mentioned earlier) that V was created (V stood for the Roman numeral five on his cell).

While Susan's worldview and tactics strike many of us as dangerous and even diabolical, it is important to note that his method of leading the country comes from his love for it. It is made clear that he does not lead in order to further his own interests. He is a lonely man, and he views his isolation from the people as a sacrifice that he makes for them: "Do I reserve for myself the freedom I deny to others? I do not. I sit here within my cage and I am but a servant. I, who am master of all that I see" (38). As with many sacrifices, Susan's is done out of love.

For such a dark graphic novel, love plays a significant role in the various story lines of *V for Vendetta*. There are some relationships where one would expect to find love, but whatever love was there is now gone or corrupted. These failed relationships generally involve people who work for the state—such as Conrad and Helen Heyer (he a weak bureaucrat and she a domineering and conniving social climber) and Derek and Rosemary Etheridge (he an angry and abusive detective and she an insecure and dependent wife).

There also are more positive love relationships, such as the one we learn about between Valerie and Ruth (a couple that is destroyed by the state's attacks against homosexuals) and Evey's love for V (more a powerful, mentoring love relationship between comrades than a romantic relationship).

But the most important love relationships are those of Adam Susan and V. Susan has a bizarre love for Fate (the computer), that seems to be a product of his isolation and loneliness. But he also has a love for his people (though it is not always clear who "his people" are) and his country (which may not be the same as "his people"). Towards the end of the graphic novel, as the government and the society are unraveling, there are scenes of mobs filling the streets and wanton vandalism. We see Susan sitting in a car, driven through a column of his citizens. He looks at them and thinks, "I'll try to love them more. They're all I have" (232). But his love for Fate, the people, and the country are all unreciprocated. Fate, in fact, cannot love—but neither can the people or the country when these are seen simply as abstractions.

In Nussbaum's terms, you cannot have compassion—a necessary complement to love—for mere abstractions. You have compassion for *real* people. But Susan seems to lack such compassion—so his love is stunted and unreciprocated by the *real* people who make up the "country" that is the object of his love and devotion. Thus, Susan's existence is lonely and emotionally vacuous. It is no surprise then that at one point, alone in the dark room with the computer, he looks up at Fate with sad eyes and asks, "Am I loved?" (184).

V too is in love with an abstraction. V is in love with justice. Right after we learn of Susan's love commitments, we see V on the roof of an old government building. It is night, overcast and foreboding, and V is looking up at a statue of a female who represents justice. He describes himself as a fan of justice, but then becomes much more personal. He says, "I loved you as a person. As an ideal" (40). But he is angry—angry that justice has been corrupted by the current regime. Indeed, he feels betrayed, and enters a dialogue with the statue. She accuses V of loving another (we get to that below), but V retorts, "It was your infidelity that drove me to her arms" (40). He calls justice a "slut" and a "whore," adding, "Deny that you let him have his way with you, him with his armbands and jackboots" (40). He then contrasts justice with his new love. "Her name is anarchy," he says. "And she has taught me more as a mistress than you ever did!/ She has taught me that justice is meaningless without freedom. She is honest. She makes no promises and breaks none. Unlike you, Jezebel" (41). He then renounces justice and, a couple of panels later, we see the top of the building blown up and the statue flying off.

While V's love of justice here seems similar to Susan's love of country (both are abstractions that both men then refer to in very personal, intimate ways), the graphic novel makes one fundamental distinction. V's love of justice always leads him back to the real flesh-and-blood lives of human beings—people like Valerie and Ruth and Evey. His love of justice leads him back to the pain, struggles, and challenges of the human condition. It leads him to identify injustices and then to eliminate or alleviate those injustices.

Much later in the graphic novel, V describes to Evey his relationship with justice in this extended monologue:

> It was not I that strayed. My love was justice, and infatuated with her truth and loveliness, I worshipped her./ ... until, behind my back, she took up with a man who violated and abused her [Adam Susan]; someone fierce and brutal with burned children on his breath. He changed her. She acquired a taste for leather, chains, and whips./ The justice that I loved was gone; who had such kindly eyes; who took such small and careful steps ... Transformed, she glared through narrow slits and ground good men beneath her vicious heel./ Imagine when I learned of her affair ... my anger and my shame to think how they'd made mock of all that I loved. My justice and her bestial swain, cavorting in their blood-stained sheets. (201)

No wonder V turned to the comforting arms of anarchy. But note, the love of anarchy in the end is a result of what she teaches him about liberty or freedom. Anarchy simply is a means to an end, so it really is liberty or freedom that V loves.

But we still are at the level of abstraction. So we must look at V's love for Evey—a love relationship starkly absent in Susan's life. The graphic novel opens with V saving Evey from harm (perhaps rape and murder) by undercover policemen. It is November 5, the day in which the exploits of Guy Fawkes are remembered (in 1605 he was part of the Gunpowder Plot to blow up the Houses of Parliament). V, who throughout the graphic novel is behind the famed Guy Fawkes mask, takes Evey to a rooftop where they witness the destruction of the Houses of Parliament—succeeding where Fawkes had failed.

Through much of the graphic novel, Evey comes to learn more about V. Her family story (her parents eventually succumbed to the abuses of the state) makes her sympathetic to his cause. She, in fact, becomes an accomplice to his efforts to throw the society into chaos in order to get the people to rise up against the leaders. And in the process, they come to love one another—the kind of deep love formed between people fighting in a just war for a righteous end.

At one point, V pulls off an elaborate hoax in which he convinces Evey that she has been imprisoned and soon will be executed (V, in fact, does engage in some level of physical and psychological torture of Evey). The goal (one that is achieved) is to bring Evey to the point where she no longer fears death. Liberated from that fear, she then can hold tight to her principles (principles of love, justice, freedom, etc.) regardless of the threats against her. Of course, she very reasonably is shocked and angered by the hoax. V tries to explain himself to her. When she asks him why he did it, he says simply, "Because I love you. Because I want to set you free" (167).

The love of V for Evey (and vice versa) is not inconsequential. Neither is her love for Gordon or Valerie's for Ruth. These are critical to the message of the graphic novel, for they represent what a just and free society should nurture. They represent an intrinsic good in human life that is threatened by the kind of oppressive state we see with Susan and his henchmen. They lack such love relationships, and that lack contributes to their capability to commit terrible crimes against the people. Love, then, needs to be an important consideration when thinking about the social contract. In the OP, we certainly do not know whom we will love in the future. But Rawls allows the parties to know basic psychological and sociological facts about human nature and societies. Perhaps here he needed to say more about how the parties' understanding of love would and should shape their choices about the fundamental principles of justice and the institutions of a well-ordered society. Given that love relationships are some of the most important goods for human beings, the basic structures and principles of society should serve to foster and preserve such relationships.

While social contract theorizing largely is implicit in the graphic novel, V makes explicit reference to it during a long broadcast to the population after he commandeers the state run television station. Chapter 4 of Book Two is V's history of the social contract—and a long history it is. It begins with an image of a monkey and V talking about dinosaurs. In the next several pages we see drawings of tanks, the first human walking on the moon, the Buddha, and suffering children—the highs and lows of human history. Throughout the panels, V is describing the failures of the people to live up to their end of the bargain, to truly govern themselves and hold their leaders accountable. With images of fascist dictators like Hitler and Stalin in the background, V says,

> We've had a string of embezzlers, frauds, liars and lunatics making a string of catastrophic decisions. This is plain fact./ But who elected them?/ It was you! You who appointed these people! You who gave them the power to make your decisions for you!/ While I'll admit that anyone can make a mistake once, to go on making the same lethal errors century after century seems to me nothing short of deliberate./ You have encouraged these malicious incompetents, who have made

your working life a shambles./ You have accepted without question their senseless orders./ You have allowed them to fill your workspace with dangerous and unproven machines. You could have stopped them./ All you had to say was "No." You have no spine. You have no pride. You are no longer an asset to the company./ I will, however, be generous. You will be granted two years to show me some improvement in your work. If at the end of that time you are still unwilling to make a go of it . . . / You're fired. (116–118)

In short, the people need a good lesson in Rousseau and Rawls. They need to reaffirm their role in the social contract. They need to recognize that the power of the government comes from them. They need to remember that justice is what the government *should do* and how the government *should be measured*.

The people also need to remember that human integrity—corporeal, psychological, and social—is a boundary that the government must never cross, and that crossing that boundary demands that the people then rise up against their government. Early in the graphic novel, as he tries to get Evey to share her story with him, V says that "Everybody is special. Everybody. Everybody is a hero, a lover, a fool, a villain. Everybody" (26). This sentiment is not just about making us feel good. It is the basis or the first principle of our political being. Each person is special, so each person has an intrinsic integrity that is inviolable. We can see this truth most starkly in the heartbreaking story of Valerie in Book Two.

While Evey is imprisoned by V (again, without her knowing that V is behind it), she begins receiving messages on toilet paper that is rolled up and slid through a little hole in her cell wall. The messages are from a woman named Valerie in the next cell (of course, she is not really there). She describes her childhood, her grappling with her sexuality, and her love affair with Ruth (some of the very few panels that have blue skies and green grass occur here). We see teachers and parents who pressure Valerie to be someone she is not, even if being other than she is would make her life easier (at least in one conventional sense). Valerie writes that "it was my integrity that was important. Is that so selfish? It sells for so little, but it's all we have left in this place [the prison]. It is the very last inch of us." Then, in the very next panel, with Evey having her head thrust into a bucket of water in order to get her to provide information to the authorities about V, we see Valerie's next words: "but within that inch we are free" (156). Valerie goes on to say of that inch, "It's small and it's fragile and it's the only thing in the world that's worth having./ We must never lose it, or sell it, or give it away. We must never let them take it from us./ . . . / I know every inch of this cell. This cell knows every inch of me. Except one" (160). The last panels of this quotation show Evey kissing the toilet paper with the text on it and then just her sad yet determined face.

Though Valerie is not in the next cell, she is not fictional in the context of the graphic novel. The "real" Valerie *was* in the cell next to V when they both were at the detention camp. And she was able to describe for V in a passionate way what we might say we find in an abstract way in Rawls's first principle of justice—the fundamental value and integrity of the human person that must never be violated and that forms the very basis of our freedom. When governments respect human integrity, then their citizens can be free and can form powerful love relationships. When that most precious "inch" of us is forsaken (for wealth, security, power, or whatever else our leaders seek) and even violated, then we no longer are free and love becomes so much more difficult to achieve.

As he is explaining to Evey why he imprisoned and tortured her, V argues for the priority of freedom (a freedom based on human integrity) over everything else—even happiness. In what might be seen as a critique of utilitarianism, V says that "Happiness is a prison, Evey. Happiness is the most insidious prison of all" (169). It is insidious for many reasons. Our pursuit of happiness may lead us to all sorts of manipulations and violations of others in order to achieve it. It also can lead us to accept passively less freedom in order to obtain some paltry measure of happiness (safety, consumer goods, fleeting entertainment, etc.). Such a trade-off is an example of a bad social contract from V's point of view. Indeed, this is why Rawls affirms freedom or liberty in the prioritizing of the first principle of justice over the second principle. We *must* begin with freedom, freedom for everyone. Only then can we pursue happiness. Perhaps V's more radical claim is that freedom is not only the fundamental condition for happiness but also the most fundamental form of happiness.

But these facts about human integrity, freedom, and the genuine pursuit of happiness are precisely what the population has forgotten.[3] That is why V wants them to remember—to remember the 5th of November when a small band of men sought to put the government back in its place (under the thumb of the people) and to liberate those who were being oppressed. By remembering, his hope is that people will act and a new better social contract can be established—a constract built on respect, love, and trust for and among real human beings rather than mere abstractions.

Early in the graphic novel, V tells Evey, "Just trust me . . . and we can wipe it all away. All the pain, all the cruelty, all the bereavement. We can start again" (29). To start again, however, V must wake up the population from their political and moral slumber. His terrorist activities are part of the effort to psychologically jolt the population, to agitate them into action. For this reason, he turns to anarchy.

Anarchy is not the same as chaos. V explains to Evey that chaos means "without order," whereas anarchy simply means a "true order" that is "without leaders"—because in the anarchic state the leaders and the people are one and the same (195). Nevertheless, chaos is a prelude to genuine anarchy. As he tells Evey, "Anarchy wears two faces, both creator and destroyer. Thus destroyers topple empires; make a canvas of clean rubble where creators can then build a better world" (222).

V's plan works to perfection. As the society falls into disorder, he again seizes a government broadcasting instrument (this time a city-wide speaker system) to appeal directly to the citizens: "Since mankind's dawn, a handful of oppressors have accepted the responsibility over our lives that we should have accepted for ourselves. By doing so, they took our power. By doing nothing, we gave it away./ We've seen where their way leads, through camps and wars, towards the slaughterhouse. In anarchy there is another way. With anarchy, from rubble comes new life, hope reinstated" (258). Then, echoing the famous lines of Rousseau's work on the social contract, V tells the people, "Tonight, you must choose what comes next. Lives of our own, or a return to chains" (258).

In the end, we are left with a society that has jettisoned its leaders (oppressors) and that is beginning to create a new order. V has died, but there is hope. There is hope for an order that manifests justice, love, and liberty, characteristics that are required for any order to survive (198).

Conclusion

Social contract theory is an important and effective way of thinking about the organization of society and the relationship between the people and their leaders. From Hobbes to Rousseau to Rawls, theorists have grappled with the trade-offs involved in the social contract—liberty versus security, order versus chaos, and much more.

The social contract is central to the plot of *V for Vendetta*. But in this graphic novel we get so much more. We get passion, energy, excitement, and love. Indeed, we learn from V that love is critical to the social contract. We must love our country for the social contract to work, but even more we must love one another. Only then will we be able to create the kind of society where love then thrives and where powerful love relationships can grow and survive.

We should recall here what we learned from Nussbaum. Political emotions like love and compassion (the latter a necessary part of the former) are "to engender and sustain strong commitment to worthy projects that require effort and sacrifice" (3). In a striking way, V reveals this truth to us. His efforts are significant, and he is willing to make the most ultimate sacrifice for the principles and *real* people that he loves. In addition, such political emotions "keep at bay forces that lurk in all societies and, ultimately, in all of us; tendencies to protect the fragile self by denigrating and subordinating others" (3). We all are fragile, even V. It is only through love and compassion, however, that we are able to avoid the temptation to build a fortress around our fragility by "denigrating and subordinating others"—in a sense, building ourselves up by tearing others down. Again, V does much to show us the way.

Towards the end of the graphic novel, as she contemplates a world without V, as she tries to come to grips with who V was, Evey says "I know who V must be" (250). A few panels later we see her facing a mirror, and a knowing smile crosses her face (251). She knows who V must be—it is her. Indeed, we all are V. At least we should be. At least we should be if we hope to live in a world that is just and free and loving.

Notes

1. The classic works on Utilitarianism are: Jeremy Bentham, A*n Introduction to the Principles of Morals and Legislation* (1789) and John Stuart Mill, *Utilitarianism* (1861). Modern application of this school of thought can be seen in the writings of philosophers such as Peter Singer *Animal Liberation* (1975) and *The Life you Can Save* (2010).

2. Rawls includes a discussion of love in *A Theory of Justice*, and of particular importance is what he calls "love of mankind." However, it does not work out in detail the connection of such love to his theory of justice and its role in a well-ordered society—at least not as thoroughly as does Nussbaum.

3. Moore shares in a short preface to the novel that he is concerned about the current state (1988) and future of England. Clearly, he wants his fellow citizens to remember V as well.

Bibliography

Hobbes, Thomas. *Leviathan*. New York: Penguin Books, 1968.
Moore, Alan, and David Lloyd (with Steve Whitaker and Siobhan Dodds). *V for Vendetta*. New York: DC Comics, 2005.
Nussbaum, Martha. *Political Emotions: Why Love Matters for Justice*. Cambridge, MA: Harvard University Press, 2013.
Rawls, John. *A Theory of Justice*. Cambridge, MA: Harvard University Press, 1999. Revised edition.

Rousseau, Jean-Jacques. *The Social Contract*. Translated by Charles Frankel. New York: Hafner Publishing, 1947.

Further Reading

Moore, Alan. *Voice of the Fire*. Marietta, GA: Top Shelf Productions, 2009.
Moore, Alan, and Brian Bolland. *Batman: The Killing Joke*. New York: DC Comics, 2008.
Moore, Alan, and Dave Gibbons. *Watchmen*. New York: DC Comics, 2014.
Moore, Alan, and David Lloyd and Tony Weare. *Absolute V for Vendetta*. New York: Vertigo, 2009.
Moore, Alan, and Kevin O'Neill. *The League of Extraordinary Gentlemen*. New York: Vertigo, 2013.

Asterix, Carnival, and the Wonder of Everyday Life

Jeremy Barris

René Goscinny and Albert Uderzo's *Asterix* novels present us with a charmingly silly world. Their shared premise is that, during the time of the Roman Empire, a tiny Gaulish village has a magic potion that makes its inhabitants extremely strong and fast, and this allows the village to keep the entire Roman Empire at a hopeless disadvantage. The main character is a wily little warrior named Asterix who, with his good, very large, and not very bright friend Obelix, has many absurd adventures as he travels in the Roman world and beyond. I shall explore *Asterix at the Olympic Games*, in which Asterix and a group of the villagers compete in the Olympic Games in ancient Greece. I shall try to show that the charmingly silly, unpretentious humor of *Asterix at the Olympic Games* does not just offer us escapist entertainment, but also embodies and so offers us a deep appreciation of the ordinary and everyday. (I should say that I have no objection to purely escapist entertainment; I just think that more is going on in this particular case.)

Because the style of humor is the same in all of the *Asterix* novels, I could have chosen any of them to explore this point. As a result, if what I say about this particular novel is right, it should help us to recognize some of what is to be appreciated in the others too. I shall try to show that *Asterix at the Olympic Games* achieves the possibility of this deeper insight into our everyday world paradoxically, by departing from the most basic functioning of that world and so by taking us radically out of the ordinary and everyday. This paradoxical achievement has strong similarities with that of the carnival tradition that the Russian scholar Mikhail Bakhtin describes in connection with medieval folk festivals, in which, for example, a peasant is made to be mock lord for a day, and the festivities include making undignified fun of the nobles. The comedy of this carnival tradition, Bakhtin argues, turns the everyday world thoroughly topsy-turvy, with the result that we are given a holiday from, and a fresh perspective on, the familiar structures and proceedings of our lives and of the world as a whole.

Carnival and the Paradoxical Perspective on the Everyday World as a Whole

Bakhtin argues that "carnival celebrated temporary liberation from the prevailing truth and from the established order" (1984 [1965], 10), creating "a special condition of the entire world, of the world's revival and renewal" (7).[1] Carnival does this in the form of humor, of "a continual shifting from top to bottom, from front to rear, of numerous parodies and travesties, humiliations, profanations, comic crownings and uncrownings" (11). As we shall see, all of these elements are also present in *Asterix at the Olympic Games*. As a result of this liberation from established truth, "The entire world is seen in its droll aspect, in its gay relativity" (11): we see the world as one in which nothing is absolutely fixed, nothing is the way things always have to be. But part of this liberation is that while this "folk humor denies [the world it parodies], ... it revives and renews at the same time" (11). The carnival spirit "offers the chance to have a new outlook on the world, to realize the relative nature of all that exists, and to enter a completely new order of things" (34). And in the humor of this kind of carnival, Bakhtin argues, "each image is subject to the meaning of the whole; each reflects a single concept of a contradictory world of becoming" (149).

Generally, in order for us to be aware of something, we need to be at some distance from it, not entirely immersed in it. For example, if we are completely absorbed in reading a book, we stop being aware that we are reading and instead become lost in the content of what we are reading. When we are interrupted, we often get a little startled at the reminder that the regular world, where we are reading, is the one we are actually in. The idea that we need some distance to be aware of something is also true of our general awareness of the everyday world; we can only be aware of the everyday world to the extent that we are not wholly immersed in it. In regular everyday life, for instance, when we are thoroughly absorbed in what we are saying, we are not usually aware of the grammar of our sentences as we talk. We only notice how we are forming our sentences when, say, we have difficulty expressing ourselves, and are then pulled out of being absorbed in what we are saying and so can reflect on how we are saying it.

Unlike with most other things, however, being unreflectively immersed in the ordinary and everyday *defines* a great deal of the ordinary and everyday and, with it, the bulk and substance of our lives and world. Reality, after all, is exactly what we take for granted as independent of our perspective and reflection, what we take as what we can rely on without having to think about it. As the great Austrian philosopher Ludwig Wittgenstein points out, "I did not get my picture of the world by satisfying myself of its correctness; ... No: it is the inherited background against which I distinguish between true and false" (1969, 15e), a picture or background that is already in place before I start reflecting on and making sense of things. That background picture of the world consists in a host of meanings and their relations. For example, before I can decide whether an idea about or perception of a tree is true or false, I first have to have at least the idea of a physical thing, and to have that idea I must have the ideas of three dimensions or more generally of space, and of solidity, and of a surface or ground that the tree or object can be located on, and of various kinds of materials that the tree and ground can be composed of, and so on. If there are meaningful objects to ask questions about, and meaningful questions to ask, then the world is already divided into a variety of objects and the kinds of connections they can have with each other, and also the kinds of thoughts that compose the questions we are asking. Without such a general, basic outline of the world already in place before I start reflecting, I cannot reflect on anything, because there is not yet anything meaningful to reflect on.

Our reflection, then, depends on a pre-existing grasp of the sense of the world or reality, a grasp that must have been in place before we began to reflect on that sense. And this necessarily unreflective grasp of the sense of reality is part of what makes up our everyday experience of the world, in which we take for granted that, for example, there is a world, and objects in it, and that those objects operate in certain ways, and that we ourselves operate in certain familiar ways.

The everyday world, then, is partly defined as what we are unreflectively immersed in. As a result, in giving us a perspective on and so a distance from the everyday as a whole, the humor in *Asterix at the Olympic Games* takes us thoroughly and altogether out of our familiar lives and our world as a whole. In particular, as I have noted, the everyday includes the basic sense that the world makes, that is, the basic ways in which the world is meaningful, logically coherent, and therefore understandable. Consequently, in taking us thoroughly out of the ordinary, the book's humor in fact takes us not only out of what is familiar, but out of the most basic ways that the world and our lives make sense. As Bakhtin notes about carnivals too, their language, for example, builds on "intentionally absurd verbal combinations, a form of completely liberated speech that ignores all norms, even those of elementary logic" (422).

Let me clarify that I do not mean that *Asterix at the Olympic Games*, like all fiction, takes us into an alternative, fictional world, and that this alternative world gives us a perspective on our everyday world and life through the contrast it makes with it. I mean that the humor of this book takes us outside of the most basic ways that the world as a whole, or reality in general, makes sense, with the result that the sense of *any* part or kind of reality becomes unclear and uncertain, including the sense of any imaginary realities we might come up with. In other words, what the book's humor contrasts with is all sense, in general, whatever it might be the sense of. As a result, the perspective it offers us is on the nature of sense itself, that is, on meaningfulness and coherence and logic themselves, in general. This perspective is therefore also on the sense—the meaningfulness and coherence—of reality in general or as a whole. As Bakhtin argues, this kind of humor turns the whole world topsy-turvy, and allows us a fresh perspective on *everything*, nothing excepted, not even stories or imaginations of contrasting realities—and not even what it means and how it works to have a perspective! In other words, with Bakhtin, I am proposing that the perspective the book offers us is so deep that it allows us freshly to reconsider the meaning and so the truth of things in the most fundamental and all-inclusive way (including even the meaningfulness and value of engaging in this kind of deep reconsideration or reflection). Not bad for a deliberately silly cartoon novel!

Of course, we can and should ask how such a radical reflection is possible, how we could conceivably reflect on things when the sense of our own reflections themselves is made uncertain. A little below, I will discuss how this might be possible.

As I shall try to show, then, the humor of *Asterix at the Olympic Games* repeatedly violates the principles or logic that structure the world's sense. And in doing so, it brings our attention to this sense. As a result, we can come to recognize and wonder at the fact simply that the world is as it is: that there is a world, that there is a sense to things, and that this particular world with its particular meanings and sense happens to be the one we are given. (In fact, I would argue that this kind of humor not only can but *does* give us this perspective, this wondering recognition that the world is as it is; I would argue that the particular pleasure this type of humor gives us is exactly this experience of charmed wonder at the world, and perhaps a sense that the world is a better place for having such works in it. We usually would not think of our amusement that way, but I suggest that is because we usually just do not realize that this is what we are experiencing. But I will not insist on this now. My discussion of the specific working of our book's humor, though, should give some support to this view.)

Bakhtin's own concern is primarily with awareness of our social world as a whole, but the Western philosophical tradition takes up the same theme of reflecting on the world as a whole in a way that goes beyond the social world. In the Western philosophical tradition the recognition simply of the existence of the world and of its sense is the basis of metaphysics: the recognition of and wonder at, not this or that reality, but reality or being itself. As Plato explains in his dialogue *Theaetetus*, philosophy "has no other origin" than the "sense of wonder" (1969, 155D), and in pursuing the sense of wonder, the philosopher's thought "takes wings, as [the poet] Pindar says, 'beyond the sky, beneath the earth,'... everywhere seeking the true nature of everything as a whole" (173E–174A). This recognition of existence is also what, in the twentieth century, Wittgenstein identifies as insight into the mystical. He writes, "It is not *how* things are in the world that is mystical, but *that* it exists.... Feeling the world as a limited whole—it is this that is mystical" (1961 [1921], 73).

It is not accidental that something like silly humor can be connected with the same kind and depth of insight as metaphysical reflection. For the same reasons that a perspective on the everyday puts us at a distance from familiar sense, serious metaphysical reflection, or reflection on the whole of reality, moves beyond all given sense, and so, like silly humor, involves all sorts of obvious failures to make complete or proper sense. As Karl Jaspers argues, the words and concepts we use in reflecting on the nature of reality in general "had their original meaning for definite things in the world," but "now ... they are used to go beyond the limits and are not to be understood in their original sense" (1997 [1935], 111). As a result, he writes, "Through reason I catch sight of something which is only communicable in the form of contradiction and paradox. Here a rational a-logic arises, a true reason which reaches its goal through the shattering of the logic of the understanding" (112). Similarly, Wittgenstein famously argues at one point that his own metaphysical statements are in fact "nonsensical" and must be used "as steps—to climb up beyond them," and that is what allows us to "see the world aright." The reader of his statements "must, so to speak, throw away the ladder after he has climbed up it" (1961 [1921], 74).[2]

As I noted, we could and should ask whether this kind of reflection and perspective on reality as a whole is really possible. If this reflection involves our stepping outside of the whole of sense, then, surely, it simply does not make sense. In addition, a perspective on the whole of reality includes a perspective on ourselves, and this means we need to be entirely outside of ourselves, which is clearly impossible. I will not attempt to offer an adequate defense of this kind of metaphysical, ultimate insight into reality here. I will only point out that this very objection, that insight into the whole of reality is impossible, itself decides that something would not make sense with respect to the whole of reality, and so in fact reflects on that same whole of reality that it claims we cannot reflect on. For instance, this objection claims to understand what "the whole of reality" means; otherwise it could not draw conclusions about what makes sense in connection with that concept. As a result, it claims the kind of insight that it argues we cannot possibly have. By its own conclusion, then, we cannot take it seriously.

My point here is not that insight into the whole of reality definitely is possible, but that this is a very difficult question to answer one way or the other—that *either* answer lands us in illogicalities. As a result, then, we can at least keep open the possibility that, as inconceivable as metaphysical insight or insight into the whole of things may seem to be, its inconceivability is not the last word, and that it *might* be conceivable and achievable. We certainly cannot rule it out in a way that clearly makes sense.

In other words, this question about whether metaphysical insight is possible is exactly the kind of question, about the whole of sense, that metaphysical reflection asks, and it has exactly the kind of deeply conflicted and uncertain sense that I have argued this kind of reflection has. (I should clarify that this is not a victory for my argument. A perspective like the one I am exploring here has built into it that it might not always be making sense and so its prima facie success might be overturned. This kind of perspective succeeds by giving us a fresh consideration, even of itself and its own value, and so does not work by winning or losing. The ending of *Asterix at the Olympic Games* will illustrate this nicely.)

It might help us a little to conceive how this kind of insight might be possible if we bear in mind that we are in the territory of paradox, and that as a result, not making sense in this logically paradoxical context might be compatible with also making sense. For example, if we are wholly outside sense, we cannot be making no sense at all, because then what we are doing *would* make sense as being simply and clearly nonsense. (In fact, this is how the view rejecting the possibility of metaphysical insight in the previous paragraph understands it and so makes sense of it). We know what nonsense is; it is the opposite of sense, whose nature we also understand. In other words, being wholly outside sense is also being outside the sense even of "being wholly outside sense," and therefore includes making or being inside sense!

Another way to see this is that in this context of trying to get a perspective on the sense of the whole of things, the only reason we step outside sense is that we are trying to make sense of sense, and this requires us to get a distance from it and see it to some extent from the outside. In other words, it is the commitment to making sense itself that requires us to depart from sense. Consequently, when we leave sense in this particular context, we are also obeying the requirements of sense.

I have argued that either answer to the question about whether reflection on reality and sense as a whole is possible seems unable to make clear sense. And I have suggested that the deep difficulty of this question leaves it open for us reasonably to explore this type of reflection and awareness as a real possibility. If it is a real possibility, it is, I think, also an important one that is worth trying to understand and achieve. In that light, I now return to exploring and proposing it as part of what *Asterix at the Olympic Games* offers us.

While the metaphysical awareness of existence is interesting and valuable enough, the humor of *Asterix at the Olympic Games* also brings about an appreciation and celebration specifically of the *unquestioningly taken for granted* character of the everyday and of the basic sense of things. In other words, it allows us to notice and appreciate the meaningfulness of the everyday as what is just ordinary and so as specifically what we do *not* notice and reflect on! And even more oddly, it does so in the very act of removing us from the everyday and its sense and so removing our taking them for granted. (This reflection that, illogically, does not interfere with not reflecting is again possible, I suggest, because in the territory of logical paradox, what genuinely does not make sense does not exclude also making sense.) It achieves this paradoxical maneuver by couching its violations of the world's basic sense in a humorous and charming atmosphere and in the context of very familiar, everyday aspects of our lives. As a result, the destabilizing of the everyday and its sense only brings out, by contrast, their safely unshakeable solidity. In this way, the very ordinary, familiar world as we unreflectively live it is opened up to our reflective awareness and appreciation, without in that process losing the homey, taken for granted character that is essential to it.

In this respect, the awareness offered by *Asterix at the Olympic Games* is the extreme opposite of another typical aspect of metaphysical insight, in which the experience of the familiar world as unfamiliar makes it unsettlingly strange. Here, nothing we know is quite as it is supposed to be, and this creates a dream-like, uncanny alienation from our world and lives. In fact, a number of Russian literary scholars contemporary with Bakhtin, known as Formalists, argued that the central function of literary art was to allow us freshly to see the world exactly by "defamiliarizing" or "estranging" us from our familiar experience of it.[3] Even in the case of the charming world of *Asterix*, this uneasy dimension perhaps comes into play when we put the book down and at some point are struck by the gulf between the charm of the fantasy world of the book and the drearier aspects of real life.

But as I have noted, and as I shall discuss further at the end of the next section, the wonder that *Asterix at the Olympic Games* brings about is not just a fantasy, but is an insight into the basis or foundations of reality and truth, into the presence and solidity of reality that we otherwise take for granted. In fact, both of these dimensions of metaphysical insight, the sense of the world as uncanny and the sense of it as wonderful, are legitimate and in the end essential to a full metaphysical awareness. But I suggest further—in keeping with the violation of everyday sense that occurs in this perspective from "outside the world"—that even though these insights thoroughly conflict with each other, still, because each of them is an insight into the nature of the *whole* world or the *whole* of reality, each is also true in a way that is entirely unaffected by the other. Each by its very nature is an insight into the whole of things, and so leaves nothing out to conflict with it That is, the truth that each insight succeeds in capturing is wholly the truth, without need for qualification or emendation, even though the conflicting truth the other insight captures is also wholly and without qualification the truth.

In fact, this is sometimes illustrated in the case of putting the book down that I mentioned above, since in the lingering context of the appreciative perspective the book gives us, even the contrast with unpleasant aspects of life that might strike us when we put the book down can be experienced as a kind of poignant wonder, for example, wonder at a world that, despite often being dispiriting and harsh, can still include such heartwarmingly transporting experiences as a book like this can provide. In this experience of being transported, we feel a delight completely independent of and unaffected by the harsh aspects of life; as a result, when we become aware of those aspects again, they can strike us, at least for a moment, as less important in the larger scheme of things.

Exactly how it might be possible to put together conflicting and in fact mutually exclusive metaphysical perspectives (or, in other words, conflicting wholly true views about the same whole reality) is a story for another time.[4] In the meantime, I have proposed that the *Asterix* books offer the dimension of metaphysical awareness that is the sense of the wonder of things; and I have argued that even though this is only one dimension of metaphysical insight, it will remain an unqualified and undiluted insight even when we take contrasting dimensions of metaphysical insight into account. It is therefore an insight that we can legitimately explore in its own right without considering those other possible dimensions of metaphysical awareness.

It is also important to note that a number of the essays in this book, true to one of the most important roles of graphic novels and comic books, highlight some of the politically skewed or otherwise deeply troublesome aspects of life. While I argue that *Asterix at the Olympic Games* shows us the wonder or meaningfulness of things, I should emphasize that this is not at the cost of neglect of or collaboration with suffering and social wrongdoing.[5] I shall return to this issue in the final section of this essay.

The Topsy-Turvy World of *Asterix at the Olympic Games*

I have hinted at, but not yet shown, that the humor of *Asterix at the Olympic Games* brings about an appreciation of the meaningfulness of the unquestioningly taken for granted character of our everyday lives and of the familiar sense of things, and that it does so by violating that sense in the context of a humorous and charming atmosphere. I have also suggested that the unsettling of the everyday and its sense brings out, by contrast, their safely unshakeable solidity. I will now try to show that the book establishes these violations of sense and also its charming atmosphere through word, image, and story structure.

For a start, the premise of the whole series of *Asterix* books is topsy-turvy. As I described it earlier, a tiny Gaulish village has a magic potion that makes its inhabitants extremely strong and fast, and this allows the village to keep the entire Roman Empire at a hopeless disadvantage. The legend to the frontispiece, present in all the *Asterix* books, reads, "Gaul is entirely occupied by the Romans. Well, not entirely ... one small village of indomitable Gauls still holds out ... And life is not easy for the Roman legionaries who garrison the fortified camps of Totorum, Aquarium, Laudanum and Compendium."[6]

The plot of *Asterix at the Olympic Games* is paradoxical as well. First, our heroes' life-mission is to resist the Romans' conquest of their country, but because only Greek and Roman citizens are allowed to participate in the Olympic Games, our heroes enthusiastically enter the games as the citizens Rome claims them to be. Then, when the Gauls find out that using magic potion is against the rules of the games, they trick the Romans into stealing their potion and using it. As a result, all the Roman competitors, fuelled by the potion that has always given the Gauls the advantage over them, win their race against Asterix, the lone Gaul running against them. Asterix himself comments during the race, "This is all topsy-turvy!" (2004 [1968], 46).[7] But Asterix then exposes the Romans and they are disqualified for using the potion, leaving Asterix as the winner. The outcome, in other words, is that the Gauls win as a result of the way in which they lose. Finally, at the end of the novel we discover that Asterix has given his victory palm to the Gauls' traditional enemy, the Romans, in sympathy. As Asterix explains, "I gave it to someone whose need was greater than mine" (48). The final panel in the book, usually devoted to celebration in the Gaulish village, instead shows us the bad guys ending up happy and promoted, and "For once . . . Caesar is pleased!" (48). (As I mentioned in the previous section, the deep perspective the book's humor offers does not work by winning or losing, by simply either succeeding or failing!)

The logical and rhetorical substance of the whole novel is also topsy-turvy. The conversations between the characters and the presentation of the story are each a tissue of contradictions, non sequiturs (completely irrelevant leaps of thought), equivocations (expressions that mix up mutually irrelevant meanings, here often in the form of puns), conceptual confusions (mistaking one type of meaning or situation for another), and circularities (supporting an idea's truth on the basis of its own claim to truth).

For example, when centurion Gaius Veriambitius[8] discovers that the fearsome Gauls are going to claim Roman citizenship and enter the Olympic Games against the champion who is supposed to bring him victory and promotion, he fumes indignantly, "I ask you! You fight people, you massacre them, you invade and occupy their territory, and then they turn against you for no reason at all!" (14). The joke here turns on an emphatic contradiction, or perhaps an extreme conceptual confusion: a cluster of glaringly good reasons is taken not to qualify as any reason at all. A less elaborate version of this kind of combination occurs later, when they have all arrived in Athens and Asterix says, "Speaking of foreigners, here come our fellow countrymen!" (25).[9]

Non sequiturs are a particularly prominent feature of the novel's humor. Early on in the story, Asterix, our hero, and Obelix, his trusty comrade, come across the Roman champion, Legionary Gluteus Maximus, training in the forest.[10] When Obelix was a baby, he had fallen into the cauldron of magic potion, and so he is permanently very strong and fast (e.g., 16). He is also very large. He and Asterix casually overtake the sprinting Roman without apparent effort and accidentally show him up in other ways. Gluteus Maximus is furious, and confronts Obelix: "You fatty! I'll take you on at ordinary wrestling, all-in wrestling, boxing! I'll wallop you at those! I'm the greatest! I'm . . ." (9). He is interrupted at that point because Obelix, without changing his casual posture, hits Gluteus Maximus so hard that he disappears from the panel altogether and lands high up in a nearby tree. As Obelix hits him, he comments quietly, "I'm not fat!" (9). That is, Obelix, both in word and in the casual posture we see in the drawing, disregards the threats and all the emphatic claims about skilled strength in the statement he is responding to, and instead responds only to what is a trivial side-issue with respect to what that statement focuses on communicating. In other words, he responds with a non sequitur. The next panel consolidates this non sequitur. Obelix turns to Asterix and asks earnestly, "Tell me straight, Asterix, once and for all: do you think I'm fat?" Asterix replies, "Of course not, Obelix. Your chest has slipped a bit, that's all. Come on, are we going to get those boars?" And in the following panel we see them stroll off (9). The actual issue the Roman raised so elaborately has now completely disappeared from their attention.

At the same time, however, Obelix has very thoroughly refuted those claims—and he has done so in the very act of disregarding them so completely. Because he beats Gluteus Maximus thoroughly but for a reason that entirely ignores his claims to skilled strength, Obelix's actions both show his superior strength and point us away from paying attention to the issue of skill or strength at all. And in this way they bring out even more starkly and clearly how trivial the Roman's claimed abilities are. Gluteus Maximus's abilities are entirely disregardable.

By its humorous exaggeration, then, the non sequitur actually works to make the centrally relevant aspects of the original topic especially clear: in relation to our Gaulish heroes, Gluteus Maximus's superior skills and strength are only imagined.

In the following example, things get interestingly complicated. At the start of the story, the aged Geriatrix[11] reports that he was picking mushrooms near the Roman camps, and was puzzled by overhearing the Romans engaged in some kind of high-spirited celebration. When the chief of the Gaulish tribe, Vitalstatistix,[12] muses that he does not "know what to make of them," Obelix (who is very large and always hungry), comments, "Mushroom soup is very nice" (6). In the next panel, Chief Vitalstatistix turns red with rage and roars, "Soup?! . . . Is that all you can think of, Obelix?!" But then, in the following panel, he declares, "When you get mushrooms you should make an omelette. That's how the real gourmet eats them!" (6). And in a further panel Obelix, Vitalstatistix, and Geriatrix are walking off while debating how to prepare the mushrooms. "I was thinking," says Geriatrix, "perhaps on toast" (6).[13]

Obelix's comment is a non sequitur, which is made explicit in the next panel; but in the following panels it is turned into and remains the main issue, so that the original issue is altogether abandoned in favor of the non sequitur. On the one hand, this sequence ignores the logic of what is relevant to the issue under discussion. On the other hand, however, its humor involves tripping us up, and this depends on our expectation that the sequence will follow the logic of what is relevant. In other words, the sequence also relies on that same logic of relevance.

The visual separation of the panels helps to achieve and underline this combination of emphasizing the mistaken nature of the logic and yet also disregarding that mistake. The chief's furious focus on the mistake has a panel to itself, isolating it so that it captures our attention in its own right; but treating the non sequitur as not a mistake then also occurs in its own panels, and so in its turn is isolated from the recognition of the mistake.

In the light of this combination, then, this kind of humor does not simply violate the sense of the world, but as Bakhtin points out, it both disregards it and also at the same time takes it seriously. This kind of humor gives us a perspective on the world—on what the world is and how it is—that has not yet made up its mind. "Each image," Bakhtin writes, "reflects a single concept of a contradictory world of becoming" (1984 [1965], 149). Consequently, the perspective this humor opens up allows and requires us to contemplate the world without stable preconceptions, to be aware of it simply for what it is or might be, even down to the still undecided possibilities of its fundamentally making sense or of its not making sense at all.

Asterix and the wise druid, Getafix,[14] have witnessed this exchange about the Romans and the mushrooms. Getafix comments, "Sometimes I get the impression our friends don't take things seriously enough. . . . It may be a bad sign for us if the Romans are in a good mood" (6). When Asterix asks what he would suggest, Getafix says, in the next panel, "Let them stew in their own juice!"[15] In the context of the serious concern about the Romans he has just expressed, we naturally take this to be a metaphor, though it also mischievously makes a kind of pun on its literal reference to the topic of cooking that sidetracked the other Gauls. But in the following panel, he adds, "It brings out the flavour" (6).[16] So we are still talking about mushrooms after all! Getafix's last comment has no exclamation point, and he makes it with a deadpan expression, suggesting that he is not joking, and this is confirmed by Asterix's deeply startled reaction in the same panel. That is, Getafix, the very embodiment of wisdom and good sense, who of all people should know better, immediately repeats the same recognition and then commission of the logical error we have just seen happen with the other characters.

But in this case, Getafix repeats the combination in a sort of pun. In logical terms, a pun is a humorously meant equivocation, an expression that works with mutually irrelevant meanings without differentiating them.[17] As a result, it initially looks as though Getafix is joking, and so creating nonsense only in order to direct us good-humoredly to the sense that contrasts with it. Seen in this context, perhaps this apparent maneuver even works, as we have said this kind of humor can do, to bring that contrasting sense out into relief so that we appreciate its solidity all the more. But then he turns out not to have been joking after all. The joke, like the other responses to Obelix's non sequitur, turns out to have been the same mistake we thought it was helping to correct. As a result, in this case, the joke now is that the original joke was not a joke after all.

If the apparent pun really had been a joke, its nonsense would have worked to confirm the contrasting sense; but because it turns out not to have been a joke after all, its straightforward nonsense simply commits the logical mistake that the joke had originally appeared to avoid. But as we saw in the combination of recognition and then commission of the mistake above, in order for the discovery that the original joke was not a joke to surprise us and so to constitute a joke of its own, we first had to react to the original joke as genuinely a joke. In other words, in this case, the humor of its turning out not to have been a joke depends on reliance on it as originally working as a joke.[18]

In the panels preceding Getafix's comments, the humor combined reliance on and disregard of logic, and in this way suspended our clarity about the contrasting roles and contributions of sense and nonsense. Here, our clarity about the contrasting roles in and contributions to sense that humor and seriousness themselves provide, too, is suspended. As Bakhtin writes about carnival humor, "It is also directed at those who laugh.... The people's ambivalent laughter ... expresses the point of view of the whole world; he who is laughing also belongs to it" (1984 [1965], 12). The "sense of the gay relativity of prevailing truths and authorities" (11) that Bakhtin argues the carnival spirit embodies is radical, and applies also to its own humorous and relativist truths.

As silly as Goscinny's and Uderzo's humor is, then, it should be clear at this point that it is also doing something radical. It goes down to the roots of sense, including the sense of its own process and achievement in doing so. And again, this coincidence of extremes, of silliness and profundity, is not an accident, but results logically from the paradoxical nature of making sense of sense. The substance of the serious metaphysical perspective consists exactly in suspending our most basic preconceptions about how sense works, and putting us in a position where it is not yet settled what is what.

Bakhtin argues that only the mutual contrasts of "an active plurality of languages" allow one to "place oneself outside one's own language" and so give one "the ability to see one's own media from the outside" (1984 [1965], 471). This allows "the modern time," or the time we are currently in, to become "conscious of itself" (468). The humor of *Asterix at the Olympic Games* brings about this awareness of our own particular historical culture too. Different languages and cultures are juxtaposed throughout the novel: for example, the

Romans intersperse their conversation with exclamations and proverbial sayings in Latin, each cultural group constantly invokes its own gods, and Egyptians talk in images made to look like hieroglyphics.

The nonsensical humor intensifies this contrast and the bringing into relief of our own culture that the contrast produces. When the Gauls arrive in Athens, they behave like modern tourists. The Parthenon "reminds me of Burdigala," one says. "No," says another, "there's a little square in Massilia" (25). At dinner at an open-air restaurant, Obelix muses, "D'you remember that little restaurant near Lugdunum where we had that delicious veal?" (26). These anachronisms are a kind of conceptual confusion. In another, one of the Gauls poses for a portrait (to be painted on a Grecian urn), and the painter holds up his brush and says, "Hold it there!" (25),[19] in the way a photographer might who can capture the instantaneous pose.

In a nice touch, our authors make fun even of themselves, and in a similarly mixed-up way. Behind the registration desk for entry into Olympia, where the games will be held, a wall panel shows two characters arguing. It is the only place where actual Greek language and lettering is used, but it is used to indicate speech in a way similar to the "speech bubbles" of modern comics and that is not at all characteristic of Greek painting. One character is saying "*Tyrannos*" to the other, and the other is saying "*Despothe*" back, and underneath the respective characters are carved "*Goscinny*" and "*Uderzo*" (29).

All of this topsy-turvyness is presented in connection with very ordinary, familiar aspects of our lives, and in a way that is charming. It is all endearingly silly rather than judgmental or biting, with quaint figures and caricatures, and shown in warm and pleasing colors. Even the violence is safe and too silly to be distressing. As Bakhtin writes of the carnival tradition, because of their "participation in the whole" of things, the images of carnival humor "are devoid of cynicism and coarseness in our sense of the words" (1984 [1965], 149). They express an appreciation of the elements of the world as each a part of the whole, and not a rejection of any of them. Because of the charming character of this perspective, it confirms our feeling safe and at ease in the world or, in other words, our taking the sense of the world for granted.

In fact, I suggest that it is only at this point, when we confirm our grasp of the sense of the world as that grasp is *before* deep reflection on it, that we genuinely achieve the metaphysical perspective that grasps the whole of things. For that unreflective taking-for-granted is itself part of the whole of things, and until it is included, we have not yet grasped the whole. In other words, in proper keeping with the paradox of stepping outside of sense to grasp sense as a whole, metaphysical or deep reflection is only complete when it includes what *it* in turn automatically, and so unreflectively, excludes from itself: the unreflective or shallow awareness of unconsidered life.

Differently expressed, to get a perspective on sense as a whole, we also need to step outside the sense of "being outside sense." But if where we are is outside of everything that makes sense, and we aim to step away from there, the only place left over from the "outside of everything" is the inside of everything. So if we step outside of being outside all sense, this means stepping back into the "inside" of sense. Truly to step outside of sense and the world, then, is in fact partly to relax unquestioningly and so entirely (because no longer with any reflection from the "outside") within it.

Even expressed in this deeply paradoxical way, this is one of the central insights of, for example, Zen Buddhism. As the modern Zen teacher Shunryu Suzuki expresses it, "When you are trying to give up everything, you haven't given up everything yet" (2003, 117). For instance, the Buddhist goal of not being attached or limited to your self or ego "does not mean to give up your own individual practice.... As long as you believe, 'My practice is egoless,' that means you stick to ego, because you stick to giving up ego-centered practice [for example, you are still there in the form of your commitment to an idea of how the practice should best be; and you also conduct the practice with reference to avoiding your self, which means that your self is still indirectly shaping your activity].... True egolessness . . . is not just egolessness. It also includes ego practice, but at the same time it is the practice of egolessness that is beyond ego or egolessness" (86, my insertion).

This appreciative awareness of the meaningfulness of unreflective, regular life, I think, is also the deep metaphysical lesson that the humor of *Asterix at the Olympic Games* (and with it the humor of the other *Asterix* novels) offers.

Verbal/Visual, Abstract/Concrete, Meaning/Matter

All of the logical carnival in *Asterix at the Olympic Games* occurs as much in image as in word. I have already noted the ways the separation of the panels and the drawings of posture and activity help to make and consolidate some of the logical connections and disconnections. The drawings also often portray physical impossibilities in the speed, force, and boundaries of activities; for example, they show characters shaking their heads so fast that there is just a blur of motion.

There is a nice example of the combination of visual and verbal conceptual confusion when the Gauls are competing among themselves to decide who their champions in the Games will be. Obelix tells the brawny blacksmith, Fulliautomatix, that Obelix's little dog, Dogmatix, is better than Fulliautomatix; this consternates Fulliautomatix, and Obelix asks, "Well, can you scratch your ear with your hind leg?" (16).[20] Several panels later, we see Fulliautomatix, in a doglike posture, proudly confounding the villagers by scratching his ear with his foot (16). In addition, as I have mentioned, the charm that is crucial to expressing the meaning that the carnival spirit shows us in the world is largely conveyed in the warm colors and endearing or quaint appearance of the images.

Will Eisner (1985), in his seminal book on the art of comics, explains about one of his own panels, which includes several different events, that "a description of the action in this panel can be diagrammed like a sentence. The predicates of the gun-shooting and the wrestling belong to separate clauses. The subject of 'gun-shooting' is the crook, and [the victim] is the object direct. The many modifiers include the adverb 'Bang, Bang' and the adjectives of visual language, such as posture, gesture, and grimace" (10, insertion added).[21] He also points out that "the visual treatment of words as graphic art forms is part of the vocabulary" (10). In *Asterix at the Olympic Games*, for example, heavily bolded lettering expresses great emphasis, anger, or alarm, and Greek characters "speak" in the kind of angular lettering we might find on ancient Greek carvings in stone. In fact, this last example consists not only in a visual expression of meaning but also in several different kinds of conceptual confusion (letter shapes do not play a part in sounds, the requirements of carved letters do not apply to penned writing, and carved Greek lettering does not make modified shapes of French or English script).

It is not, however, simply that images and words cooperate with each other. Something much deeper is made noticeable here. Because the art of graphic novels shows that words and images are so plainly capable of doing closely related things—the words can describe physical objects, and the pictures can express logical connections and disconnections—we can recognize that what makes this possible is that they *are* closely related things. The world we experience by seeing it, the world of physical images and equally, for that matter, the world of physical things, makes *sense* in certain ways and not in others; and, reverse-wise, the meanings of our statements and thoughts express the sense of the physical things or states of affairs that they are, after all, often statements *about*.[22] It is true that the meanings of particular words and the particular things they mean or refer to are very different from each other. Nonetheless, as Peter Winch (1958) very helpfully explains, when we are concerned with the ultimate nature of things in general—in his words, when we are concerned with "the nature of reality as such and in general" (8)—we should remember, for example, that "when we speak of the world we are speaking of what we in fact mean by the expression 'the world'" (15). In other words, in the end, "The world *is* for us what is presented through those concepts" given in our language (15). When we talk about things, we refer to something that we *mean*—even when we talk about things that are separate and different from our words, or about reality that is separate from our concepts—and this meaning *is* what our words and concepts express.[23]

Consequently, the intimate cooperation of words and images helps us to see that, when we "step outside" the sense of the world as embodied in words and images to get a perspective on and reflect on that sense, what we are seeing freshly is not just a theoretical interpretation of the world, not just our concepts, separate from the world, but the sense of the world itself that those concepts express. The kind of carnival in which the *Asterix* books consist, then, truly gives us insight into the very reality of our everyday lives and of the things of our world, and not just into our views about them.

A Note on Metaphysical Wonder, Political Injustice, and Suffering

As I mentioned in the first section, while I argue that the *Asterix* books show us the wonder or meaningfulness of the everyday world, it does not do so at the cost of neglect of or collaboration with suffering and social wrongdoing. In fact, for Bakhtin himself, the medieval folk festival tradition to which I argue the spirit of *Asterix* is similar was fundamentally political, in that it expressed the equality of the people at large in opposition to the established hierarchies of social power and privilege. These festivals, he writes, "were linked to moments of crisis, to breaking points in the cycle of nature or in the life of society and man.... They were the second life of the people, who for a time entered the utopian realm of community, freedom, equality, and abundance" (1984 [1965], 9).

Further, although I focus on the ways in which the comprehensive or cosmic perspective that Bakhtin shows in this festival tradition includes all of our basic structures of sense or meaning, that perspective still remains fundamentally political even in this extended context, in that the sense of the everyday world that it is a perspective on is partly structured or informed by political norms. As, for example, the political philosophers and cultural critics Louis Althusser (1971), Roland Barthes (1972 [1957]), and Michel Foucault (1980) have very powerfully argued, political ideology in fact works most effectively by becoming part of our taken for granted ways of understanding our world. In this way, that ideology seems simply to express reality and not to be an ideology or interpretation that serves particular interests at all.[24]

But precisely because the metaphysical perspective takes us fundamentally out of the familiar world as a whole, including out of sense itself in general, and not only out of the political dimensions of our lives, it puts us in a position to reconsider the potential biases on all sides. After all, political perspectives that aim for justice and truth have their assumptions too, and the role of what we perhaps unjustly take for granted, without realizing it, cuts both ways, and affects how we understand justice and the issues on both sides of each political divide.

This position of general re-examination also helps us to resolve a problem that has become fundamental to political debate in the last half-century or so. On the one hand, in the light of the influential idea I have mentioned that ideology and the favoring of particular interests that it disguises are built into our most basic ways of making sense, injustice is built into our fundamental structures of understanding the world, so that any political alternatives we can conceive, no matter how apparently just or supportive of equality and freedom, are themselves inescapably still shaped by the unjust assumptions and logic of those structures of sense. For example, Jean Baudrillard (1975) argues that Marx's concept of production, which is the main instrument of Marx's critique of capitalism and of his proposed movement beyond it, still embodies some of the basic, untransformed presuppositions of that same capitalism. It was in the context of capitalism, after all, that Marx learned how to think and make sense of the world. As a result, precisely to carry out Marx's liberatory goals, we would need to come to think in a way that is unavailable even to Marxism. In fact, Marx himself insisted on this same point, which is why he wrote very little about what the future state of society would look like.[25] The problem, however, is that if the biases of ideology are built into our most basic structures of sense, it is hard to see how we could possibly come to think in a way that is free of those biases.[26] Unless, to anticipate my point, we can in some way "step outside" our ways of making sense as a whole.

On the other hand, in the light of the same idea that injustice is built into our fundamental ways of making sense, even if we do somehow succeed in establishing genuinely alternative ways of understanding the world and carry them out, we will then, by definition, be operating with an altogether different way of making sense from the old one, sharing none of its basic ways of making sense. As a result, as our many-cultured and many-subcultured world has brought into sharp focus, the two ways of understanding the world will have no common ground that would allow us to compare them and establish which way of understanding things is right or better. We will no longer mean the same things by the same issues, or understand the relevant logic and evidence the same way, and there is then no way to establish our way of making sense as more legitimate than the old one, or than alternative new ways of understanding the world. As a result, we run the risk of arbitrarily and unfairly imposing our own commitments on others, those whose way of making sense of the world is still the old one, or those with yet other alternative new ways of understanding the world.

Still, the metaphysical stepping outside of sense in general helps us to move toward resolving both sides of this problem. It does so by allowing us to reconsider even the most fundamental structures of sense in our society, and to do so without first pre-deciding which are oppressive and in what ways, in what contexts, and to whom they are so.[27]

That being said, this problem is not the main concern of this essay. I am concerned here with the meaningfulness of life and our world—not excluding its politically unjust and otherwise negative dimensions, but including these in all the many diverse meaningful dimensions of life and reality. In the carnival tradition too, as Bakhtin emphasizes, even death "is not a negation of life seen as the great body of all the people but part of life as a whole—its indispensable component, the condition of its constant renewal and rejuvenation. Death is here always related to birth; the grave is related to the earth's life-giving womb" (1984 [1965], 50). In this perspective "death and renewal are inseparable in life as a whole, and life as a whole can inspire fear least of all."

But even without going as far as that thoroughly and confidently positive viewpoint, the bad sides of life require our recognition in their own unmitigated, sometimes terrible right, the wonder of life is also fundamental to reality, and this is the dimension of reality that, I believe, the metaphysical perspective of the *Asterix* books brings out. What is more, as I have suggested, in doing so it does not avoid the bad things, but in fact can help us to be sure that we are seeing them truly and so can help to put us on the path to doing justice to them. The issue is not to know what is what in advance—since, for the reasons of ideological bias I have discussed, this is something we cannot be sure we can do—but to come to sort out what is truly positive and negative, good and bad. And what allows us to do this, rather than, without realizing it, to begin already guided by our taken for granted assumptions about what the answers are, is the perspective that wonders about life and reality as a whole, and as a result steps outside of settled sense so that we genuinely do not know definitively one way or the other. In the end, if possible, I think the issue is also to come to see what place the bad aspects of the world have in a meaningful life. To arrive at all of these decisions responsibly, we first need to unsettle our sense of all of these things so that we are no longer immersed in their taken for granted familiarity, but can see them, as it were, from the outside. And this is part of what the humor of the *Asterix* books allows us to do.[28]

Notes

1. I have put the original date of publication of the works I cite in square brackets after the date of the edition I have used when there is more than a few years' difference between the two dates.

2. Wittgenstein's friend and student Norman Malcolm reports that Wittgenstein also suggested that "a serious and good philosophical work could be written that would consist entirely of *jokes*," although he also insisted that the jokes should not be "facetious" or with "no serious purpose" (1958, 29).

3. For a helpful introduction to formalism, see Bennett 1979, 20–25.

4. I explore the possibility and nature of this kind of coordination of mutually exclusive, equally legitimate overall perspectives in Barris 2015.

5. Many political theorists argue that what I have described as the homey, everyday sense of things that we do not reflect on is the most insidious operation of political ideology, since we do not even notice that this unreflective sense of things embodies biases and agendas, but simply see it as expressing the way things are. Roland Barthes, for example, argues that middle class ideology "transforms . . . History into Nature. . . . Bourgeois ideology yields an unchangeable nature" (1972, 141–142). As I have suggested, however, and as the Wittgenstein quotation in the first section argues, our unreflective sense of things is also the basis for truth, whether political or otherwise, and so has a much wider significance than just a political one. I shall discuss this further in the final section.

6. In the original French, "Totorum" is *Babaorum*, a phonetic spelling of *baba au rhum* or "rum baba," a small cake soaked in rum; and "Compendium" is *Petitbonum*, a phonetic spelling of *petit bonhomme*, which is both "little fellow" and bread cut in the shape of a little person.

7. In French, "*C'est vraiment le monde à l'envers!*" (1968, 46), which translates straightforwardly as "this is truly all topsy-turvy!"

8. In the French, *Tullius Mordicus* or "Obstinate Tullius."

9. "*À propos d'étrangers, voici des compatriots!*" (1968, 25).

10. An obelisk is both a kind of tall pillar and the typographical dagger that is used as a sign for a footnote once an asterisk has already been used: it is the asterisk's sidekick! "Gluteus Maximus" in the French is *Claudius Cornedurus* or "Claudius Hardhorn."

11. In the French, *Agecanonix*, or "Very Advanced Age."

12. In the French, *Abraracourcix*, a phonetic version of *à bras raccourcis*, "with arms raised ready to fight," or more colloquially, "with fists flying."

13. In French, Geriatrix is "rather thinking of a mushroom salad" ("*moi, je verrais plutôt les champignons en salade*" [1968, 6]).

14. In the French, *Panoramix* or "Wide View."

15. "*Il faut les faire sauter!*" (1968, 6), or roughly, "let them jump!" or "let them fry!"

16. "*Les champignons gardent toute leur saveur quand ils sont sautés*" (1968, 6): "Mushrooms keep all their flavor when they're fried (sautéed)."

17. In this case, in the English version, it is an amphiboly, or an ambiguity set up by the grammar of the sentence and not located in any of the words on their own. In French, we could think of it as an equivocation on *sauter* ("jump" and "fry," or perhaps, alternatively, on "fry" taken both literally and metaphorically).

18. This suggests that there is a sense in which, at the time of the original joke, it *was* a joke, and only retroactively, in the subsequent panel, became what was never a joke (!). This is in keeping with the general paradox at work in "stepping outside of sense in general," that sense and logic are both taken seriously and disregarded: things are not what they are, but they also are just what they are. The humor of the discovery that Getafix's statement was not a joke after all depends on reliance on it as originally working as a joke; but once we reject it as a joke, of course, it turns out originally really *not* to have been a joke at all. The sense of the humor requires that both are true, and that both are not true.

In other words, when we are reflecting, as we are, on a metaphysical perspective that suspends (while also not suspending) the functioning of sense, our own reflection or commentary on that metaphysical exploration is itself working at the level of suspended sense that belongs to the perspective that is its topic, and so our own reflection or commentary shares its illogical (and also logical) texture.

For a technical defense of the legitimate sense of this kind of retroactive and paradoxical shift of truth over time, in the context of "backward induction" in rational choice theory, see Dupuy (2000).

19. "*Ne bougeons plus!*" (1968, 25), or very literally, "Let's not move anymore!"

20. In the French, "Fulliautomatix" is *Cétautomatix*, or "It's Automatic," and "Dogmatix" is *Idéfix* or "Obsessively Unchangeable Idea." Although *Idéfix* does not make a corresponding pun to Dogmatix's pun on "dog," it does make a sort of bilingual pun on different written expressions of part of the name's sound. It is a phonetic spelling of *idée fixe*, and as a result very neatly fits the regular French "-*ixe*" to the "-ix" ending of the Gaulish name.

21. In the context of linguistics and cognitive science, Neil Cohn (2013) argues that "the mind/brain treats all expressive capacities in similar ways," so that certain "general properties of cognition emerge in the visual-graphic modality just as they do in verbal and signed languages" (195), although they occur with differences that result from the nature of "the channel and properties of the behavior itself" (196).

22. There are some very reasonable objections to the idea that words and images are closely related in this kind of way. Eric Vos (1998), for instance, quite rightly argues that words and images work in some ways that are so different as to be mutually exclusive (144), so that we cannot simply treat them as expressing the same sense. And for a very helpful and subtly nuanced book-length defense of the essentially different natures of words and images in the context of comics—and also for a very fine account of what comics distinctively do and how they do it—see Miodrag (2013). I suggest, however, that meaning or sense itself is not fully a simple, self-same "thing." This is why, for example, it is not only possible for us "step out" of sense to get a good grasp of it, but why sense itself *requires* us to "step outside" of it to get a good grasp of it. After all, we cannot be sure what sense we are making or

whether it really is the appropriate sense until we have a perspective on it; and as I argued in the first section, we can only have that perspective on something by being at some kind of distance from it. It is built into meaning or sense, then, that it works by being at some kind of a distance from itself, or by not being fully the same as itself. Because of this, I suggest, even fundamentally unlike forms of expression, such as words and images, can after all express the same meaning or sense. I explore this "non-self-concidence" of sense in detail in Barris 2015, most directly in the concluding chapter or Coda.

23. In addition to the contemporary lines of thought of which Winch's argument is an example, there is a long-standing Aristotelian tradition, from Aristotle's own work to the late medieval taking up of Aristotle, that explores the idea that concepts succeed in connecting with their particular objects and expressing them because both the concept and the object are shaped and in fact made to be what they are by one and the same "form" or structuring principle. This form provides the defining character of both the object that the concept expresses and of the concept itself, and so is more or less what I am describing as their "sense." For a brief contemporary defense of this kind of idea, see Bonjour 1998, 149–151, and 180–185.

Scott McCloud (1993) describes the cartoons that are a central element of the art of graphic novels and of other comics as "stripping down an image to its essential 'meaning'" by "focusing on specific details" (30), and he argues that "by de-emphasizing the appearance of the physical world in favor of the idea of form, the cartoon places itself in the world of concepts" (41). (Notice that McCloud draws on the idea of "form" here, our contemporary sense of which came about partly in the Aristotelian tradition mentioned above. This is also true of the connected idea of "essence" that he makes use of in this passage.) I have argued in this section, further even than this very illuminating point he makes, that cartoons can do this because the physical world itself is already partly in the world of concepts. McCloud writes a little later, "There's a lot more to cartoons than meets the eye" (45), and I would add that this helps us to see that there is a lot more to whatever we see than meets the eye.

In this light, McCloud's description of cartoons as expressing an image's essential meaning or concept implies that cartoons also express what is essential about the things or situations that the images or concepts reflect. In other words, cartoons can capture the essences of things, and so are in fact one form of the most deeply realistic and accurate kind of representation.

24. For instance, see the quotation from Barthes in note 5.

25. David McLellan (1975) writes, "on Marx's own principles . . . any detailed predictions were bound to be baseless. For all ideas were rooted in the socio-economic soil of their time, and descriptions of the future would thus be rootless ideas without any foundation in reality" (66–7). As Marx himself insisted, for example, when communist society first "emerges from capitalist society," it is "in every respect, economically, morally, and intellectually, still stamped with the birthmarks of the old society from whose womb it emerges" (1977 [1875], 568).

26. An alternative approach to dealing with this problem, one form of which was very influentially argued by Michel Foucault, is to embrace this situation. In this view, since it is inescapable that our structures of sense shape us in ways that support particular interests at the expense of others, we should all accept this and exercise our freedom by creating novel ways of making sense of our lives and so of shaping them, and encourage others to

do the same. But in that light the people who prefer to oppress us are equally justified in making sense of the world as they do and in shaping their lives as oppressors, as are any others whom our ways of understanding and living may conflict with. We fight for what we want, and they fight for they want, and there is no basis beyond that on which to defend our aims—even to ourselves—or to criticize theirs. The result is that we still have not avoided the injustices, but instead are ignoring them and in fact actively participating in them. For this kind of criticism of Foucault, see, for example, Michael Walzer, who argues that Foucault's approach to political wrongs does not "give us any way of knowing what 'better' might mean" (1986, 61).

27. In a wonderful account of radical social change that is in several ways closely related to the themes of this discussion of *Asterix*, Paolo Virno (2008) argues that fundamental political change requires an escape from our entire system of meanings to a completely different one. Because these systems of meanings are mutually exclusive, the transition between them involves radical shifts in the meanings of what we are talking and thinking about. In other words, this transition consists in a tissue of logical errors (in fact, all the standard fallacies that critical reasoning textbooks teach us to avoid). And as Virno argues, these errors correspond to different types of jokes.

28. I would like to thank Jeff McLaughlin for his thorough and very helpful comments, which have helped me to clarify and deepen my discussion considerably. I would also like to thank Steve de Wijze for his careful and encouraging reading of the essay, as well as for his illuminating insights into the world of *Asterix*. And I thank Paul Turner for helping me to get clear on and so to try to avert some likely misunderstandings of my in many ways counter-intuitive theme.

Bibliography

Althusser, Louis. "Ideology and Ideological State Apparatuses." In *Lenin and Philosophy and Other Essays*. Translated by Ben Brewster. London: Monthly Review Press, 1971. 127–186.

Bakhtin, Mikhail. *Rabelais and His World*. Translated by Hélène Iswolsky. Bloomington: Indiana University Press, 1984 [1965].

Barris, Jeremy. *Sometimes Always True: Undogmatic Pluralism in Politics, Metaphysics, and Epistemology*. New York: Fordham University Press, 2015.

Bennett, Tony. *Formalism and Marxism*. London: Routledge, 1979.

Barthes, Roland. *Mythologies*. Translated by Annette Lavers. London: Granada, 1972 [1957].

Baudrillard, Jean. *The Mirror of Production*. Translated by Mark Poster. St. Louis: Telos Press, 1975.

Bonjour, Laurence. *In Defense of Pure Reason: A Rationalist Account of A Priori Justification*. New York: Cambridge University Press, 1998.

Cohn, Neil. *The Visual Language of Comics: Introduction to the Structure and Cognition of Sequential Images*. New York: Bloomsbury, 2013.

Dupuy, Jean-Pierre. "Philosophical Foundations of a New Concept of Equilibrium in the Social Sciences: Projected Equilibrium." *Philosophical Studies* 100 (2000): 323–345.

Eisner, Will. *Comics and Sequential Art*. Paramus, NJ: Poorhouse Press, 1985.
Foucault, Michel. *Power/Knowledge: Selected Interviews and Other Writings 1972–1977.* Edited by Colin Gordon. Translated by Colin Gordon et al. New York: Pantheon, 1980.
Goscinny, René, and Albert Uderzo. *Astérix aux Jeux Olympiques*. Paris: Dargaud, 1968.
———. *Asterix at the Olympic Games*. Translated by Anthea Bell and Derek Hockridge. London: Orion Books, 2004 [1968].
Jaspers, Karl. *Reason and Existenz: Five Lectures*. Translated by William Earle. Milwaukee, WI: Marquette University Press, 1997 [1935].
Malcolm, Norman. *Ludwig Wittgenstein: A Memoir*. London: Oxford University Press, 1958.
Marx, Karl. "Critique of the Gotha Programme." In *Karl Marx: Selected Writings*, edited by David McLellan. Oxford: Oxford University Press, 1977 [1875]. 564–570.
McCloud, Scott. *Understanding Comics: The Invisible Art*. New York: HarperCollins, 1993.
McLellan, David. *Marx*. Glasgow: Fontana/Collins, 1975.
Miodrag, Hannah. *Comics and Language: Reimagining Critical Discourse on the Form*. Jackson: University Press of Mississippi, 2013.
Plato. *Theaetetus*. In *Plato: The Collected Dialogues*. Edited by Edith Hamilton and Huntington Cairns. Translated by F. M. Cornford. Princeton: Princeton University Press, 1961.
Suzuki, Shunryu. *Not Always So: Practicing the True Spirit of Zen*. Edited by Edward Espe Brown. New York: Quill, 2003.
Virno, Paolo. "Jokes and Innovative Action: For a Logic of Change." In *Multitude between Innovation and Negation*. Translated by Isabella Bertoletti, James Cascaito, and Andrea Casson. New York: Semiotext(e), 2008. 67–167.
Vos, Eric. "Visual Literature and Semiotic Conventions." In *The Pictured Word: Word and Image Interactions* 2, edited by Martin Heusser et al. Atlanta: Rodopi, 1998. 135–147.
Walzer, Michael. "The Politics of Michel Foucault." In *Foucault: A Critical Reader*. Edited by David Couzens Hoy. Cambridge, MA: Basil Blackwell, 1986. 51–68.
Winch, Peter. *The Idea of a Social Science and Its Relation to Philosophy*. London: Routledge & Kegan Paul, 1958.
Wittgenstein, Ludwig. *Tractatus Logico-Philosophicus*. Translated by D. F. Pears and B. F. McGuinness. London: Routledge & Kegan Paul, 1961 [1921].
———. *On Certainty*. Edited by G. E. M. Anscombe and G. H. von Wright. Translated by Denis Paul and G. E. M. Anscombe. New York: Harper & Row, 1969.

Further Reading

The Adventures of Tintin novels, by the Belgian cartoonist Hergé (this was his pen name; his given name was Georges Remi), also include a lot of charmingly silly humor and so establish a space that is partly outside of logical sense, but they make an interesting contrast with the *Asterix* books. The *Tintin* stories have a contemporary setting, and typically involve suspenseful and dangerous adventures, often in the world of international intrigue. As a result, the silliness often also partly serves as comic relief. But because their art work, although it is impressively precise and detailed, is that of comics, and in particular has much of the same kind of cartoon-work and of pleasingly charming coloring and quaintness of characters as we find in the *Asterix* books, it constantly reminds us that it is a pleasurable fantasy, and so largely takes the reality out of the danger and suspense, and, like the *Asterix* books, confirms that the familiar world it shows so charmingly is safe to relax into and take for granted. But this still remains a more serious and dangerous world than that of the *Asterix* books and, as a result the *Tintin* books bring about a strange and interesting combination of the delightful wonder of the everyday and the unsettling defamiliarizing of the world that are both dimensions of metaphysical awareness.

Queering Epistemology and the Odyssey of Identity in Alison Bechdel's *Fun Home*

Ian MacRae

> Although there are other ways of making sense of the world,
> ... the method of personal narratives has become the pervasive everyday philosophy in postmodern Western culture.
> —Gary D. Fireman, "Narrative Selves: Our Philosophy for Everyday Life."

Alison Bechdel is a well-known cartoonist and graphic novelist whose bimonthly strip, *Dykes to Watch Out For*, launched in 1983 and has appeared for many years in large numbers of gay and lesbian papers across the United States and Canada. Bechdel is by now a bona fide cultural phenomenon, and one of the most famous lesbian artists in America; the adaptation of her first graphic memoir, *Fun Home*, debuted as a musical on Broadway in New York in April 2015, and won five Tony Awards in June of that same year. The first graphic novel ever published by the large, mainstream house Houghton Mifflin in 2006, *Fun Home* has spawned pilgrims who travel to Beech Creek, Pennsylvania, to see the house in which Alison grew up and the site where her father was killed. Subtitled "a family tragicomic," this is an autobiographical text. It tells Alison's story of growing up and coming out, and of her relationship with her family, and above all with her father, a queer man who may have committed suicide, and who apparently lived a closeted, unhappy existence. His death, we are told, was "a queer business" (57).

Alison is scrupulous and honest both in recording the "facts" of her family life, and in engaging in their analysis and interpretation. As she documents in *Fun Home*, Bechdel developed an obsessive-compulsive disorder at the age of ten, in which she would the count number of water droplets falling from the bathtub faucet, and the number of edges of flooring at doorways. She sensed an "invisible substance" lingering in thresholds, and would recite a "special incantation" to keep this "noxious" miasma from clouding her lungs (135–36); she grew anxious over odd numbers and the dreaded number thirteen. Her mother took to reading to her in the bathtub to soothe her nerves, while her father gave her a wall calendar with instructions to "Just write down what's happening" (140) as a way of ordering her thoughts and experience, and of resisting anxiety and flux. As Rhiannon Goldthorpe observes in "Literature as Philosophy," "the diary form is *par excellence* a medium of reflection, designed to stabilise and shape the self" (719)—and so it would prove for Alison. The first words in her diary are her father's, to get her started: "Dad is reading." Thus begins Bechdel's "compulsive propensity to autobiography" (140), as a gift from her father, with reading and writing and a shared faith (but also a profound doubt) in the signifying power of language at the core of their relationship.

Alison starts out as a diarist by recording the daily quotidian, banal events such as who made popcorn or the day's weather, and is "obsessed with making sure my diary entries bore no false witness" (169). Soon enough, however, she begins to insert a small, "minutely-lettered phrase I think" after each entry (141). She recognizes that "all I could speak for was my own perceptions, and perhaps not even those," and her "simple declarative sentences begin to strike me as hubristic at best, utter lies at worst" (141). Under this sort of verbal and psychological pressure, even "The most sturdy nouns faded to faint approximations under my pen" (141). And so she comes to ask a simple if profound philosophical question: "How did I know that the things I was writing were absolutely, objectively true?" (141). Thus begins what Alison understands is "a sort of epistemological crisis" (141)—a recognition of the complexities of subjectivity and the fallibility of memory and perception, the inadequacies of language to the task of representation, and even a loss of faith in consensual, objective, material reality itself.

Alison has stumbled, as a ten-year-old child, onto "the gaping rift between signifier and signified" (142), "the troubling gap between word and meaning" (143), the rupture at the heart of the verbal sign. This crucial insight remains at the structural centre of modern semiotics, and is the basis of Ferdinand de Saussure's dyadic (two-part) theory of language, published in *Course in General Linguistics* in 1916.[1] In that we cannot think outside of signs—humans are a "signifying monkey," in Henry Louis Gates Jr.'s phrase—young Alison is riddled with anxiety, beside herself with uncertainty and doubt. In order to supplement her memory and align her representation more closely with the truth of her experience, the qualifying phrase *I think* begins to multiply in her diary. In order to "save time" she invents a graphic (visual) symbol for the phrase, "a shorthand version of *I think*, a curvy circumflex" (142), and begins to insert this elongate, quasi-inverted *v* after each sentence. Alison then takes to "drawing it right over names and pronouns," and finally sketches the symbol in large format over *entire pages* of her diary, thereby overriding the "objective" text with the overwhelming subjectivity of herself as writer and perceiver (143). As she tells us in her follow-up graphic memoir, a second genealogical and autobiographical riddle titled *Are You My Mother? A Comic Drama* (2012), "By far the most heavily obliterated word is 'I'" (49). It is a twinned catastrophe: the loss of faith in the objective world, coupled to the dissolution of an emergent, fragile subjectivity.

Alison's "crisis" of knowing and representation signals a *visual turn* in her life writing, in which the graphic arts come to work alongside the verbal text to create a structure of knowledge that aligns more closely with what she knows and how she knows it, which includes how she feels and what she perceives, and myriad other non-verbal cues. It is important that the formal properties of the graphic novel seem able, for young Alison, to present the complexities of her "epistemological crisis" more quickly, effectively, and efficiently than words alone could do. The young diarist also develops visual shorthands for menstruation and masturbation, which are also among those embodied knowledges that *Fun Home* privileges (169).[2] This combination of text and image, of words and images juxtaposed and read in sequence to create autobiographical meanings, begun early and compulsively if also shot through with uncertainty, remains at the heart of Alison Bechdel's creative practice today.

This chapter takes Alison's epistemological crisis as its point of departure in treating *Fun Home* as a philosophical text, where by *philosophy* we simply mean, in the first instance, an approach to truth, a way of apprehending reality, a search for understanding and meaning. Along with Alison, we are interested in philosophy, and particularly in epistemology, in the sense of a moral approach to life, as a way of constructing and representing a just and true life, and in this case, a just and true personal and family history; like Alison, we pay close attention to gendered identities and sexual expression. At the heart of her graphic novel, Alison's "successful" story, an "entwined political and sexual awakening" (81) of a young homosexual person growing up and becoming an artist, is contrasted in with her father's closeted, suicidal anguish, a "solipsistic circle of self, from autodidact to autocrat to autocide" (140). These two narratives are closely linked in *Fun Home*, and revolve around each other "in the tricky reverse narration that impels our entwined stories" (232). In that the book models its central father-daughter relationship on the axis of Leopold Bloom and Stephen Dedalus's relationship in James Joyce's modernist novel *Ulysses* (1922), which is itself modeled on Homer's *The Odyssey*, we need to read *Fun Home* as a hybrid, inclusive work that addresses important philosophical questions while also being carefully calibrated as a literary form. In *Fun Home*, Alison Bechdel deploys a range of literary texts as intertextual referents in order to structure her questions and inquiries. In this way the text treats its subjects with a questioning and allusive playfulness that refuses to foreclose possibilities, and is unwilling to rule, once and for all, on someone else's—her father's, in particular—"erotic truth" (230). It is precisely this literary *form*, and the range of *Fun Home*'s literary intertexts, references and meanings, that undergird and organize this graphic memoir's structure of knowing, its epistemology. The overriding argument here is that literature and epistemology are indissolubly linked in *Fun Home*, in which we cannot understand one without the other.[3] *Fun Home* is a literate, sophisticated text which incorporates a broad cultural inheritance while wearing its learning lightly, playfully, comically, even queerly. Alison's words and pictures poeticize and politicize her relationship to her father, and through a series of intertextual references and literary discussions generate a series of queered relationships to inherited philosophies, histories, and ways of knowing.

In taking up these ideas, this essay will move to define and discuss the concept of "queer philosophy," and the notion of an "epistemology of literature" in Bechdel's work. It will consider notions of artifice and desire in Alison's family life, the body's role in the construction of knowledge, and the role of memory and subjectivity in reconstructing a genealogical *and* historical past. We will address ways of knowing in the graphic novel, with an understanding that gaps between verbal and visual signifying systems, and within knowledge structures themselves, are exploited by the genre and made to signify by Bechdel. We read *Fun Home* as an "open" text, chock full of other texts, signs and referents; and trace a few of its more concrete literary intertexts, while assuming no prior knowledge of these writers, to examine how with them Alison constructs an order of knowledge that is literary, philosophical, and queer. In the end we are interested in the ways of knowing Alison produces in *Fun Home*, that is, in the *epistemology* of the text, the ways in which she creates structures of meaning in which to locate the life narratives of her father, Bruce, and of her own sexuality, gender, and experience. We will finally suggest that *Fun Home* works to create a resistant, subjective, compassionate, provisional, literary means of knowing, a knowledge of and through the body—in a word, a *queer* epistemology. This structure and method provides

Alison with one way, as she has observed in a recent interview, "to get at feelings with ideas" (2014, 216).

Memory, Epistemology, History

Philosophers are typically concerned with the establishment of concrete definitions and abstracted, rational categories, with questions of taxonomy, structure and order, and so we begin with three succinct definitions of our key philosophical term. For Nicholas Rescher, "The mission of epistemology, the theory of knowledge, is to clarify what the conception of knowledge involves, how it is applied, and to explain why it has the features it does" (xiii). For Matthias Steup, "Defined narrowly, epistemology is the study of knowledge and justified belief.... [E]pistemology is concerned with the following questions: What are the necessary and sufficient conditions of knowledge? What are its sources? What is its structure, and what are its limits?" (2014). As Jonathan L. Kvanvig explains, "The history of epistemology centers on the concept of knowledge, especially on the difficult questions of whether knowledge is possible and, if it is, how much of it there is" (ix). This is Alison's principal subject and epistemological problem in *Fun Home*: what is it possible for her to know about her father's life, death, identity and sexuality; and what (and when, and how) does she know about her own gender identity and sexual expression? Further, what does the conception of this knowledge involve, how is it applied (by herself, her father, her family and society), and why does it have the features that it does? Are her beliefs justified? Alison is interested, as an adult, in "knowing," but also in studying this knowledge, and in developing a theory of sexuality, identity, family, and suicide. This theory of knowledge is also a brief social history, embodied in actual human lives, of changing social structures—of an epistemology of sexuality. What then are the limits and conditions of this knowledge, what are its sources and its histories, and how can Alison order and structure what she does and does not know in order to communicate all of this to her reader?

Alison's reconstruction of memory in *Fun Home* is anchored in two specific events, to which the book's non-linear, recursive structure almost obsessively returns: the self-discovery of her own sexuality, her coming of age and coming out to her parents; and the death of her father, some four months later, either from accident or suicide. This is social and family history, not fiction, and if it is to be truthful, the past cannot be altered. In this telling the personal details, as well as the larger patterns (economic, social, sexual, psychological) that we call *history* are revealed. But each re-telling is also already an understanding and an interpretation, and the idea that the interpreter is a singular, unchanging self is itself "an illusion that we all strive to maintain but can never truly achieve" (Fireman 476). In this way *Fun Home* as graphic memoir offers a model for the presentation and analysis of memory and its role in identity construction and in our knowledge of social history.

Alison is witnessing, remembering, and reconstructing both her identity and that of her father's, but it is not her same "self" who is narrating and being presented (see Brockmeier 2010). If the traditional sense of autobiography is to create a stable and coherent sense of self, here is a gap in the structure of the text's knowledge of the past which comics are able to open up and exploit: the temporality of the experiencing young Alison, and of the adult author who illustrates and narrates her. This plurality of voices allows for a more in-depth portrayal of the past, and also creates a distancing, analytical and critical vision, as Alison can both be engaged in dialogue and event (as a youth) in a panel, and comment upon it (as an adult artist, some twenty-seven years after the fact) in the text's voice-over narration.

The graphic novel as genre, with its interplay and tension between text and image, as Scott McLeod made clear in his seminal study of "closure" (1994, 63), is in fact exemplary in its ability to create and ramify this "gap" between time depths and signifying systems, which Alison is able to deploy in the construction of multi-temporal and multi-perspectival knowledge structures. As Robyn Warhol observes, "A close look at *Fun Home* shows that this text operates through many more layers—on many more narrative levels—than two, because both the visual and the verbal subdivide into multiple separate and overlapping narrative tracks, creating narrative elements that 'work with' the space between image and words" (2). This notion of a "space between" in the graphic narrative is important, in that it enables Alison to overcome her epistemological crisis in the first place as a child (with a graphic icon), and then a second time as an adult graphic novelist. It is not that this space is ever completely filled or "closed," or that identity becomes equivalent with memory and its representation, but that the space between reality and its representation becomes populated with signs, images, words, with various perspectives and interpretations, artists and authors—with a range of literary intertexts, and with what an "archive of family documents" (Chute 175)—all of which add to our understanding of Bruce's life and death, but none of which can "close" these questions or their meanings completely.

It is this epistemological multiplicity and ambiguity that drew the young Alison to drawing in the first place, with the graphic symbol intervening to represent the unavoidable subjectivity of the perceiving subject. As Alison explains in an interview, "it was this bridging of symbol and reality, of the label and thing itself, that was so exciting. The endless slippage between signifier and signified that was so troubling to me in my diary entries seemed somehow to come to rest here—or at least pause . . ." (2007; in Warhol, 10). The reader is also involved in this process of making meaning, in filling in gaps and asking and partially answering (or moving to "close") questions that the text finally and permanently leaves open. As Gillian Whitlock observes, comics are replete with "blank spaces where new meanings can be generated . . . This is a meaning produced in an active process of imaginative production whereby the reader shuttles between words and images" (978). The ultimate "blank space" in the Alison's family saga is the "irresolvable problem of her father's closeted homosexuality" (Warhol, 11).

The social-historical context of *Fun Home* reveals something like the "progress of love"—the way homosexual identities are actively embodied and socially performed by Alison in ways they were not a generation earlier by her father. We can then approach the notion of "queering epistemology" through a short story of that name by the recent Noble Laureate Alice Munro, "The Progress of Love," in which a father calls his daughter to tell her his wife has just died: "I think your mother's gone," he says. As his daughter observes, "The word 'gone' seemed full of nothing but a deep relief and even an excitement—the excitement you feel when a door closes and your house sinks back to normal and you let yourself loose into all the free space around you. That was in my father's voice, too—behind the apology, a *queer* sound like a gulped breath" (3). An elderly woman dies peacefully yet unexpectedly and her husband is relieved, released, excited even to perceive a new freedom, a new life. These are not the normative, naturalized emotions of loss and mourning one might expect to accompany the loss of a life's partner. For Munro, these are *queer* emotions that find expression in a sound beyond syntax, a sound that conveys a sort of hermeneutic of desire and that lurks beyond language, even beyond conscious recognition itself—"a queer sound like a gulped breath."

Alison dedicates an entire page in *Fun Home* to this "*multi-valent*" word, complete with Webster's dictionary definition, context, and analysis (57), clearly signaling its importance. As David Halperin explains, "Queer is by definition *whatever* is at odds with the normal, the legitimate, the dominant. *There is nothing in particular to which it necessarily refers*. It is an identity without an essence. 'Queer' then, demarcates not a positivity but a positionality *vis-à-vis* the normative" (62). Cherry Smith argues that queer "defines a strategy, an attitude, a reference to other identities and a new self-understanding. . . . Both in culture and in politics, queer articulates a radical questioning of social and cultural norms, notions of gender, reproductive sexuality, and the family" (280). In a "Pink Paper" cited by Smith (277), Keith Alcorn suggests that "queer is a symptom, not a movement, a symptom of a desire for radical change." For Annamarie Jagose in *Queer Theory: An Introduction*, "Queer is an ongoing and necessarily unfixed site of engagement and contestation" (11). What is important to both Munro and Bechdel is that queerness has "neither a fundamental logic, nor a consistent set of characteristics" (Jagose, 11). In *A Critical Introduction to Queer Theory* (2003), a useful overview and analysis of the term's critical history, Kerry Sullivan comments that Queer Theory has been "constructed as a sort of vague and indefinable set of practices and (political) positions that has the potential to challenge normative knowledges and identities" (43–44). Queer then is a slippage in the (heteronormative) works, an ambivalent element that resides on the margins of language and meaning, where it exerts a subtle if persistent pressure on conventional structures of knowing, even moving slowly over the past few generations from the margins into the mainstream—from Beech Creek, say, to Broadway.

As Judith Butler (1990), Halperin (1995), Smith (1996), Jagose (1997), Sullivan (2003), and other theorists of gender and sexuality have shown, heterosexuality itself is a complex matrix of discourses, institutions, and so on that has become normalized in the culture, thus making particular relationships, lifestyles, and identities seem natural, ahistorical, and universal. But the discursive nature of heteronormativity also makes these concepts contestable, and open to change. Queer theory is rooted in a rhetoric of resistance and a provisional politics, and seeks to examine power relations by which the matrix of heteronomativity has been constructed as universal, timeless, and true. As Munro suggests, in a case that itself is contra-orthodox, queer can also be heterosexual, is not restricted but open, and can be taken up by anyone who feels marginalized—that is, outside the norm or ideal, particularly (but not only) as a result of their sexual practices (see Halperin 1995). In Munro's story, an older white heterosexual male, newly widowed and not quite mourning, in defying the norms and codes of the quasi-sacred family unit, and indeed of the sanctity of life itself, can feel queer, can sound queer, and can realize that his subjectivity has always been an inter-subjectivity, his autonomy a partial fiction. Part of himself has died as well.

So how then does Alison Bechdel apply the provisional, resistant, transformative nexus of subjectivity, power, and identity known as queer theory or "queer philosophy" to her own life story; and how does she order and structure this knowledge with respect to language, memory, sexuality, gender, the body, visual arts, even Western literature and critical theory at large? When Bruce dies only four months after she has come out to her parents, Alison feels at first responsible, then upstaged, and then experiences a second epistemological crisis in which she responds to the tragedy of her father's death with "ghastly, uncontrollable grins" (46). Truth is, part of herself has died as well.

Fun Home's first section, "Old Father, Old Artificer," introduces the central relationship between Alison and her father, and clearly associates creativity with forgery, images with counterfeits, and genealogy and inheritance with both blessing and curse. A high school English teacher, Bruce is a maker of labyrinths and mazes in which he himself has become trapped. His house, a restored Gothic mansion, is itself a grand illusion, a masterpiece which he works tirelessly to maintain, possibly his "greatest achievement" (4). This is the eponymous Fun Home, Beech Creek's funeral home, with Bruce as the town's third-generation undertaker, yoked to the family business in small town America when, say, a coastal city—and a less tightly circumscribed social context—could have offered his life other directions. The family house furnishes the text with its central paradigm of representation without substance, of artifice and aestheticism in place of honesty and truth. It is home to a family united in its will to pursue the auto-gratification of creativity and solitude at the expense of community, kinship and love, an "artists' colony" of compulsive creators "absorbed in our separate pursuits" (134).

Bruce's artifice is that he appears on the surface to be an ideal husband and father, a provider and homemaker with three children, a consummate heteronormative patriarch. Yet reality itself is strangely inverted behind the curtain of this comprehensive façade; as Alison observes, he "treated his furniture like children, and his children like furniture" (14). Below the surface, Bruce's marriage is a sham; he is violent and prone to rages, mercurial, selfish and self-absorbed, and he entangles others in his dilemmas. His family life is an unreasonable facsimile of such, a theatre of the absurd which unfolds in period rooms filled with props and not people. His children are never sure "if the minotaur lay around the next corner" (21)—he is a monster come to life as a "normal" man. This is the epistemological crux of the book, and of Alison's life: is Alison's father "legitimate?" Is their family life, and his marriage, "true?" If Bruce's identity and erotic truth is a lie and a shambles—what about her own? As Alison asks her reader: "Would an ideal husband and father have sex with teenage boys?" (17).

For Bruce, the carefully maintained illusion of an ideal family will not stop him from cruising for sex with other men in New York City (194), having sex with his high school students (17), or plying them with liquor (173). The heteronormative surface obsessively erected over a life riven with repressed queer desire is an illusion he cannot maintain. These irresolvable tensions ultimately drove him to suicide—at least in the most probable of Alison's interpretations of his death. This is the dark secret at the heart of an autobiographical comic:

her father's relationship with his gardener, his babysitter and his students, with sailors and other young men, and the court cases, family and professional tensions, shame, STDs, and disturbed and abused teenage boys that resulted. Given this, as Alison observes, that Bruce's death was officially classified as an accident "was quite possibly his consummate artifice, his masterstroke" (27).

Literature as a Way of Knowing

Bruce—like the text that represents him, and like his daughter, who majored in English at university—understands and structures his life through literary references. He seems to prefer fiction to reality. Her parents met performing a play, her mother is likened to Isabel Archer in Henry James's *A Portrait of a Lady*, and Bruce himself, it is suggested, is a monster in a labyrinth; as Alison explains, "My parents are most real to me in fictional terms" (67). In high school English class father as teacher and daughter as pupil get along swimmingly, and are able to communicate fluently through textual intermediaries; in the car outside after class they are cold and distant (198–99). Bruce identifies with the drunken recklessness of F. Scott Fitzgerald, "the colossal vitality of [Gatsby's] illusion" (64), and with Oscar Wilde, the well-known queer writer whose life and fortunes were doomed as he was persecuted for his defense of "the love that dare not speak its name."[4] This queer love that Bruce dared not speak of or productively embody is the love which Alison articulates subtly, even beautifully, in *Fun Home*.

Alison for her part identifies with Shakespeare and Company in Paris, the bookstore owned by lesbians who published *Ulysses* in London and in French translation; with an entire stack of lesbian literature in the library; and with the spiritual eroticism, even the erotic truth, of Joyce's novel *Ulysses*. Alison discovers that she is a lesbian, fittingly enough, while reading in the campus bookstore (74); she tells us that her own private course of reading at university could have legitimately been called "contemporary and historical perspectives on homosexuality" (205). She is an autobiographical heroine on an odyssey of self-discovery and self-realization. Her memoir constructs a counter-memory, a secret and intimate history, not as a grand narrative but as something individual, subjective, and deeply personal—the story of a single life that also speaks to the history of the constructions of gender and sexual expression in Western literature and culture at large.

In addition to Wilde, Fitzgerald, James, and Joyce, *Fun Home* offers quick and accessible sketches of Proust, Camus, Tolstoy, Ruskin, Homer, Salinger, Faulkner, Hemingway, Collette, and others. *Mad* and *GQ* magazines also appear, as does the Batman logo, the Addams family, and Jimmy Stewart films (icons of popular and cinematic culture)—this is a graphic novel with a highly resolved if mongrel, burgeoning form. The playful patina of comics seems to leaven the freighted material of suicide, paternity, sexuality, mortality, and provides a sheen of the unserious, the simply-colored, the informal and two-dimensional that is capable of treating serious concerns with a light touch. This is, in part, how comics *know*. Bechdel does this in spare, two-tone drawings, and with simple lines that are both economical and incisive. The blue wash of the image also signifies, as does its absence. "Midnight blue" is her father's favourite colour (130), and we see the colour drain from Alison's mother's face as genuine feeling drains from her marriage, with Alison observing that "my mother's luminous face has gone dull" (72).

In its verbal and visual representations of photographs, film, television, letters, books, calendars, radio chatter, colouring books, audio tapes, westerns, drive-in movie screens, newspapers, more letters and more books, *Fun Home* assembles and orders an archive of personal, popular, and family culture. This is an "open work," in Umberto Eco's sense (1976)—a text that is chock full of libraries, dictionaries, encyclopedias, gravestones, of artifacts to be read and that operate as text within the domain of the image. The realms of text and image are brought into deep and dialogic contact in this work, in which they overlap and intersect in all kinds of venturesome ways, and call us to an "active" reading of both visual and verbal art as sequential narrative. These "texts within the text" lead us outward into an expansive network of other writers, readers, and works, to literary and cultural histories that are often eroticized, and almost always queered. In this way canonical works are rewritten, reinscribed, and recontextualized as part of the "queer business" that is *Fun Home*. This is an epistemological property as well, of course, which reminds us of the fundamental quality that no artistic text is a discrete, closed off entity, unique or utterly original—and that the same holds for any human life or mind. In this structure of knowing, the "self" as fully autonomous agent uncoupled from social relations is itself rendered illusory. Given these interlocking networks of relations, the type of knowledge Alison seeks (like the dynamics of an active reading) can never be final, and will always be subject to future qualification and revision.

In *The Myth of Sisyphus* (1955), the French writer Albert Camus called suicide the logical solution to the absurdity—the irrationality and lack of purpose—of life. Bruce had been reading Camus' *A Happy Death* the summer of his death, and had been leaving the text "around the house in what might be construed as a deliberate manner" (27). A year earlier, he had been reading Marcel Proust's well-known masterwork *The Remembrance of Things*

Past, luxuriating in its literary and horticultural effects, and in its treatment of memory and search for truth—a truth which for Proust included error and equivocation, the fallibility of memory and the particularities of subjectivity, perception and sensation: in short, those faulty, unstable, individualized constructions of knowledge through which each of us constructs and makes sense of the world. Proust's monumental work, published in seven volumes between 1913 and 1927, and which he was still editing on his deathbed in 1922, is another text which underlies and irrigates Alison's structure of knowledge in *Fun Home*. As Goldthorpe explains, "*A la recherche du temps perdu* ends not with nostalgia for transcendental truth or for a pre-existent essence of the self, but with a celebration of the contingent, the unstable, the provisional, the indeterminate, and with a tentative promise of continued self-creation" (716). So too does *Fun Home*. As Alison observes, with his obsession for flowers, surfaces, literature, aesthetics, and boys / young men, "If ever there was a bigger pansy than my father, it was Marcel Proust" (93). In ways like these, *Fun Home* becomes imbued with the moods and meanings—the philosophies and epistemologies—of the literary projects of Camus, Proust, Joyce, and others.

The attentive reader will notice that Bruce puts down Tolstoy's novel *Anna Karenina* to play with Alison on the memoir's first page. The book's title is visible in the illustration, though it is never mentioned in the narrative text. If we "read" this picture, we might also recall the novel's well-known first sentence: "Happy families are all alike; each unhappy family is unhappy in its own way" (1). Immediately then we will understand that here is an unhappy family, and the reader's task is simply to discover in which particular way this is so. We may also know that Anna Karenina, in emotional turmoil over the uncertainty of her lover's fidelity, and considering "her own position" as a woman with a lover "false and dishonorable" (340), commits suicide by throwing herself under a moving train at novel's end. In this way another thread of reference and meaning is woven into the fabric of *Fun Home*, clearly suggesting (without ever saying so directly, in an indirect discourse that amounts to an epistemology of literature) her father's bitter unhappiness, misplaced eroticism, vain and deceptive nature, and suicide. To be sure, these crucial meanings are brought to bear without words from the narrator, but (merely) through the appearance of a book in an illustration—such is the signifying power of comics.

Again on *Fun Home*'s first page, in another quick yet powerful and far-reaching genealogical and literary reference, the relationship between father and daughter—which a family friend defines as almost "unnaturally" close (225)—is figured as "a particular reenactment of the mythic relationship" between Daedalus and son Icarus (3). *Fun Home* begins with an image of

Icarian Games, and Bruce has put down the Tolstoy novel so that his daughter may soar on his extended legs. (And so already perhaps we realize she will fly in this graphic novel, and he will fall.) Daedalus, the "cunning worker," was a skillful artificer who was even said to have invented images; he in this sense an appropriate or *legitimate* spiritual forebear for Alison as graphic artist. Alison describes her father as "an alchemist of appearance, a savant of surface, a Daedalus of décor" (6). And yet his creations work to blur and obscure, to hide and erect a false front over the hidden paths of his queer desire: "He used his skillful artifice not to make things, but to make things appear to be what they are not" (16).

As told by the Roman poet Ovid in *Metamorphoses*, Daedalus built a labyrinth for King Minos in which to imprison the Minotaur, a monster who was half-man and half-beast, but then was imprisoned there himself. Daedalus built wings so he and his son Icarus could escape the labyrinth, but Icarus disobeyed his father's instructions and flew too close to the sun. The wax binding his wings melted, and Icarus crashed back to earth. As we learn early in *Fun Home*, "In our particular reenactment of this mythic relationship, it was not me but my father who was to plummet from the sky" (4). In this retelling, the myth of the Minotaur is both put forward and played with, or *queered*, as Bruce becomes Icarus as well as Daedalus: the father as maker of labyrinths and images (or artifices), who falls back to earth (after, in this case, being hit by a truck). But Bruce is also the Minotaur, with the mind and imagination of a man but with the symbolic hindquarters and aberrant desires of a beast—in other words, a monster trapped in a labyrinth of desire that he himself (in relation to his society) has created.

Filiation: Repetition with Critical Difference

Alison, as noted, is scrupulous in her desire to record the "facts" correctly. She likes to pose for each visual panel in her graphic work, often in costume, and then to photograph these set-ups, and uses these images as "a quick reference to draw from" for nearly every frame of her work (Bechdel 2014, 207). *Fun Home* as graphic memoir is grounded in photographs in yet another important way, in that photographs from the Bechdel family album are placed at the beginning of each chapter, where they substantiate Alison's past and lend material substance to her memories. "I want people to know it is a real photograph of something that actually happened," she has said (2014, 210). It was, in fact, one of the Bechdel family's archived images that inspired Alison to write about her father in the first place—a snapshot of the babysitter Roy which she discovered after her father's death. "Over the years," she says, "that picture persisted in memory" (2014, 210). This image appears as a two-page centerfold spread in *Fun Home* (100–101), in a visual format which recalls pornographic magazines. It depicts a young man in his underwear languorously posed, while Alison remembers being eight years old and on family vacation in a motel room next door, oblivious. It is the shock of this recognition, this gap between her knowledge of Bruce's "actual" activities and his "secret" life, that the text seeks to fill, always incompletely.

It is important to observe that the crucial moment at the core of the text—her father's suicide—is not rendered as an image. It is an absence, a gap or lacuna, an aporia in the text's general field. This is crucial to the text's conception of knowledge and of its limits, that the absolute truth of Bruce's death cannot be known; the book's way of knowing must rest upon a foundational uncertainty. The driver of the truck that hit Bruce said he jumped "backward into the road 'as if he saw a snake'" (89). The truth, Alison knows, is somewhere in the middle—in the spaces between memory and imagination, word and picture, gender identity and sexual expression, heteronormativity and queer desire, accident and suicide. What Alison *doesn't* say is as important to her approach to morality, to what is right and just and true regarding her father's death and sexuality, as what she does; absence is part of her methodology and of her approach to truth. The "true knowledge" of what happened to her father, what motivated him and to what ends, who we wanted to have sex with and why, who he did have sex with, under what conditions and why, exists outside the domain of the knowable. As does the "truth" of his sexual expression, the category the articulation of his sexual desire can be placed into, the way outsiders might wish to label and so domesticate his desire, claiming to know. Bisexual, homosexual, or an aberrant, deviant sexuality, pedophilia, even the vexed problem of a seventeen-year-old's "consent," of grooming, as well as intra-marriage cruelty and spousal abuse—none of these terms are broached in *Fun Home*. To consider these questions is not much fun at all, of course; the literal meaning of the book's title is deeply ironic. Proust called homosexuals "inverts," and Alison has "always been fond of this antiquated clinical term," while recognizing at the same time that "it's imprecise and insufficient, defining the homosexual as a person whose gender expression is at odds with his or her sex" (97). Such narrow definitions, she tells us, cannot encompass her father's "erotic truths" (230). One of the absurd paradoxes of suicide, as Camus pointed out, is that the suicide takes his or her rationale—however logical, strange, deviant or misguided—with him or her to the grave.

On the one hand, Alison's humility and reticence to overdetermine another's life constitutes a moral position, an ethical sign, and an epistemological choice. On the other hand, Bruce's quasi-confessional to the college-age Alison, that "I'm bad. Not good like you" (153), clearly signals the moral valence of the book, and of the politics of coming out, of performing and embodying queer desire—and in Bruce's own voice, no less.

All of this is to come closer to the trick in understanding Bechdel's work, that the reader must develop a theory of knowledge—an epistemological perspective—that is contingent, indeterminate, open to experience, multivalent and multi-perspectival, and that refuses to foreclose the possibilities of another's life and identity in recognizing the possibilities of being, becoming and change. *Fun Home* is less concerned with so-called objective "factives" (the positivist knowledge that obsessed Alison as a young diarist) than it is with the validity and epistemological status of memory, desire, eroticism and equivocation—those subjective states and perceptions that influence how and what we know of the world and ourselves. Alison is equally interested in what she "thinks" and in what she feels.

Finally then, *Fun Home* models its central father-daughter relationship, and its larger epistemological structure, on the axis of Leopold Bloom and Stephen Dedalus's relationship in Joyce's modernist masterpiece *Ulysses* (1922)—as the imminent consummation of a spiritual paternity that is perennially approached, even as it is perpetually postponed. In Homer's *The Odyssey*, upon which Joyce figured *Ulysses*, Telemachus opines, "Never yet did any man know his parentage of his own knowledge" (1.214-20); to which in *Ulysses*, Stephen Dedelus, Telemachus's Dublin double, replies, "Paternity may be a legal fiction" (U.9., 842-43). (We may have biological proof as to the identity of our mothers, yet before DNA testing paternity could remain a mystery, and has therefore long been taken, in this sense, as a leap of faith—a "legal fiction.") Jacques Derrida notes that this "concern ... about familial legitimation makes both *Ulysses and Finnegans Wake* vibrate" (62). *Fun Home* too is concerned with spiritual and biological fathers, with "legitimate" fathers and daughters. In *Ulysses* the crucial relationship is between fatherless Stephen and sonless Bloom—that is, with spiritual as opposed to biological filiation. In the seventeenth of eighteen chapters, the Ithaca episode of *Ulysses*, after Bloom has sought out Stephen for a good part of the day and night—the two having passed each other without connecting at the National Library earlier in the day–they repair for cocoa to Bloom's home, where they fail to make a substantial emotional connection, and Stephen wanders off into the night, the fleeting moment of potential forever lost.

Fun Home repeats this story with critical difference, and uses *Ulysses* as a basis for knowledge construction. In this "inverted" re-telling, Alison becomes—or, like Bloom to Stephen, *almost* becomes—spiritual father to her own father in one late scene, when the two almost connect on a weekend with Alison home from college, after she has come out to her parents in a letter. They drive together to a movie theater and Bruce begins to speak of his own formative queer experiences, before Alison interjects with a related story of her own, at which point he becomes quiet and withdrawn. After the movie they go to a well-known local gay bar, but are turned away because she is underage. "We had had our Ithaca moment," she concludes (221–23). It is the moment of missed connection to which their relationship has always tended: "our paths crossed but we did not meet" (211). Perhaps this absence of actual connection (while he was living) *is* symbolically achieved and redressed in the reading and writing of *Fun Home*, which is compassionate, generous, provisional and resistant (of normative, simplified meanings) in coming to know Bruce's death, and therefore in coming to understand and honour the complexities of his life and memory. One can argue that the text's ambiguous ending in fact signals that spiritual consubstantiation in the Joycean sense has in fact been achieved in *Fun Home*, as Alison learns to express her queer identity within the bounds of society, which are themselves not static, in ways her father was unable to achieve. In this sense, his own closeted life and quick, unhappy death serves as a negative example, a spur to her own evolution and gender expression. As she tells us in her the book's final phrase, "He was there to catch me when I leapt" (232).

Much like *Ulysses*, *Fun Home* combines so-called "high" and "low" cultural forms and subjects, and speaks candidly of male and female homosexuality, physical desire, masturbation and cunnilingus, of the power and pleasure of libraries and literature, of the embodied self and carnal knowledge. The comic book is full of illustrated bodies at work, rest and play, as cadavers and lovers—and in many cases, quite dead (e.g. 43, 44, 189, 224). The concrete particularly of the illustrated body seems to reinforce the notion that identity is generated in the body, and that the physical organism is the instrument through which identity is performed. As Kim Atkins argues, "Identity is articulated, not at a purely psychological level but at the level of the synthesis of the heterogeneous: at the level of my bodily perspective" (95). Alison very much incorporates "an epistemology of the body" into *Fun Home*, in which the desire the body speaks is respected as proper knowledge, a guiding structure which, to achieve a life of progressive, disciplined liberty, must in some sense be incorporated into the broader contexts of knowing. The illustrations in the graphic novel may well help draw us closer to the intimacies of the performing body, without the often clumsy and inadequate references to common nouns and familiar verbs. Comics in this sense still cross out sturdy nouns and make certain verbs unnecessary. This is another way the graphic novel knows. Bechdel's drawings seem to render even erotically charged bodies lighter and more playful, and leave room for difference, complexity and ambiguity, all without a hint of the exploitative, the voyeuristic, or the pornographic.

Bechdel is of a generation that came out as lesbians in the early 1980s and really did not have older models available. She is creating culture as she is documenting it, forging a self-legitimating and accurate cultural history not only of herself, but also for her generation. According to the conventions of gay autobiography, as codified by Bertram J. Cohler in *Writing Desire* (2007), *Fun Home* proceeds along normative lines, with coming out as a significant event. This life story is written from a point in the future, in a place of calm organization and order; it looks back over the events of a life with the retrospective glance of an ordering history. Some twenty-six years have passed from Bruce's death to the publication of *Fun Home*, and it took Alison seven years to complete the text, so deep and complex is the knowledge it structures. She states that it "was a real struggle to get to a point where I trusted myself enough to commit things to the page" (2014, 1008).

In charting the entwined lives of father and daughter, as a social history *Fun Home* manages to map a period of time in which the transition to queer positionalities has become more fluid, and however still difficult, on the whole less perilous. We can read the relationship between Alison and her father as one of repetition with critical difference, as his life ends in silence and disaster, and she "repeats" it one generation later with expressive creativity, disciplined and imaginative freedom, and a learned, conscious, politicized self-understanding. *Fun Home* is marked in this sense by continuity, symmetry, and parallelism between the generations, and by rupture and change. Alison rewrites an inherited script to achieve a different end—and her sense of a new, different ending corresponds to broader changes in social history. (This contributes to the resonance of the text and, no doubt, to its success as a musical on Broadway). This process of repetition with critical difference is repeated internally in the text, in the range of literary intertexts she incorporates, analyzes and critiques. In this way the form of the book (its structure) reproduces its contents. If the father was silenced by his choices, Alison's decision is to write, to draw, to express herself and represent her story (which is also his). She doesn't claim originality, but creates a structure of autobiographical truth through a complex form of combinatorial play. This repetition is not toward duplicity and concealment, but articulates a search for clarity and freedom, one that recognizes the limits of its knowledge with humility and grace. The structure of knowledge Alison produces by interrogating her own personal, literary and cultural history results in a graphic memoir organized and structured, to borrow from Edward Said, as "a kind of activated library whose effect is to stimulate the production of forms of disciplined, gradually actualized freedom" (139). The monster in the labyrinth is laid to rest, as more diverse gendered and sexual identities are freely embodied and creatively expressed. In the process, Alison Bechdel becomes one of the crucial voices of her generation.

Notes

1. For de Saussure, as put forward in *Cours de linguistique générale* (*Course in General Linguistics*, 1916), the sign is composed of a *signifier*, the form which the sign takes; and the *signified*, the concept it represents, a mental construct or an object existing in the world; with the relationship between the two *signification*.

2. I am grateful to Christine Poenaru-Zuziac for this insight and others, as well as for her valuable research on this project. Christine's *research apprenticeship* was sponsored by the Dean of the Faculty of Liberal Arts at Wilfrid Laurier University's Brantford campus.

3. For example, the subtitle "family tragicomic" signifies the text's engagement with literary genres (tragedy: her father's; comedy: her own) as well as its central structures of a homosexual bildungsroman (a coming of age text), moving toward the Kunstlerroman (a portrait of the artist as a young lesbian), with strong notes of the Gothic braided through.

4. On trial for "committing acts of gross indecency with other male persons" in 1895 in London, Oscar Wilde was read a poem by his companion, Lord Alfred Douglas, in which the famous phrase appears. Wilde's response brought the crowd in the courtroom to applause: "'The Love that dare not speak its name' in this century is such a great affection of an elder for a younger man as there was between David and Jonathan, such as Plato made the very basis of his philosophy, and such as you find in the sonnets of Michelangelo and Shakespeare. It is that deep, spiritual affection that is as pure as it is perfect. It dictates and pervades great works of art like those of Shakespeare and Michelangelo, and those two letters of mine, such as they are. It is in this century misunderstood, so much misunderstood that it may be described as the 'Love that dare not speak its name,' and on account of it I am placed where I am now. It is beautiful, it is fine, it is the noblest form of affection. There is nothing unnatural about it. It is intellectual, and it repeatedly exists between an elder and a younger man, when the elder man has intellect, and the younger man has all the joy, hope and glamour of life before him. That it should be so the world does not understand. The world mocks at it and sometimes puts one in the pillory for it." http://law2.umkc.edu/faculty/projects/ftrials/wilde/Crimwilde.html.

Bibliography

Atkins, Kim. "Narrative Identity and Embodied Continuity." *Practical Identity and Narrative Agency*. Edited by Catriona Mackenzie and Kim Atkins. New York: Routledge, 2008. 78–97.

Bechdel, Alison. *Fun Home: A Family Tragicomic*. New York: Houghton Mifflin Company, 2006.

———. "An Interview With Alison Bechdel." Public Conversation with Hillary L. Chute. *Modern Fiction Studies* 52.4 (2006): 203–219.

———. 2007. Script for lecture delivered at PEN/Faulkner event with Lynda Barry and Chris Ware, November 9, 2007. Unpublished manuscript.

———. *Are You My Mother? A Comic Drama*. New York: Houghton Mifflin Harcourt, 2012.

Brockmeier, Jens. "After the Archive: Remapping Memory." *Culture and Psychology* 16.1 (2010): 5–35.

Butler, Judith. *Gender Trouble: Feminism and the Subversion of Identity*. New York: Routledge, 1990.

Camus, Albert. *The Myth of Sisyphus and Other Essays*. Translated by Justin O'Brien. New York: Vintage Books, 1991 [1955].

Cohler, Bertram J. *Writing Desire: Sixty Years of Gay Autobiography*. Madison: University of Wisconsin Press, 2007.

Chute, Hillary L. *Graphic Women: Life Narrative and Contemporary Comics*. New York: Columbia University Press, 2010.

Derrida, Jacques. *Acts of Literature*. Edited by Derek Attridge. New York: Routledge, 1992.

Eco, Umberto. *The Open Work*. Translated by Anna Cancogni. Cambridge: Harvard University Press, 1989.

Fantasia, Annette. "The Paterian Bildungsroman Reenvisioned: 'Brain-Building' in Alison Bechdel's *Fun Home: A Family Tragicomic*." *Criticism* 53.1 (2011): 83–97.

Fireman, Gary D. "Narrative Selves: Our Philosophy for Everyday Life." Review of *Autobiographical Memory and the Construction of a Narrative Self: Developmental and Cultural Perspectives*. Edited by Robyn Fivush and Catherine A. Haden. *American Journal of Psychology* 118.3 (2005): 475–80.

Gates, Henry Louis, Jr. *The Signifying Monkey: A Theory of Afro-American Literary Criticism*. New York: Oxford University Press, 1988.

Goldthorpe, Rhiannon. "Literature as Philosophy." *The Cambridge History of Philosophy 1870–1945*. Edited by Thomas Baldwin. Cambridge: Cambridge University Press, 2003. 714–720.

Halperin, David. *Saint Foucault: Towards a Gay Hagiography*. New York: Oxford University Press, 1995.

Jagose, Annamarie. *Queer Theory: An Introduction*. Melbourne: Melbourne University Press, 1997.

Joyce, James. *Ulysses*. Annotated students' edition. With an introduction and notes by Declan Kiberd. New York: Penguin, 2000.

Kvanvig, Jonathan L. *The Value of Knowledge and the Pursuit of Understanding*. New York: Cambridge University Press, 2003.
Lemberg, Jennifer. "Closing the Gap in Alison Bechdel's *Fun Home*." *Women's Studies Quarterly* 36.1 (2008): 129–40.
McCloud, Scott. *Understanding Comics: The Invisible Art*. New York: Harper Perennial, 1994.
Munro, Alice. "The Progress of Love." *The Progress of Love*. New York: Knopf, 1986.
Ovid. *Metamorphoses*. Translated by John Dryden et al. Edited by Sir Samuel Garth. Wordsworth Classics of World Literature. Hertfordshire: Wordsworth Editions Ltd., 1998.
Rescher, Nicholas. *Epistemology: An Introduction to the Theory of Knowledge*. Albany: State University of New York Press, 2003.
Rich, Adrienne. "It Is the Lesbian in Us . . ." In *On Lies, Secrets, and Silence: Selected Prose 1966–1978*. New York: Norton, 1979. 199–202.
Said, Edward. *The World, the Text, and the Critic*. Cambridge: Harvard University Press, 1983.
Saussure, Ferdinand de. *Course in General Linguistics*. Translated by Roy Harris. London: Duckworth, 1983 [1916].
Steup, Matthias. "Epistemology." *The Stanford Encyclopedia of Philosophy* (Spring 2014) Edited by Edward N. Zalta. <http://plato.stanford.edu/archives/spr2014/entries/epistemology/>. 2 June 2015.
Smith, Cherry. "What Is This Thing Called Queer?" *The Material Queer: A Lesbigay Cultural Studies Reader*. Edited by Donald Morton. Boulder: Westview Press, 1996. 277–285.
Sullivan, Kerry. *A Critical Introduction to Queer Theory*. New York: New York University Press, 2003.
Tolstoy, Leo. *Anna Karenina*. New York: Vintage Books, 2012.
Warhol, Robyn. "The Space Between: A Narrative Approach To Alison Bechdel's *Fun Home*." *College Literature* 38.3 (2011): 1–20.
Whitlock, Gillian. "Autographics: The Seeing 'I' of the Comics." *Modern Fiction Studies* 52.4 (2006): 965–79.

Further Reading

Are You my Mother? A Comic Drama is the 2012 follow up to *Fun Home* by Alison Bechdel.

The Minor Machinery of Animal Packs: Becoming as Survival in Spiegelman's *Maus*

Corry Shores

Spiegelman on His Use of Mice

One of the most striking features of Art Spiegelman's *Maus* are the characters' cartoon animal forms: Nazis are cats, Jews are mice, Poles are pigs, Americans are dogs, Brits are fish, the French are frogs, and Swedes are deer. Spiegelman intentionally placed his work into a tradition of animal cartooning widely known by Warner Brothers, Hanna-Barbera, and Walt Disney animations (Spiegelman, *MetaMaus*, 118, 121, 135). Nonetheless, his purpose was not to sanitize or "banalize" the Holocaust (Spiegelman, "The 5,000 Pound Maus," 193).[1] Rather, the implementation of the animal forms serves as a shockingly evocative device that attests to the power of graphic novels as a means of persuasive communication and artistic expression. Yet perhaps it is not immediately obvious what makes the animal forms so effective. Let us first look at Spiegelman's own stated motivations. Then afterward we will turn to the ideas of French philosophers Gilles Deleuze and Félix Guattari ("D&G") to add to Spiegelman's theories. We will elaborate two main theses in this essay. One is that the content of *Maus* displays not simply humans that have taken the forms of animals, but more specifically, it examines what D&G call "becoming animal" and "minorization." As we will see, a person's or a people's "becoming animal" is not something that degrades them, but is rather an instance of their having admirable skills at survival in trying circumstances. The second thesis, which we develop more briefly in conclusion, is that *Maus* itself is a work of minorized literature, namely, a "minor documentary." Thus in sum, we will find that *Maus* both depicts graphically and also demonstrates a sort of self-variational "becoming" that bears the political power of resistance or revolution.

Since *Maus*'s publication, Spiegelman on numerous occasions has addressed the specific question, "why mice?" He explains that it all began when he was tasked with writing a short comic using animal characters for a one-shot entitled *Funny Animals* (*MetaMaus*, 111). At the time, Spiegelman was also learning about American racist animal cartoons, where "blacks were cheerfully represented as subhuman, monkeylike creatures with giant minstrel lips," and he also examined less overtly racist animations like Disney's "Steamboat Willie," in which the mouse characters "had 'darkie' rhythms and body language" (*MetaMaus*, 112; "Art's Father," 81). His first idea was to do a Tom and Jerry-style cat and mouse cartoon with blacks depicted as mice being harassed by the "Ku Klux Katz." But later he settled on something more related to his own life, namely, the Holocaust experiences of his father Vladek, a Polish-Jewish immigrant who raised Art in the United States (*MetaMaus*, 112–114, 118). Then on the basis of interviews Spiegelman conducted with Vladek, he wrote a three-page "Maus" story with Nazi cats who imprison Jewish mice in "Mauschwitz" (Spiegelman, "Maus," 9–12).[2] This becomes the template for his two longer *Maus: A Survivor's Tale* graphic novel volumes, *Maus I: My Father Bleeds History* (1986) and *Maus II: And Here My Troubles Began* (1991), with the second winning a Pulitzer Prize.

Spiegelman names other important influences as well for his idea to use animal forms. One source he cites is Franz Kafka's short story "Josephine the Singer, or the Mouse Folk," which is "a metaphor of the Jews as mice" (Spiegelman and Gaiman, "Conversations"), since it serves as a "dark parable and prophecy about the situation of the Jews and Jewishness" ("Art's Father," 82).[3] Spiegelman's other "collaborators" in his decision to use animal forms were Nazi propagandists and even Hitler himself, whose quotation, "The Jews are undoubtedly a race, but they are not human," is found at the opening of the first volume of *Maus* (*MetaMaus*, 114). Spiegelman says his animal characters are "humans with animal heads" who "stand up and insist on their own humanity," even though they are capable of profoundly and incomprehensibly inhumane treatment of others. The Nazis, Spiegelman notes, "slated Jews for extermination, which is not something that is done to people. It is done to pests, to vermin" (Spiegelman, "The Holocaust through the Eyes of a Maus"). Yet what he considers the "most shockingly relevant anti-Semitic work" is the 1940 Nazi propaganda film *The Eternal Jew* [*Der Ewige Jude*], directed by Fritz Hippler (*MetaMaus*, 115). By drawing branching lines on a world map, the film portrays the Jews as following the same general migration pattern that rats had taken, beginning first in Asia and "infesting" from there all corners of the world. "Rats," the film says, while showing them in dense packs chewing through sacks of grain and scurrying up out of sewer drains, "represent the elements of *sneakiness* and *subterranean* destruction among animals, just as the Jews do among mankind," with a hard cut to images of Jews. And it continues, "The *parasite* nation of Judah is responsible for a large part of international crime" (Hippler, *The Eternal Jew*, emphasis mine). Note that the visual composition of the rat images, as for example in one shot where a mass of them are crawling over one other, stands in stark contrast to the portrayals of the immense body of geometrically arranged and mechanically organized Nazi soldiers in the earlier, 1935 propaganda film *Triumph of the Wills* [*Triumph des Willens*] by Leni Riefenstahl.

Spiegelman, a "veteran deconstructionist," also subverted this animal metaphor that he appropriated from the Nazis. He "wanted it to become problematic" by including "all sorts of paradoxes in the text" ("Art's Father" 82). They are thus "self-destructing metaphors . . . meant to fall apart" (Spiegelman and Gaiman, "Conversations"). For example, he cites as one instance a scene where there is a mixed "species" couple—a Jewish mouse wife and a German cat husband—whose children are drawn with mouse heads but also with cat stripes (*Maus II*, 131; *MetaMaus*, 131–132). In another case where the metaphor "breaks down" (*MetaMaus*, 133), Vladek and his first wife, Art's natural mother Anja, are hiding from the Nazis in a basement. Anja becomes distressed and yells while pointing into the darkness, "Aiee! Th-there are *rats* down here!" Vladek calms her by claiming, "Those aren't rats. They're very small. One ran over my hand before. They're just *mice*!" But then Vladek confides in Art that really they were rats, and in fact Spiegelman draws the rat in its normal animal form walking on all four feet down on the basement floor. Later the Polish woman who owned the house finally comes down with food, and Anja complains, "There are *rats*, giant rats! They're *horrible*!" The Pole replies, "Well—you're better off with the rats than with the Gestapo. . . . At least the rats won't *kill* you!" And Vladek agrees, admitting to Art, "She was right. We were happy even to have *these* conditions" (*Maus I*, 147–148; *MetaMaus*, 134–135).

Spiegelman offers yet another instance where he makes use of the instability of his animal metaphors. While Vladek is being marched out of Auschwitz to another camp, he witnesses a fellow prisoner being shot to death. He describes the victim "jumping, turning, rolling 25 or 35 times around. And stops." Then Vladek recalls immediately, "When I was a boy our neighbor had a dog what got mad and was biting. The neighbor came out with a rifle and shot. The dog was rolling so, around and around, kicking, before he lay quiet."

For two panels Spiegelman cuts to this earlier scene, showing a dog, in its normal animal form, being shot in one panel and lying dead on the ground, bleeding, in the next. Then in the following and final panel on the page, Spiegelman draws again the prisoner likewise lying dead on the ground, with Vladek commenting "how amazing it is that a human being reacts the same like this neighbor's dog" (*Maus II*, 82; *MetaMaus*, 133–134).

In both of these cases, it becomes visually and narratively ambiguous what is a real animal and what is a "human" animal. And this ambiguity is paralleled by the inhumanity of the Nazis' treatment of the Jews in each instance. Thus as Spiegelman puts it, these scenes are part of *Maus*'s "inquiry into what it means to be human in a dehumanizing world" (*MetaMaus*, 133). What we might note in Spiegelman's deconstructive strategy is how his appropriation of the animal cartooning tradition reverses the roles implied in the Nazis' animal metaphor. *The Eternal Jew*, along with other propaganda, portrays the Jews as rodents, which justifies acting inhumanely toward them in order to eradicate them.[4] In a way, the Germans are thus presented as the victims of Jewish selfish destructiveness. However, by critically appropriating the cat and mouse cartoon format, the Jews become the victims of Nazi harassment, which forces them to take rodent-like strategies of "burrowing" in hiding places like basements, behind false walls, in construction holes, and in barns with other animals (*Maus I*, 110–113, 121, 140), scavenging for and hording precious food scraps (*Maus I*, 112; *Maus II*, 49), and even gnawing on wood to stave off hunger (*Maus I*, 123). Spiegelman accomplishes this reversal by making only subtle manipulations to the Nazis' own metaphorical imagery.

There is finally one last motivation for the animal forms that Spiegelman mentions. Since he was working with his father's memory, Art could not know exactly what each remembered person looked like. So, the generic animal forms allowed him to leave out all that unknowable detail. Another advantage of "despecifying the faces," he explains, is a "defamiliarization" that allows for a stronger "empathic response" and thus a greater sympathetic proximity to the characters and their experiences ("The Holocaust through the Eyes of a Maus"; *MetaMaus*, 132). His term for this phenomenon is the "Little Orphan Annie's Eyeball Effect" (Spiegelman and Gaiman, "Conversations"). Little Orphan Annie was drawn with white hollow eyes that ask the viewer to "project the expression and ultimately the face through these blank pieces of paper that were inside those oval eyeballs" (Spiegelman and Gaiman, "Conversations"). So although this is a story of Art Spiegelman, his parents, and their own unique traumas from the Holocaust, when seeing the animal caricatures, we might project onto them our own personal "inner sets of associations" (*MetaMaus*, 150). Thus Vladek is not just Art's father, but someone more like our own father, or any father. "Paradoxically," then, "while the mice allowed for a distancing from the horrors described, they simultaneously allowed me and others to get further inside the material in a way that would have been difficult with more realistic representation" (*MetaMaus*, 149).

In the following, we will take for granted that the animal forms create this intense proximity to the story's events and to the characters' experiences. But we will expand upon Spiegelman's account of their "deconstructive" function. While it is important for us that the animal forms effect a reversal in the hierarchies, what interests us even more is the nature of the sorts of variation that serve to undermine such rigid and oppressive structures. As we will see, it is the power of self-variation that allows *Maus*'s deconstructive reversals to occur in the first place.

Spinozistic Composition

Our argument will be that Spiegelman's use of the animal forms, in addition to their deconstructive and sympathetic powers, also exhibits and demonstrates D&G's "becoming animal" and "minorization." To arrive at how this is so, we need first to detour through their notion that the composition of entities is based on the interactions of their parts or participating members, which is a concept that they draw from the Dutch philosopher Baruch Spinoza.[5] One way to begin this account is with an examination of the "economics" of this constituting interactivity. For this, D&G have us consider their distinction between limits and thresholds. Deleuze himself was once an alcoholic, and he explains how knowing one's limit of tolerance actually enables one's alcoholism to continue. Drunkards are ridiculed, Deleuze explains, because they claim they know when to stop, yet seemingly to everyone else they have no self-control at all. But they really do know just when they have reached "the last drink," even with a refined sense of precision, since they know exactly the greatest quantity they can drink before they create a situation that can completely end their habit, as for example, getting hospitalized, arrested, losing a job, becoming abandoned by loved ones, or attempting suicide. This would be going beyond their limit and crossing a threshold that would make the cycles of behavior and the flow of alcohol cease, since it causes the alcoholics to change internally on account of physical or psychological damage and likewise to break supportive relations with others around them. But since attaining up to but not past their limit enables the patterns and relational bonds to repeat the next day, the "last drink" is both an ending and a beginning point (Deleuze and Guattari, *A Thousand Plateaus*, 437–439, henceforth *TP*; Deleuze and Parnet, "B comme boisson").

This assessing of limits, D&G argue, is what is at work when two parties enter into a renewing exchange relation that keeps a flow of goods and services passing between them and that binds them as well into a larger entity. In their illustration, one group produces seeds and the other one, axes. Each party assesses the maximum amount they can expend of their own supplies and also receive from the other one, before they must radically alter their own composition and functioning and as well break off their mutually beneficial exchange relation. For example, if the ax-makers buy too many seeds, they will have to change their agricultural system or take a damaging loss from the wasted expenditure. Or if the seed-makers demand too many axes, then the axe-makers might need to over-stretch their resources and productive capacities. Thus, they both assess each other's and their own limits, past which they themselves and their partnership will decompose, and it is partly on this basis that they determine the relative values of the goods they exchange. D&G illustrate with another example, namely, the way that married couples conduct their arguments with one another. Each spouse wants to have "the last word," which would allow that person to win the dispute. They assess that limit by knowing what they must stop themselves before saying, since crossing this threshold would be so damaging as to mean divorce (*TP*, 437–438). Under this view, then, the relationship is more symbiotic than contractual, because what each party always keeps in mind is maintaining the mutually beneficial bond between them.

There is another element of this notion of Spinozistic composition that this example of marriage and divorce will illustrate, namely, the nesting of composition: any part is itself a whole made up on a smaller scale of other parts internal to it, and any such whole as well combines with still other ones on its scale, together composing a larger unit. Furthermore, alterations in composition are to be understood as somehow involving changes that happen at all scales at once. To illustrate this, let us look at an example in *Maus*. There is a section in the first volume that reproduces a short comic Spiegelman wrote years prior about his mother Anja's suicide (*Maus I*, 100–103). She had a nervous breakdown, so we might view this situation internally as the parts of her physical and emotional systems having crossed certain thresholds of stability. In neurological accounts perhaps this could be understood simplistically for example as certain portions or functions of her brain not providing sufficient neurochemicals for the other parts to maintain normal operations. This internal decomposition leads to her severing herself from Vladek and Art through suicide. That event harms her two survivors internally by deeply traumatizing them, Vladek especially. Although he continues living, the damage was so great that he had to make major changes in the working of his own mind to repress memories of Anja, going as far as to burn very important diaries she wrote during the Holocaust, which were meant specifically for Art and would have made a vital contribution to Maus (*Maus I*, 158–159). Yet the chain of causation does not so clearly begin within Anja and work outward to her relations with other people. We also learn throughout *Maus* that Vladek is extraordinarily difficult to live with, and perhaps his impossible demands on Anja contributed strongly to her internal decomposition (*Maus I*, 43–44, 131–132). We could view the breakdown of relations between Jews and Nazis during the war in similar terms. Anja's family is well-off, and Vladek, by means of his business skills and help from Anja's father, heads a successful textile factory (*Maus I*, 29). Jews were no doubt important and productive contributors to the nations they lived in. However, under Nazi rule, they were dehumanized and divorced from society, leading to a physical decomposition of Jewish groups and individuals, parallel to the moral decomposition among the Nazis. In both cases, we see the same dynamic in the changes of structure. The integrity of something's internal composition has much to do with its external relations, and vice versa. And thus the processes of decomposition likewise occur dually on inner and outer levels. In these examples above, the decomposition was detrimental to all those involved. Yet we now will explore a mode of "decomposition" that in fact strengthens internal and external relations, since it is a form of continuous recomposition that allows metamorphosing things and groups to adapt better to trying situations while at the same time making it harder for oppressive powers to harm them.

Animals and Packs

With these concepts in mind, we may turn now to the notion of becoming-animal. We will examine two main components to it. The first is the self-variation of the parts, and the second is the flexible composition of the group or "pack" of animals. When discussing this second point, D&G turn to Elias Canetti's distinction between crowds and packs (*TP*, 33–34). Both are groups of individuals. But packs tend to be smaller, and any differences between the members are vital to the strength and well-being of the group as a whole. Crowds, on the other hand, would then be larger, and internal differences are made irrelevant, since there is a sort of equalization that comes in part from the group submitting to a common purpose. Thus, packs are heterogeneously composed while crowds' participants are more homogeneous (Canetti, *Crowds and Power*, 29–30, 93–97). D&G use the concepts of filiation and alliance to describe the two different ways that participants relate in these unities. Homogeneous groupings could be ones for example with blood ties, since the members are related by common descent and shared family features (*TP*, 246). When bonds are filial like this, the unity is based more on an assimilation of the parts. Sometimes this conformity is compelled upon a population, as seen for example by totalitarian governments through their propaganda campaigns and laws against outsiders or minority cultures and political affiliations. The bonds in packs, however, are based on alliances and pacts, which bring together heterogeneous elements into coordinated functioning with each other (*TP*, 241–242).

In *Maus*, for example, we see how family relations become less binding than opportunistic temporary alliances between strangers. Anja's family before the war is depicted as a strong unit of mutually supporting members (*Maus I*, 74–76). As Nazi rule takes over Poland, however, we watch those family relations erode. Art is confused at one point when Vladek explains that he needed to pay cousins, whose last name was also Spiegelman, to help himself and Anja escape transport to Auschwitz. Art asks, "Wouldn't they have helped you even if you couldn't pay? I mean, you were from the same family." Vladek exclaims, "Hah! You don't understand . . . at that time it *wasn't* anymore families. It was everybody to take care for *himself!*" (*Maus I*, 114). Instead of such fixed relations that once structured their communities, interpersonal alliances during the war are portrayed as being formed spontaneously through temporary agreements that are ambiguously both trusted friendships and pure business relations. We know that trust and friendship are important in these agreements, since very often Jews in *Maus* pay others for certain services, only to be sold out to or betrayed by the Nazis (*Maus I*, 124; *Maus II*, 83), which is in fact how Vladek and Anja were finally captured and taken to Auschwitz (*Maus I*, 155). Before that, they were hiding at a Polish woman's house. Vladek made this arrangement after buying goods from her numerous times at a black market. In one instance he generously gave her extra money for the sake of her child, and she then offered him her place as a safe house (*Maus I*, 141). Vladek and Anja then seemingly become almost like members of the Polish woman's family, with Anja even voluntarily helping the son with his schoolwork (*Maus I*, 142). However, one day Vladek does not have enough change to pay the woman the full amount for bread that she was supposed to go to town to buy, and so he promises her the rest later. The woman returns sometime after saying she could not buy it for him, since she was unable to find any. Vladek is pretty certain she was lying, but he says she was a good woman anyway. As Vladek explains in answer to Art's question if he had to pay the woman to stay at her house, "Of course I paid . . . and *well* I paid. . . . What do you think? Someone will risk their life for nothing?" (*Maus*

I, 142). Even Vladek himself, instead of charitably saving a person who needed water, does so only by receiving some sugar from him in exchange (*Maus II*, 86).[6] In another scene, Vladek tries to gain favor with the head tinman at Auschwitz. He was a Russian Jew who hated capitalists like Vladek once was, telling him, "Hah! You never did an honest day's work in your whole life, Spiegelman! ... You owned big factories and exploited your workers, you dirty capitalist!" (*Maus II*, 47). However, after Vladek begins supplying the communist with food, their ideological differences are put entirely aside, and they continue working for each other's benefits (*Maus II*, 47–48).[7] As Vladek observes, "If you want to live, it's good to be friendly!" (*Maus I*, 62). All this, of course, is not unique to these exceptional circumstances but is rather the way things often work in life. Yet what is notable here is that the Jews under these conditions lost their normal fixed relational structures and had to adapt to a situation of high variability in the composition and structuring of their social groupings, thus making them more like a pack than like a crowd or State.

Another feature of packs according to Canetti is that they have a dynamic structure where members' statuses may change, like a stellar constellation whose stars somehow constantly vary their relative positions, thereby altering the character of the whole formation.[8] As D&G write, a pack is "continually transforming itself into a string of other multiplicities, according to its thresholds and doors" (*TP*, 249). But for individuals to change in relation to one another, they need to change over time in relation to their own selves as well, by means of a "metamorphosis" of sorts. This is one reason D&G also take interest in Kafka's "Josephine the Singer," since she "sometimes holds a privileged position in the pack, sometimes a position outside the pack, and sometimes slips into and is lost in the anonymity of the collective statements of the pack" (*TP*, 243). To elaborate, we could here consider Deleuze's notion of "infinite identity" (Deleuze, *The Logic of Sense*, 2–3). Often we understand the infinite in quantitative terms as being something larger (or smaller) than anything with a finite value. Yet since the finite is something with limits, we might also think of the infinite simply as something without bounds that limit it. In instances of quantity, it would be something limitlessly large (or small). But in the case of compositions, we could conceive of things with "infinite identities" as ones with flexible definitional boundaries, such that their internal constitution and relations to other participants can undergo wide variance while still maintaining the heterogeneous cohesion of the internal and external groupings. For example, Vladek was a prisoner of war during Poland's war with Germany, yet he and other captured Jewish soldiers still maintained their religious practices by modifying them in accordance with their limited means in the camps (*Maus I*, 54).

Also, during the Nazi's policy of "the final solution," in order to escape notice, Jews in *Maus* are often shown as concealing their heritage and pretending to be non-Jewish members of their nations. To represent this, Spiegelman depicts Vladek and other Jews as wearing pig masks so to appear like all other non-Jewish Poles. For example, when hiding at a house far away from the town with the black market Vladek frequented, he rode in using the streetcar meant for German and Polish Nazi officials, saying "Heil Hitler" as he entered, all while shown as wearing his pig mask. For, on that car "The Germans paid no attention of me," while in the car for normal Poles, "they could *smell* if a Polish Jew came in" (*Maus I*, 140). In another remarkable scene, Polish children are playing outside, and they detect that Vladek is a Jew, even though he is trying to disguise himself as a regular Pole, again depicted as wearing his pig mask. The children run home in fear, with one screaming, "Help! Mommy! A Jew!!" Their mothers come out, and Vladek greets them saying "Heil Hitler" and assures them all that he is no Jew. Although he "came out well from this," he says, "the experience cost me really a lot of hairs" (*Maus I*, 149).[9]

And so, what D&G call "becoming-animal" is not simply changing to an animal form, but rather more generally it has to do with the flexing of limits that define oneself (*TP*, 238).[10] But we might then wonder, why do D&G use this notion of "animal," if all they really mean is self-variation? One reason is because this flexing of one's own limits is something they characterize in terms of animal territorial behaviors. But what will make this association somewhat confusing is that we need to think of "territories" as having a broader sense than we conventionally give it, and another issue is that a plant in one of their main examples is exhibiting this territorial behavior. Yet since it illustrates the concepts well, let us begin with plants and consider a garden with a variety of species. Some of which, like trees, have evolved to capture sunlight from up high, while others, like grasses, from below. Mushrooms do not even compete for the light and in fact thrive especially where it is lacking. And the flower species do not all bloom at the same time and in the same way, but rather they have evolved to take-up their own unique place in relation to each other. In this way, a plant can be said to be territorializing not just in the sense of one mature plant taking up and dominating a physical location in the soil, but as well the plants territorialize evolutionarily by differentiating their traits in ways that give them their own relational place among other plants, based on the unique properties they developed. What interests D&G, however, is the mutational movement that takes something past its own relational boundaries into foreign territory, thereby creating both a variation of itself and at the same time new alliances with other creatures. They illustrate with the example of orchids and wasps (*TP*, 10; 293). Certain orchids have evolved to visually resemble female wasps and also to emit their pheromones, which causes male wasps to be especially attracted to the flowers and to land on them enthusiastically. This results in the orchid's pollen being disseminated more readily, and as well it benefits the wasps by loading them with the pollen they seek. So over the course of its gradual evolution, this orchid species has departed from its prior relational place among the other flowers and creatures and entered the foreign territory of insects, by taking on wasp traits and participating in wasp mating behaviors. D&G's term for this transgression of one's own territorial boundaries is "deterritorialization," which Deleuze says can be understood as becoming "outlandish" (Deleuze and Parnet, "A comme animal"). The orchid is both going outside its native place or "land" into foreign territory, and as well it is becoming outlandish in the sense of being freakish or strange in comparison to what it once was.

But the reason why it is called "becoming-animal" and not "becoming-plant" or "becoming-creature" it seems is because animals especially are much more actively and spontaneously engaged in deterritorializing activities, rather than only being so in their evolutionary development, like plants perhaps are. Deleuze says that animals are always on the lookout for signs indicating that they need to vary their behavior in relation to other creatures' actions and to changing situations in the world (Deleuze and Parnet, "A comme animal"). Nonetheless, their term "becoming-animal" can still be confusing for a couple reasons. The first is that even though animals are willing to alter themselves to adapt to changing situations, even going as far as to chew off a limb to escape a trap, their spontaneous behaviors are perhaps not as radically mutational as is the orchid's evolving so to look less like a flower and more like an insect. Thus, D&G seem to be narrowing their focus on a certain tendency in some animals' behavior, and then conceiving it in a more essential form. The second confusing thing has to do with the fact that for them becoming-animal involves both deterritorialization and yet as well the formation of packs. They write, "A becoming-animal always involves a pack, a band, a population, a peopling, in short, a multiplicity" (*TP*, 239). Yet when something mutates, it presumably is breaking away from its group rather than integrating with it. However, such self-variations create new alliances, like with the orchid forging an alliance with the wasps. Thus, the "pack" in this example is not the orchids being grouped with each other but rather the orchids being allied with the wasps, and as well of course with such other creatures as the worms and bacteria that nourish the soil, and so on. As such, packs should be thought of as combining very heterogeneous members. Hence, we will understand becoming-animal to mean a sort of self-variation by which one leaves one's proper "territory" while in the same act producing novel groupings by forging new relations.

D&G further characterize the deterritorialization involved in becoming-animal with the notions of escape and flight. Animals of course can flee an enemy, and D&G write that rodent burrows are structured in such a way that every turn is like another escape route, with the whole structure being a network of evasion (*TP*, 6–7). But flight also has the meaning of escape from one's own self, in the mutational sense we discussed above (Deleuze and Guattari, *Kafka*, 36). D&G call it "stationary flight," since it is an escape without changing location (*Kafka*, 13). In the second book of *Maus*, there is a section where Spiegelman depicts himself as a human cartoonist wearing a mouse mask (*Maus II*, 41–47). And in the introduction to *MetaMaus*, he likewise draws himself as a cartoonist with a mouse face, but at the end, he struggles to pull off his "mask," only to reveal a bare skeleton behind it (*MetaMaus*, 9). What this might suggest is that there is no absolute fixed identity, and instead it is just one mask or another. The important distinction we need to make here is whether or not someone wears the "mask" (that is, pretends to have an alternate identity) for the purpose of concealing what one regards to be a deeper fixed identity that one has, or if instead one regards the new masks as authentic selves that one is really in the process of becoming. In the first case, the falsity only has the power to deceive others, but it changes nothing with regard to one's identity. In that sense, the person never was, nor never will be, what they are pretending to be. But in the second case, the falsity of the mask has the power to transform one's own identity, since although the person never had that identity before, they adopt it now as being a presentation of a self they sincerely intend to become and actively takes steps to transform into (Deleuze, *Cinema II*, 143–147). While in the camps, Vladek exercises this "power of falsity," as Deleuze calls it, by spontaneously adopting new occupational identities. Up to this time, we only know of him having two such identities, namely, factory owner and merchant. But when living in the ghettos, he needed working papers to prevent him from being taken to the camps. He obtained them not by actually becoming a workman of one sort or another, but instead by bribing officials at workshops. He was not actually expected work while at these places, but when Nazi officials made visits, he needed merely to pretend to be working. However, matters became different after he was taken away to the camps. Jews there were killed if they could not really serve some important occupational function that would help maintain the camp's operations. So then it becomes necessary for Vladek not only to appear like he is a worker of some kind, but he actually needed to instantaneously adopt these other identities in an authentic way so that he could serve a useful function. To accomplish this, he first falsely proclaims he has a particular occupational identity, following which he puts his heart into the task of actually becoming that sort of workman. For example, before the camps, his father-in-law bribed the overseer of a tin shop to give Vladek working papers that claimed he worked there, but really he was never expected to perform any tasks. However, the overseer instructed Vladek, while pointing to a shop room with actual tinsmiths hard at work, that "if there's ever a round-up, run in here and pretend you're working" (*Maus I*, 78). Yet despite this privilege of his, he carefully observes what the tin workers are doing. For, he explains, "You must know everything to survive" (*MetaMaus*, 54). Then later, when in Auschwitz, he falsely claims to be a tinsmith, but he instantaneously becomes one by getting right to the job, working just on the basis of his prior observations (*Maus II*, 47). And before the camps, Vladek also worked at a factory that repaired German boots. Again, he was only expected to pretend to work whenever Nazi officials made an inspection. Nonetheless, he was taught how to perform the repairs so that it would appear convincing that he was an actual worker there (*Maus I*, 117). Then in Auschwitz, he heard that they needed a shoemaker, and so he falsely claimed to the official in charge of the camp's shops, "You know, I've been a shoemaker since childhood" (*Maus II*, 60). And like before, he worked only with what he recalled from observation, and he immediately demonstrated that he had the abilities of a shoe repairman. Even though this was merely his first real attempt at the craft, the officer was quite impressed with Vladek's work, exclaiming, "You're better than our *last* shoemaker!" (*Maus II*, 60). Here we see how self-falsification, when combined with an earnest effort to flee from oneself and become something new, is in fact productive of new authentic identities. Vladek also in this instance built a new alliance with the officers at the camp, which helped expand the limits of the Jewish "pack" by building advantageous relations with the Nazi officials.

Thus, those cases when Vladek is depicted wearing a pig mask while trying to deceive others into thinking he is a non-Jewish Pole are not really instances of him taking flight from himself and hence are not examples of him becoming-animal (*Kafka*, 13). However, what does constitute becoming-animal is the fact that Vladek fluently mutates himself in ways that create heterogeneous packs on the basis of him forming new alliances. Yet many of those who could not so readily adapt themselves in these trying situations did not survive like Vladek was able to do with his extraordinary luck and skill. And even Vladek himself may have been traumatized so much by his Holocaust experiences that he lost the ability to modify himself to suit the very different post-war circumstances in the U.S. For example, his traumatic experiences of starvation and living with very limited means may have made him permanently tight with money and other resources, which often infuriates the people around him who suffer from this behavior.[11] In one scene, the older Vladek tries to return opened and half eaten food boxes to the grocery store. Art and his wife stay in the car, not wanting to be present at such an embarrassing interaction. Art's wife says she would have killed herself before undergoing that much trauma, and in fact it is a "miracle" that Vladek survived. Art replies, "In some ways he *didn't* survive" (*Maus II*, 90). One way to interpret this is to say that Vladek was changed so much by his experiences that his older, "real" self died. However, on the basis of our ideas regarding becoming-animal, we would say that the reason he did not survive is because he was unable to mutate again after the war in a way that successfully builds and maintains his relations with other people rather than constantly straining them.

Maus and Minor Literature

We turn now to the concept of minorization, and we begin by clarifying the distinction between "minority" and "minoritarian." Note first that what D&G mean by "majority" is not just any group of a larger size. Rather, when they use this term, they refer to a state or standard by which other individuals can be judged so to determine whether or not they deserve certain rights afforded only to a privileged group. As such, majority groups often have a fixed structure and a rigid system of values that all members must conform to. Yet this also means that even groups with relatively few members can be majorities, so long as they are homogenized in accordance with certain rigid standards and are also oppressive toward those who are excluded from their group. To illustrate, D&G explain that while there might be fewer humans in the world than flies, humans are still a majority when they consider themselves as a "standard in the universe" against which flies are denied the rights granted to humans. And even within human society there are civil majorities which are such because they presuppose their right to vote and exercise that right over those whom they deem unworthy of it (*TP*, 291). Now, groups excluded from the majority are of two types: minority and minoritarian. Minorities are those that cling to a fixed group identity in the face of oppression, while minoritarian groups are ones with a "politics of becoming-animal," by which the members individually, and hence as well the group as a whole, deterritorialize in a process of self-variational becoming (*TP*, 247–248, 291–292). Thus Jews, D&G explain, constitute a minority if their only concern is forming a state. However, they are minoritarian when they instead "become-Jewish," meaning that they open their identity to mutation, on both the levels of the individual and as well of the pack or "machinic assemblage," as part of a strategy to undermine the oppression of majorities (*TP*, 291).[12] Our purpose for taking up this new terminology is to account for the "mechanics" and dynamics of the political relations between the majority and the minoritarian. The majority tries to establish and enforce values, meanings, and identities, which adversely affect minoritarian groups. We have seen this already with the Nazi propaganda that wanted to affix to the concept of Jew the notions of pest and selfish destruction by means of the metaphor of rats.[13] Minoritarian packs, however, "continually work [upon families and States] from within and trouble them from without, with other forms of content, other forms of expression" (*TP*, 242). One strategy for accomplishing this is creating what D&G call a "minor literature" on the basis of minorizing the major language. The idea is that you do not invent a new language, but rather you use the language of the majority group and intensify its expressive powers by misusing it in politically advantageous ways. We saw already how *Maus* minorizes two major languages, namely, the animal metaphoric language of the Nazis and the visual conventions of animal cartoons, with the result being a reversal of which group is made the guilty party.

Yet there is still another way that *Maus* creates a minor literature within a major language. D&G write that one way to minorize the "arid" major language is to "make it vibrate with a new intensity. Oppose a purely intensive usage of language to all symbolic or even significant or simply signifying usages of it. Arrive at a perfect and unformed expression, a materially intense expression" (*Kafka*, 19). A purely intensive, non-signifying use of language could be expressive animal-like sounds (*Kafka*, 22), which automatically call out to one's pack, since "what is a cry independent of the population it appeals to or takes as its witness?" (*TP*, 239). In fact, whenever Spiegelman draws mouths on the mice characters, "They're almost always there as cries and screams" (*MetaMaus*, 145), with one notable example being a scene where a group of Jewish camp prisoners were burned alive in a pit, depicted with their mouths wide agape, screaming in agony and terror (*Maus II*, 72).

There is also a way that the language is intensified while still using English words and basic syntax rather than just animal-like sounds. D&G note the problem that immigrants have in living in a region that speaks a language quite foreign to their own. Their problem as well is surviving in such a society whose different values are built into its language, institutions, and conventions, without themselves becoming victimized by those structures (*Kafka*, 19–20).[14] The question, then, is "how to tear a minor literature away from its own language, allowing it to challenge the language and making it follow a sober revolutionary path?" (*Kafka*, 19). To accomplish this, one must write "like a dog digging a hole, a rat digging its burrow ... finding his own point of underdevelopment, his own *patois*, his own third world" (*Kafka*, 18). In such a "minor utilization" of a major language, one embraces the fact that they are a "sort of stranger" within the language, because the aim is to make the language itself "emigrate" by warping its grammar and filling it with "vocables that are fleeting" and nomadic (*Kafka*, 25–26). As we may have noticed from prior quotations, Vladek's English is written in a Polish immigrant's sort of dialect, with its many "mistakes" and other oddities. Spiegelman explains that Vladek's "English is broken English. He came and cobbled together his English after another lifetime had been built and destroyed. So to hear the story through language that isn't structured through the way you usually hear it, you hear something freshly" (Spiegelman, "The Holocaust through the Eyes of a Maus").[15] In fact, Spiegelman insisted that all translations of *Maus* have Vladek speaking a "broken" version of whatever language it was changed to (*MetaMaus*, 152–153). Alan Rosen, in his examination of Vladek's dialect, notes how English has been argued by some as inadequate for telling the story of the Holocaust, since it was not a commonly used language among the people involved and thus would fail to give the most accurate possible testimony to the events (Rosen, "English as Metaphor," 123). Vladek's broken English, however, gives his account an authoritative voice, because it is truer to one of the actual languages that was used (Polish), and because it presents the events in their foreignness to English speakers ("English as Metaphor," 124, 130–133).[16] Rosen also cites one case where the misusage profoundly intensifies the impact of the sentence. Vladek was marched from Auschwitz to another camp at Dachau, and he says, "Here, in Dachau, my troubles began" (*Maus II*, 91).[17] Rosen argues that on one level, this statement is ironic, because it is absurd. We just learned of the horrific troubles Vladek endured in the ghettos and in Auschwitz. Thus, by using "an idiom that is inappropriate for the circumstances to which it refers, Art calls attention to both Vladek's foreignness—the difficulty of mastering English idioms—and to the foreignness of the experience—a degree of suffering that resists idiomatic formulation" ("English as Metaphor," 127). But at the same time, it is not merely a misusage, since Vladek wanted to convey the intensity of "a new dimension of anguish" that enters his experiences at this time ("English as Metaphor," 127). When one encounters Vladek's statement that his troubles only began in the *second* concentration camp, one might be shocked into disbelief, having already learned of unspeakably and unimaginably dehumanizing horrors prior to it. So by misusing English, Vladek makes this sentence "vibrate" with emotional intensity, and it conveys the shock that the Jewish victims must have experienced with each successive higher dimension of suffering they endured. Thus, he minorizes English and thereby is able to add an expressive level of intensified meanings that testify to the horrible crimes the Nazis inflicted upon the Jews.

Conclusion: *Maus* as a "Minor Genre"

These, then, are the ways that the content of *Maus* can be said to exhibit becoming-animal and minorization. Yet its form itself, we suggested before, actively demonstrates a sort of minorization as well. D&G call Kafka's personal letters a "minor genre" (*Kafka*, 31). What we finish by considering is the minorizing role *Maus* may have played in the context of mass media in the twentieth century. Spiegelman notes that the Comics Code Authority of the 1950s made seemingly more adult-friendly (or adult-appropriate) genres like horror, crime, and science fiction become no longer financially viable.[18] For the most part, this left on the stands only children's comics, such as animal themed ones, and juvenile superhero comics. Yet there was as well an underground movement of more adult themed comics of which Spiegelman was a part (Spiegelman and Gaiman, "Conversations"). *Maus* as we noted takes up the conventional animal traditions, and at the same time it brings the underground style into the mainstream. But in the process, Spiegelman creates an interesting genre. Now note that in documentary film, a director can strive to incorporate a large portion of "objective" materials, for example by using stock news reel footage of the events or by filming artifacts like documents, photos, and so on. A director might also choose "subjective" materials, especially eye-witness testimony. Claude Lanzmann's *Shoah* (1985) is a film documentary of the Holocaust that is notable for its near exclusive use of subjective materials, being made of a series of interviews with Jewish survivors, Nazi SS officers who worked at the camps, and others who witnessed the horrors of the ghettos and camps.[19] The film demonstrates that documenting these subjective elements of past events is vital for understanding the human experience that is fundamental to our history. So although *Maus* can be classified for example as an autobiographical work,[20] it can also be seen as a documentary graphic novel.[21]

Perhaps before *Maus*, few would have considered comics and graphic novels as legitimate means of historical documentation, since cartoon drawings are so heavily contaminated with the subjectivity of the artist, and because they were often not regarded as a serious art form. Of course, many hand drawings serve as historical documents when photographs are unavailable, and Spiegelman himself made use of such spontaneously made drawings by people in the camps who drew "with a real urgency," since they witnessed something they felt needed to be documented but cameras were unavailable (Spiegelman, "The Holocaust through the Eyes of a Maus"). And other comics artists had made cartoon documentations before *Maus*, like Will Eisner's *Last Day in Vietnam* and Keiji Nakazawa's *Barefoot Gen*. Yet while *Maus* is not the first comics documentary, it has played a leading role in successfully minorizing the language and conventions of comics and graphic novels such that they came to be recognized by the public as an art form with the power to give deeply compelling and historically valuable documentations of the past. In that sense, we might consider documentary graphic novels like *Maus* as belonging to a minorizing genre, with the works of such cartoonists as Joe Sacco, Marjane Satrapi, and many others demonstrating the vitality of the genre and the importance of the graphic novel and indeed of the general continued significance of comics among mass media.

Notes

1. See Spiegelman and Gaiman, "Conversation"; Spiegelman, "Art's Father," 72; and Spiegelman, *MetaMaus*, 120 and 135. Spiegelman considers Don Bluth and Steven Spielberg's animated film *An American Tale*, in which "cute" Russian-Jewish mice are chased by menacing Cossack cats (Katsacks), to be a sanitization of his ideas in *Maus* ("Art's Father," 72; *MetaMaus*, 78–79). Yet Spiegelman's critical appropriation of this animal cartoon tradition, he explains, stems more specifically from Bill Elder's parody of Disney's Mickey Mouse, entitled "Mickey Rodent!" in Harvey Kurtzman's *Mad Magazine* (January 1955). Spiegelman writes that the message of *Mad* was "The media—the whole damn adult world—is *lying* to you, . . . and we here at MAD are part of the media" (*Breakdowns* 6). *MAD* produced an "antidote to the 1950s, which was a certain kind of ironic distance from what you were looking at. . . . Without Kurtzman we would not have had protests against the Vietnam War, because it taught you to question . . . the monolithic authority of images." And so, "When he did ["Mickey Rodent!"], he was telling you that the Disney universe was not so squeaky clean" (Spiegelman and Gaiman, "Conversation").

2. I will use "Vladek" to refer to Art's father, and "Spiegelman" or "Art" for his son, Art, the author of *Maus*.

3. It might not be immediately apparent what the Jewish element of this story is. Some commentators claim that Josephine's odd singing, which is really more like whistling, is to be understood as her speaking Hebrew or Yiddish (Suchoff, *Kafka's Jewish Languages*, 183–184, 206–209), since "both [the mouse folk and Jewish] cultures may be described by lost traditions, histories, and cultures and by collective persecution" (Baer, "Performative Emotion in Kafka's 'Josephine,'" 155).

4. Spiegelman notes "how regularly Jews were represented literally as rats" in, for example, the cartoon caricatures of Philippe "Fips" Rupprecht (*MetaMaus*, 115–116).

5. I provide a more detailed account of how Deleuze obtains these concepts from Spinoza in Shores, "Body and World in Merleau-Ponty and Deleuze," 197–203.

6. Not all of Vladek's generosity can be explained as pure self-interest, however. For example, he helps a friend in Auschwitz get proper clothes and eating implements, seemingly just out of sympathy (*Maus II*, 29–34).

7. There are numerous other examples in *Maus* of these temporary alliances that are built through exchange relations. See for example *Maus I*, 151; and *Maus, II* 31–33. But again, the matter is not so simple. In one scene, Vladek is talking secretly to Anja at the camps, and he tells her not to give her food away to friends, since "they don't worry about you. They just worry about getting a bigger share of your food" (*Maus II*, 56). One of Vladek's survival skills is his ability to know whom to trust and whom not to. Other Jews even pay him to give advice regarding whom to make pacts with and when, in order to escape the ghetto (*Maus I*, 124).

8. "In the changing constellation of the pack, in its dances and expeditions, he will again and again find himself at its edge. He may be in the centre, and then, immediately afterwards, at the edge again; at the edge and then back in the centre" (Canetti, *Crowds and Power*, 93).

9. There are many other notable examples of the Jews using pig masks to alter their cultural identities. See for example *Maus I*, 64, 125, 136, 138–139, 141, 144.

10. "Becoming can and should be qualified as becoming-animal even in the absence of a term that would be the animal become.... A becoming lacks a subject distinct from itself; but also ... it has no term, since its term in turn exists only as taken up in another becoming of which it is the subject, and which coexists, forms a block, with the first" (*TP*, 238).

11. We also learn that other Jewish friends of Vladek and of his second wife Mala, who also survived the camps, did not develop Vladek's problem (*Maus I*, 131), so perhaps this element of his personality was not so much changed as it was accentuated and made permanent.

12. Although we might normally make a strong distinction between the concepts of animal and of machine, for D&G these notions are much more entangled. As with packs and becoming-animal, machines are heterogeneous systems whose parts are under variance with themselves and in relation to one another: "The line of escape is part of the machine. Inside or outside, the animal is part of the burrow-machine. The problem is not that of being free but of finding a way out, or even a way in, another side, a hallway, an adjacency" (*Kafka*, 7–8); and in "a *machinic assemblage*," just as in an animal pack, "the parts ... are independent of each other, but [it] functions nonetheless" (*Kafka*, 37).

13. D&G also distinguish types of animals, with the second type functioning like the Nazis' use of the rat metaphor, and the third being like Spiegelman's deconstructive appropriation: "There is a second kind: animals with characteristics or attributes; genus, classification, or State animals; animals as they are treated in the great divine myths, in such a way as to extract from them series or structures, archetypes or models.... Finally, there are more demonic animals, pack or affect animals that form a multiplicity, a becoming, a population, a tale" (*TP*, 240–241).

14. Among their numerous examples is Franz Kafka, a Czech Jew who lived in Prague and wrote in German (*TP*, 98; *Kafka*, 19–20).

15. D&G explain how Kafka's German, by being "incorrect" in certain ways, intensifies its expressive powers:

In the lovely pages where he analyzes the Prague German that was influenced by Czech, Wagenbach cites as the characteristics of this form of German the incorrect use of prepositions; the abuse of the pronominal; the employment of malleable verbs (such as *Giben*, which is used for the series 'put, sit, place, take away' and which thereby becomes intensive); the multiplication and succession of adverbs; the use of pain-filled connotations; the importance of the accent as a tension internal to the word; and the distribution of consonants and vowels as part of an internal discordance. Wagenbach insists on this point: all these marks of the poverty of a language show up in Kafka but have been taken over by a creative utilization for the purposes of a new sobriety, a new expressivity, a new flexibility, a new intensity." (*Kafka*, 23, citing Wagenbach, *Franz Kafka*, 78–88)

Kafka, in his diaries writes, "Almost every word I write jars up against the next, I hear the consonants rub leadenly against each other and the vowels sing an accompaniment like Negroes in a minstrel show" (*Kafka*, 23, quoting Kafka, *Diaries*, 15 December 1910, 33). Thus by means of these misusages, "Language stops being representative in order to now move toward its extremities or its limits" (Kafka, 23).

16. Rosen also argues that at the same time, the imperfections in Vladek's misusage indicate that English has limitations to its authority in this task, perhaps because the mistakes suggest inaccuracies in the descriptions ("English as Metaphor," 132).

17. In the recordings and transcriptions, there is a part that is similar: "And finally we came to Dachau. And this was a camp—terrible. Then it started my misery, in Dachau. I went through this much, that I cannot even tell anybody what I went through in Dachau" (*MetaMaus*, 269).

18. For more on the Comics Code and its effects, see Amy Nyberg's *Seal of Approval: The History of the Comics Code*, or see her variation on this treatment, "'No Harm in Horror': Ethical Dimensions of the Postwar Comic Book Controversy," where she discusses the issues from an ethical point of view.

19. In many cases, the most powerful moments arise when the witnesses cannot continue speaking, as they are unable to utter the atrocities they saw. Here language also breaks down, and yet expressive intensities in the speakers' body language and vocal modulations say more than words can.

20. See for example Chaney, *Graphic Subjects*, part 1.

21. For more on documentary comics, see Hillary Chute's forthcoming book *Disaster Drawn: Visual Witness, Comics, and Documentary Form*.

Bibliography

Baer, Andrea. "Performative Emotion in Kafka's 'Josephine, the Singer; or, the Mouse Folk' and Freud's 'The Creative Writer and Daydreaming.'" In March Lucht and Donna Lucht (eds.), *Kafka's Creatures: Animals, Hybrids, and Other Fantastic Beings*. New York: Lexington, 2010. 137–156.

Canetti, Elias. *Crowds and Power*. Translated by Carol Stewart. New York: Continuum, 1973 [1962].

Chaney, Michael (ed.). *Graphic Subjects: Critical Essays on Autobiography and Graphic Novels*. Madison, Wisconsin: University of Wisconsin, 2011.

Deleuze, Gilles. *Cinema 2: The Time-Image*. Translated by Hugh Tomlinson and Robert Galeta. Minneapolis: University of Minnesota/Athlone, 1989.

Deleuze, Gilles. *The Logic of Sense*. Translated by Mark Lester and Charles Stivale. Edited by Constantin V. Boundas. New York: Columbia University, 1990.

Deleuze, Gilles, and Claire Parnet. "A comme animal" and "B comme boisson." In *Gilles Deleuze from A to Z*. Directed by Michel Pamart. Translated by Charles J. Stivale. France: Semiotext(e), 2012. DVD.

Deleuze, Gilles, and Félix Guattari. *Kafka: Toward a Minor Literature*. Translated by Dana Polan. Minneapolis: University of Minnesota, 1986.

Deleuze, Gilles, and Félix Guattari. *A Thousand Plateaus: Capitalism and Schizophrenia, 2*. Translated by Brian Massumi. Minneapolis: University of Minnesota, 1987.

Der Ewige Jude [*The Eternal Jew*]. Directed by Fritz Hippler. Germany: Deutsche Film Gesellschaft. 1940.

Nyberg, Amy Kiste. "'No Harm in Horror': Ethical Dimensions of the Postwar Comic Book Controversy." In Jeff McLaughlin (ed.), *Comics as Philosophy*. Jackson: University Press of Mississippi, 2005. 27–45.

Nyberg, Amy Kiste. *Seal of Approval: The History of the Comics Code*. Jackson: University Press of Mississippi, 1998.

Rosen, Alan C. "The Language of Survival: English as Metaphor in Art Spiegelman's *Maus*." In Deborah R. Geis (ed.), *Considering Maus: Approaches to Art Spiegelman's "Survivor's Tale" of the Holocaust*. Tuscaloosa: University of Alabama Press, 2003. 122–134.

Shores, Corry. "Body and World in Merleau-Ponty and Deleuze." *Studia Phaenomenologica* 12 (2012): 181–209.

Spiegelman, Art. "The 5,000 Pound Maus: On the Anniversary of Kristallnacht, Art Spiegelman Revisits His Legacy." Interview by Ella Taylor in 1998. In Joseph Witek (ed.), *Art Spiegelman: Conversations*. Jackson: University Press of Mississippi, 2007. 191–195.

———. "Art's Father, Vladek's Son." Interview by Lawrence Weschler in 1986. In Joseph Witek (ed.), *Art Spiegelman: Conversations*. Jackson: University Press of Mississippi, 2007. 68–83.

———. *Breakdowns: Portrait of the Artist as a Young %@&*!*. New York: Pantheon/Random House, 1972.

———. "The Holocaust Through the Eyes of a Maus (Art Spiegelman)." Television interview. University of Washington Television (UWTV), 1991.

———. "Maus." In Terry Zwigoff (ed.), *Animal Funnies* [or *Funny Animals*, issue 1]. San Francisco: Apex Novelties, 1972. 9–12.

———. *Maus: A Survivor's Tale, Book I: My Father Bleeds History*. New York: Pantheon Books, 1986.

———. *Maus: A Survivor's Tale, Book II: And Here My Troubles Began*. New York: Pantheon Books, 1991.

———. *MetaMaus*. With Hillary Chute (associate editor and interviewer). New York: Pantheon/Random House, 2011.

Spiegelman, Art, and Neil Gaiman. "Neil Gaiman in Conversation with Art Spiegelman." Public discussion. Sosnoff Theater at the Richard B. Fisher Center for the Performing Arts at Bard College, April 4, 2014.

Suchoff, David. *Kafka's Jewish Languages: The Hidden Openness of Tradition*. Philadelphia: University of Pennsylvania, 2012.

Triumph des Willens [*Triumph of the Will*]. Directed by Leni Riefenstahl. Germany: Leni Riefenstahl Produktion. 1935.

Further Reading

Joe Sacco (writer and artist), *Palestine* (2001). Sacco documents journalistically the lives of people affected by the Israeli-Palestinian conflict.

Marjane Satrapi (writer and artist), *Persepolis* (2000–2003). Satrapi gives an account of her childhood and young adulthood growing up in Iran and studying in Austria.

Art Spiegelman (writer and artist), *In the Shadow of No Towers* (2004). Spiegelman portrays the trauma he suffered from the September 11 terror attacks in New York City, and in a sense it can be seen as a sequel to *Maus*.

Brian K. Vaughan (writer) and Niko Henrichon (artist), *Pride of Baghdad* (2006). It tells the story of lions, from their own perspective, escaping a zoo in Baghdad after an American bombing in 2003.

Simone Lia (writer and artist), *Fluffy* (2003–2005). A man takes care of a bunny as if he were its father, and the bunny behaves in all senses like a human child and inadvertently teaches the man the meaning of life.

Entangled Memories and Received Histories: Reading Sacco's *Footnotes in Gaza*

David J. Leichter

On November 3, 1956, during the Suez Canal Crisis, the Israeli Defense Force entered the city of Khan Younis in the Gaza Strip. What happened next is unclear. However, according to figures from the United Nations, 275 Palestinians—140 refugees and 135 residents—were killed. Eight days later, in the city of Rafah on the Egyptian border, another 111 Palestinians were killed.[1] Perhaps because these two events occurred outside the main theatre of the war, until recently they have been largely forgotten.

That they were forgotten is perhaps outrageous. Regrettably, however, it is not uncommon. It is impossible to remember every detail of the present; impressions left by the original experience fade away, lose clarity, and become part of an undifferentiated past. However, forgetting is not simply a dulling of the immediacy of the present or passive matter of letting events fade from memory. Rather, historians make choices about how to connect events together and how to structure the details of the past into a coherent whole. Those that cannot be meaningfully incorporated into a narrative are thus excised. In this case, forgetting is the result of deliberate, intentional action.

Joe Sacco's *Footnotes in Gaza* highlights the stakes of the politics of remembering and forgetting by investigating what happened in Gaza in November 1956 and discerning its relevance in the midst of an ongoing conflict and occupation. In this work, Sacco examines the interrelationship between memory and identity in situations of ongoing injustice by focusing on ways that memory is blocked, distorted, and prevented, on the one hand, and, on the other, how remembering can occur as a shared experience with one's contemporaries. This work of graphic journalism, then, shows why the history of injustice matters, and shows that in order to address the current situation between Palestinians and Israelis, there needs to be confrontation with a legacy of injustice.[2]

The basic claim I will be exploring in what follows is that memory does not merely transmit information; it is also a medium through which the past of others can be heard and for which we are responsible. At issue, then, is the question of working through or coming to terms with the past: what, if any, responsibilities do the living have to do with the dead? What are the proper ways to distinguish victims, perpetrators, and "innocent bystanders," as a community comes to terms with its recent (perhaps even distant) history? And finally the most fundamental of questions: who are we and what have we done or allowed to be done in our name?

Footnotes, I argue, reveals an important dimension of ethical and political discourses, namely, that, even though forgotten, the past nevertheless continues to shape present contexts and political identities, as well as to form possibilities for action. Furthermore, by highlighting the continuing significance of a traumatic history for a place with multiple ethno-racial identities, Sacco calls our attention to the ways that memory can be used to enable communities to come to terms with what it has done or allowed to be done in its name, facts it would prefer to forget but cannot, reformulating or rejecting certain values in light of the past, and with who it has been but no longer wishes to be. In so doing, the work of remembering the "footnotes of history"—the marginalized and ultimately forgotten events, actions, and people—transforms something that appeared to be completed and forgotten into a past that must be returned to, worked through, and remembered.

The paper will proceed by first highlighting a particular tension in *Footnotes in Gaza*. While the graphic and comic elements of Sacco's work enable him to depict the past, they nevertheless stand in tension with his journalistic aims. While the problem of representation is common to all narratives, it is particularly problematic when situated within the ethical aims and attempts to stand in solidarity with the dead. In order to address this tension, we need to reframe what memory aspires to and how it is able to call back the past. In addition to establishing identity, memory can be used to disrupt and challenge taken-for-granted relationships and understandings about the world. *Footnotes in Gaza* and other graphic novels can thus be used politically to enable the past to burst forth into the present by giving voice to those who are oppressed and to articulate a memory of suffering.

Toward a Graphic Journalism

Footnotes in Gaza, and Joe Sacco's other works, offers a unique entry into the medium commonly called "graphic novels." Novels, of course, commonly refer to long form fictional narratives. Graphic novels would be those novels that depict or illustrate in various ways the unfolding of the plot of the story. However, in actual practice, the boundaries of the medium are much more fluid and ambiguous. Many landmark graphic novels are memoires, journals, and other kinds of creative non-fiction. Sacco's work is not only decidedly non-fictional; it submits itself to the standards and practices of journalism. Tying together the possibilities inherent in the medium of comics with the standards of journalistic integrity, however, is not without its problems.

Like long-form journalism, his approach is to remain in an area, such as Gaza, Bosnia, or Iraq, in order to interview people and uncover the immediate causes of a conflict, the broader political and historical machinations at the root of the conflict, and its lasting impact on civilians. *Footnotes in Gaza*, specifically, has its origins in a spring 2001 collaboration between Joe Sacco and Chris Hedges for *Harper's* magazine.[3] Their goal was to provide an "on the ground" report of the ways that the residents of the city of Khan Younis were coping during the early months of the Second Intifada against the Israeli occupation. In preparing for this assignment, Sacco notes that he recalled a reference in Noam Chomsky's book *The Fateful Triangle* to a large-scale killing of civilians in the city, and discussed with Hedges whether it should be included in the article.[4] After conducting interviews, the authors decided that this event merited being included in the article. For whatever reason, however, the editors at *Harper's* decided to excise those paragraphs when the article went to press.

Because of the magnitude of this massacre—perhaps the largest one of Palestinians on their own land[5]—its implications, and because of the obscurity of what happened, Sacco returned to Gaza in November 2002 in order to conduct extensive interviews with people who witnessed the events unfold. However, because he also wanted to situate these events in a broader historical context, he also interviewed members of the Knesset, historians, Fedayeen (Palestinian guerilla fighters), and Palestinians currently living in Gaza. The primary aim of these interviews was to record these stories and thereby establish a record of what actually happened, as well as to see its lasting effects on Palestinians who continue to live in that area. This record would not only help to explain the origins of the present conflict, but it would also help to rescue the dead from obscurity.

In the process of conducting research, interviewing subjects, determining what to include and exclude, and finally organizing these into a narrative, Sacco himself comes to realize that his work is implicated in this process of forgetting, framing, and omitting details. While interviewing eyewitnesses, he becomes intimately familiar with a well-known problem with memory, namely that "memories change with the years and the memories we have excavated here are decades old. Memory blurs edges; it adds and subtracts."[6] Memory is notoriously fickle—not only do we add details to our memories or get them wrong, but also these details of our memories change over time and we often "remember" being at events that we did not directly experience. Interviewing different people about the same event will often yield slightly different accounts, even as the major details remain constant. As a result, even people who saw the same event will have different, perhaps conflicting, recollections of what happened.

Because these tensions and contradictions between witnesses often cast doubt on their knowledge of what actually happened, Sacco and his guides find themselves in the position of determining whose testimony is credible and whose testimony is not. Thus, questions of memory are not just questions about their accuracy but also they are questions of whose memories can be trusted and which memories fit the details and story already established. He writes, "In the absence of UNRWA records, of Israeli records—and could we rely on them if we had them?—it's up to us to fill history's glass with as much truthful, cogent testimony as we can. If some truth spills along the way, we apologize."[7] It would thus appear that the process of actively remembering and reconstructing the past inevitably and somewhat paradoxically entails forgetting.

Sacco's experience of gathering together these testimonies may not be ideologically motivated to distort or conceal the truth, but his organization of it into a narrative form is still problematic. The very fact that he is using images in order to represent events, people, and action. This is a classic philosophical problem: how is it possible that languages and pictures come to represent anything?[8] In his work "Narrative Form as a Cognitive Instrument," Louis O. Mink suggests that the narrative forms that historians, and by extension journalists, use to recount the past are distinct from the events themselves. He claims, "Narrative form in history, as in fiction, is an artifice, the product of individual imagination."[9] The way that we tell a story—it's tragic, triumphant, comic, epic, form—is different from the way that we experienced those events. Narratives have a beginning, middle, and end; life, by contrast, does not. Stories are told, but life is lived. They are, in short, discontinuous.[10]

This difference between narrative and life is problem for all writing that purports to recount what actually happened, but in the medium of graphic novels it is further compounded with its use of images. While Sacco's illustrations are based on careful attention to details about the world that his subjects inhabit, they are nevertheless "cartoony."[11] Even as the drawings and images of *Footnotes in Gaza* allow the story of these "footnotes" and their retrieval to be told, they are filtered through Sacco's own choices of how to represent what happened. "In essence," he notes in the forward, "I am the set designer and the director of every scene that takes place in the 1940s and 1950s."[12] This means that, as he notes in a different work, "there will always exist, when presenting journalism in comics form, a tension between those things that can be verified, like a quote caught on tape, and those things that defy verification, such as a drawing purporting to represent a specific episode."[13] Insofar as the panels, captions, frames, dialogue, and page layout are fundamentally the author and illustrator's choice, Sacco is ultimately representing events that he did not witness himself. And this means that if the eyewitness testimony is an interpretation of what happened, then *Footnotes in Gaza* is an interpretation of an interpretation, and we are doubly removed from the original scene.

As readers, our understanding and knowledge of the events that happened is highly mediated, perhaps even uncertain. It would seem, in other words, impossible for graphic journalism to accurately represent the past. If this is the case, then it appears, at least on the face of it, difficult to see how *Footnotes in Gaza* could fulfill either of its aims. There is, on the one hand, the problem of bridging the gap between the representation and the represented, and, on the other, the problem ensuring that the representation does justice to the dead.

It thus appears that Sacco's attempt to be a graphic journalist is problematic. Do the graphic elements to his journalism make his reporting suspect? Conversely, how might his journalistic commitment to truth affect how he depicts what happened? How would this ability or failure affect the possibility of doing justice to the past? In order to see the promises and risks of *Footnotes in Gaza*, we will need to get some philosophical help.

On Our Faithfulness to the Past

Sacco's graphic journalism thus appears to be caught in a serious tension. On the one hand, as a form of journalism, his work must "report accurately, get the quotes right, and check claims."[14] On the other hand, his depiction of those events will inevitably be filtered through a set of choices of what is shown and how it is shown. How the soldiers look, how the Palestinians look, what the cities Khan Younis and Rafah look like, and even how the images on the page are laid out will be filtered through a particular perspective. How would it be possible to do justice to the past and to preserve the memory of those unjustly killed, if the depiction of what happened is inevitably flawed? In order address this tension we need to consider what it means to remember something and what it means to be faithful to the past.

We often understand memory as an intensely personal and private phenomenon. Indeed, a common metaphor used to understand it is that of the archive, storehouse, or database. On this conception, memories are stored in a kind of warehouse of the mind, which are then accessed through a search that enables us to recall them on different occasions. A particular memory, then, represents the past only if it is unaffected by subsequent factors. As the French philosopher Henri Bergson puts it, "time can add nothing to its image without disfiguring it" (Bergson, 83).[15] According to this "storehouse" or "archival" model, memories are not only caused by the past, but their meaning is singular and stable, fixed and unchanging (Campbell, 54). If we remember it differently at different times, our memory of what happened is questionable or our ability to recall it is suspect.

To say that memory is a storehouse or database entails specific standards for its success and its accuracy. A memory adequately represents the past if it contains a wealth of corresponding details. Sue Campbell describes this "naïve view of memory" as being characterized by "its reproductive fidelity to a past experience through its development via a process in which the experience alone determines what is remembered."[16] If memories need to contain enough detail (exactly how much detail is enough?) that corresponds to the original experience, Sacco's graphic journalism could not be an instance of successful or accurate recall. In fact, the norms of faithfulness envisioned in this common view would likely prevent recollection or remembering from ever being successful.

What then does being faithful to the past mean, if not fidelity in creating a detailed reproduction? In his manifesto, Sacco suggests that "anything that *can* be drawn accurately *should* be drawn accurately—by which I mean a drawn thing must be easily recognizable as the real thing it is meant to represent" (Journalism, xi). There are several terms here that call for further attention. The first is the notion of accuracy: good remembering gets something right about the past. It is, in Paul Ricoeur's words, "tied to an ambition . . . that of being faithful to the past."[17] However, a commitment to accuracy and fidelity to the past does not necessarily mean that that memory needs to be measured against its ability to reproduce a number of details about the past. Wealth of detail is, after all, only one way—and rather context-specific way—that renders an accurate depiction of something, and excessive detail can overwhelm the information the cartoonist is trying to convey in the panel or on the page.

Paul Connerton, in *How Societies Remember*, argues that remembering is just as much a social phenomenon as it is a mental one. It is enacted in performances, rituals, commemorations, social norms and practices, bodily habits, and literature. What counts as "successful remembering" for each of these depends on the situation in which it is enacted. To remember the dead while laying a wreath, in other words, operates according to a different set of norms than remembering what happened on the witness stand. This effectively takes memory out of the mental domain and situates it as a set of practices, which ultimately reveals the ways meanings are shared between people and groups. Not only does this mean that the practices of remembering are much broader than just what is going on in our heads, but it also suggests that the practices of remembering are also closely aligned with telling stories—laying a wreath at a ceremony, in other words, does something akin to telling a story insofar as it highlights a particular event, situates it in the context of the present, and does so in light of the future. The ability to tell a story, in other words, is not distinct from life but arises from life itself. This means that we need to be attentive to the ways that Sacco draws out the testimonies of eyewitnesses in order to show how sharing the past can shape and disrupt our identities. Instead, we also need to attend to which details he has decided to represent, and which details are salient. By determining which features or themes to highlight, especially across a number of different panels, one can paint a picture that is just as accurate as one with a welter of detail.

Secondly, we need to understand what the notion of recognition Sacco mentions entails. To recognize something is to identify something; it is to take something *as* something.[18] Such recognition relies on seeing specific, distinguishing marks that identify the object as the kind of object or person it is.[19] Though such recognition is cognitive in nature—it deals with beliefs—there is also an important emotional investment in it. That is, it is through producing certain emotional responses that the image elicits that make manifest the meaning or significance of the past. Here, the point of memory is less to tell us what happened than what it was like to *feel* what happened (Ahmed 2004).[20] Thus, presenting the events at Khan Younis and Rafah as traumatic, fearful, uncertain is different from representing it as shameful, insignificant, or as an act of bravery. By getting readers to experience and feel the same kinds of uncertainty and fear through an image—that they experience an event as if they were there—a drawing or cartoon can be said to represent the past faithfully. The affective shifts in memory can help to form and even reshape what readers find significant, establish new patterns of saliences that connect the present and the past, and disclose new possibilities for responding to the past. Thus, the emotions and affects that Sacco uses as part of his framing of the image can help to remember the past successfully.

Being faithful to the past not only describes the relationship between the image, representation, or drawing and the event, action, or person that it represents. It is also a virtue.[21] To be faithful to the past is to be responsible and answerable for one's account of it. In an interview about *Footnotes*, Sacco puts the point thus:

> You realize these [drawing and artwork] are very powerful tools and you're careful about how you use it. I could make things look a lot worse too, but I think about how I'm going to present it. You don't want things to look spectacular; you don't want violence to somehow look beautiful. There are a lot of ways to think about what's in your hands. There is an inherent danger with subjectivity: there's a great responsibility with something on which you have a view and how you are going to present it.[22]

Sacco's point here is clear—as the illustrator and author, he is responsible for at least some of the ways that his work will reinforce or resist commonly held patterns of thinking. To be responsible with memory, to be faithful to the past, means to be answerable for the ways that its significance is made manifest by what is depicted and how it is depicted.

If Sacco's book accomplishes something important about remembering the past, it does so because it highlights several important issues about the nature of remembering. First, it identifies and develops an account of events that are significant and meaningful for understanding the present situation of the Israeli-Palestinian relationship. Second, it highlights a particular way that the relationship to the past is evaluated in terms of our emotional and affective natures. As such, it would appear that the accuracy of memory can neither be separated from questions about the significance of the past nor from questions about how to enable those whose memories differ from that told by the dominant narrative to speak. We now must see where the significance of this story lies.

Narrating Dangerous Memories

We have seen that Sacco's graphic journalism can be faithful to the past in a way that does not require it to reproduce in exact detail what happened.

In fact, because he blends words with images, his work makes it possible to recall the significance of the massacres at Khan Younis and Rafah and situate them in the present. To do so, Sacco illustrates how memory can be used to disrupt assumed identities, call into question prevailing historical narratives, and challenge the current conditions in which people live.

Learning how to be faithful to the past through processes of telling and listening to stories is central to acquiring a social identity.[23] However, practices of remembering do not only reinforce a sense of belonging and community, they can also be used to disrupt or challenge that very same identity. A "dangerous memory," as Steven Ostrovich puts it, is a adisruptive practice of and from memory" (Dangerous Memory, 239). This practice of memory is one in which, as the German political theologian Johann Baptist Metz puts it,

> earlier experiences break through the center-point of our lives and reveal new and dangerous insights for our present. They ... show up the banality of our supposed 'realism.' They break through the canon of all that is taken as self-evident ... [and] subvert our structures of plausibility. Such memories are like dangerous and incalculable visitants from the past. They are memories we have to take into account: memories, as it were, with future content." (Metz in Ostrovich, 42)

They disrupt traditional historical narratives that inform the collective identity of a group by recognizing a point of view of history from the perspective of those who have suffered, been marginalized, or victimized.[24] Rather than the triumphant march of history, which is often cast in terms of the progress of freedom, a dangerous memory arrests the linear flow of time and allows the past to burst forth into the present in order to let the voices of those who have not yet been heard speak. As such these disruptive and disturbing memories call us to identify with oppressed others, against dominant and often ideologically-motivated narratives, on the basis of shared experience of the contingencies and fragilities of human existence.

The central metaphor of the *Footnotes in Gaza*—footnotes—highlights precisely the way that dangerous memories can operate. Footnotes, of course, are notes placed at the bottom of a page that reference or add additional comment on a part of the text. These notes are not directly related to the main argument, but are instead ancillary or supplemental to the text itself. Often, one can read a text without checking the footnotes and still follow the main argument.[25] They are, as Sacco puts it, "inessential at best; at worst they trip up the greater narrative."[26] In order for the official story to take shape and become more streamlined, "history shakes off some footnotes altogether."[27] This is an inevitable process—no historical narrative can recount everything that happened and be intelligible. In order to make sense of what happened, in other words, historians need to make difficult decisions about what to include and what to exclude. In this way, an historical narrative works to glide over those footnotes in order to establish a coherent account of what happened and how the past leads to the present.

By contrast, when recounting the footnotes that history has sloughed off, Sacco narrative takes a unique form. The narrative structure reveals at once the ways that those who witnessed the original events still, in some sense, remain there, and the ways that the past nevertheless remains present even though hidden and forgotten. It does so by weaving together an account of the eye-witness testimonies of those who lived through the mass killings with a report of the conditions in which Palestinians found themselves in 2003. We can see better what the significance of dangerous memories is by examining the difference between the modes of narration that characterize the dominant narrative and the narrative that recounts Palestinian suffering.

When recounting the Suez Canal Crisis, the Sinai Campaign of 1956 (Operation Kadesh), and its immediate implications, Sacco offers a conventional, if subtly triumphant narrative. Sacco begins the story during the aftermath of the 1948 Arab-Israeli War, which turned many Palestinians into refugees. During the early years of Israel's statehood, hundreds of thousands Jewish immigrants came to the country settling land and displacing refugees. Skirmishes between the two groups were common. By 1956 between 2,700 and 5,000 Palestinians had been killed, as had 300 Israeli settlers. The primary voice of this story is Mordechai Bar-On, the Bureau Chief during the Sinai Peninsula Campaign. Bar-On explains that the initial retaliation operations were an attempt to coerce the Palestinian military into neutralizing guerilla fighters from conducting raids into Israeli territory, thereby preventing "the spilling of Jewish blood."[28] These Israeli military operations—described by Bar-On as a strategy of "deterrence"—culminated in a raid in the West Bank led by future Israeli Prime Minister Ariel Sharon, which left at least forty-two Palestinian civilians killed including thirty-eight women and children. In their attempt to control the region, NATO countries funded the Israeli army and the Soviet Union was doing the same for Egypt. The Suez Canal Crisis was a direct result of these global political machinations.

As a response to these attacks, Sacco's narrative continues, Palestinian Fedayeen conducted their own counter-raids into Israeli territory in order to redeem the deaths of those killed by the Israel Defense Forces (IDF). While these attacks were not considered as a threat to state of Israel, they did have an effect on the morale of those living on Kibbutzim near the border. Soon, however, the Israeli government, felt pressured to "escalate retaliation operations to the level which would provoke [Egypt] to begin a war, or at least would blur ... who started it" (70).²⁹ While this did not work, there were still skirmishes on the Gaza region.

Soon, however, the machinations of global politics caught up with the region. The French government protested Egypt's support of the Algerian rebellion; the British felt threatened by Nassar's pan-Arab alliances and thought that it threatened the main thoroughfare—the Suez Canal—for British traffic to their oil reserves in the region. With their own motivations and concerns in the region, the French, British, and Israeli governments met to engineer a war with Egypt and begin to determine how to divide the spoils of war. The war did not unfold as planned, and the United States soon diplomatically intervened to prevent a larger war.

This account that Sacco offers does not merely set out the background against which the massacres occurred. It highlights the dominant narrative of these events unfolding and the temporality involved in this particular kind of recollection. The temporal order of history is linear; one even follows another in such a way that the historian can retrospectively identify and situate the documentation and evidence that best draws together the outcomes and consequences of the agents' actions, which we, and not the agents acting in the moment, become privileged to know. Put in formal terms, "Of any two real events in the past, it must be the case either that one of them happened before the other, or that they happened at the same time" (Williams 2002, 162). It is, in short, a broadly historical account that draws out the causes of the events narrated.

Not only are the primary agents political actors and nations, but also the narrative, as its often told, tends to be one that recounts the ways that Israel has grown to be a global and international political entity. Appropriately, Sacco's narrative takes a detached tone. The images are captioned with the narrative, thus freezing the moment in time. This technique effectively offers an account of the past from the third-person perspective, giving the past the sheen of objectivity by effecting a detached tone, one which ultimately helps to emphasize the distance between the past and the present.

There is a further consequence of Sacco's technique of narration at this level that is worth noting. In these sections recounting the events at the historical level, the primary interviewee is Mordechai Bar-On. By interviewing Bar-On and situating his responses in terms of the historical record, Sacco presents, on the one hand, the Israeli version of the Suez Canal Crisis and Sinai Peninsula Campaign—part of which were the massacres at Khan Younis and Rafah—but on the other hand he shows the ways that the Israeli perspective of this period has also become the historically objective account. As a result, Sacco implicitly reinforces the sense that this historical account has ideologically been transformed into the dominant narrative, and that an objective account of history is often ideologically motivated.

The dangerous memory of the forgotten killings in Khan Younis and Rafah disrupts the linear and historical time that structures the conventional history of the region. The interviews that Sacco conducts with witnesses to the violence in Khan Younis and Rafah suggest a different experience of time. Rather than the historian's detached and impartial posture, the testimonies that he elicits from the Palestinians attest to the ways that past remains present.

In order to do so, Sacco takes several steps to remove his own perspective from the narrative. However, rather than take the detached third-person perspective to in order to do this, he now lets the eyewitness's story guide the images in each panel. The pace of the story slows down, and the illustrations often linger on the faces of those who witnessed the events. Despite the desire to tell a coherent narrative and to get others to understand exactly what happened, many of the interview subjects lapse into silence or express a profound frustration at their inability to articulate the experience itself. For those who lived through these events, that time stretches and condenses in non-linear ways. When recounting being round up by Israeli troops and lined up against wall, Abdullah El-Horani gets up to demonstrate how he was able to escape. In Sacco's retelling, El-Horani begins to move to the wall of his office where the interview is taking place but then shifts the scene fifty years past.[30] Rather than a past that is finished and done with, this illustration of their experience reveals the ways that the past continues to into the present.

Here we find the central claim of Sacco's work. The difficult of remembering what happened in 1956 is because, as one Palestinian put it, "events are continuous; one after another."[31] Sacco notes that the previous evening the Israeli Defense Force attacked a camp and killed eight. The night before that, two more people were killing in Khan Younis.[32] In a macabre joke, he notes that his journalist friends "could file last month's story today—or last year's for that matter—and who'd know the difference?"[33] Violence has become so commonplace that the past has almost become interchangeable with the present.

What then does it mean to say that events are continuous? The German philosopher Martin Heidegger distinguishes two senses of the past, *Vergangenheit* and *Gewesenheit*.[34] The former refers to the ways that the past is finished or over-and-done-with. When we refer to something as "ancient history," we capture a sense of the remoteness of the past and the distance of the past from the present. On this view, the past is "fixed," events are over, and it cannot be changed. By contrast, *Gewesenheit* refers to a sense the ways that the past exists as "having been."[35] The past does not live on in the present simply because of its effect on the present; rather the past exists by continuing to work on us. When we say "I am still working," or "I have been working since 8 o'clock," the past hours of work reveal our present possibilities, which themselves are manifest in light of our futures. If I have a deadline I must meet, the long hours that I work gain their significance from that obligation. In this sense, our past comes from our future.

Sacco uses several techniques to capture a sense of the way that the past remains in the present. He calls attention to tensions between temporal proximity and distance between the past and the present by juxtaposing images of the same place in different times. The most striking of these comes at the climax of his account of the Khan Younis killings, in which he presents side-by-side illustrations, the first depicting bodies piled against the ruins of a fourteenth-century castle, which now forms one side of the town square, and the second showing the same castle side in present day—it's walls covered in graffiti and posters, the bustle of the city where the dead were unceremoniously piled.[36] By juxtaposing these two panels, Sacco highlights the temporal difference between the present situation and the past violence. It compels the reader to imaginatively supply the story that lead from the past to the present and reflect on the ways that the past nevertheless remains. He'll also use the technique of overlaying a past event with an image of the person who is presently recollecting it. Doing so highlights the way that the past is never fully gone, even as it is distant and different from the present. These graphic techniques of narration helps to emphasize the role that stories play in bringing past injustice to light and it creates possibilities for addressing those historical wrongs in a way that does justice to dead.

For a history to be received, we also need to attend to the particular context in which the testimonies take place. Doing so brings us to the experiential dimension of memory transmission. If the act of bearing witness transmits a meaning over time and through time, from one generation to the next, the act of inheriting that meaning requires an understanding of the memory is shared with others in a particular historical location. In other words, we need to attend to the ways that stories come to be heard, just as much as we need to understand how they come to be expressed.

To do so, we need to attend to the ways that Sacco presents the then-current situation in Gaza and how that situation positions them to the past. While it is tempting think that the "footnotes" that eventually fall off the official narrative are lost, nothing is lost once and for all to the past. Forgetting is inevitable—as impressions recede into the distant past, the elements of the experience that initially affected us become flattened, muted, and undifferentiated. At the same time, forgetting is required for any act of explicit recollection. The loss of memory that propels and motivates the acts recollection comes with the possibility of forgetting. Thus, for Sacco's recollection or retrieval of the past to work, the kind of forgetting that makes the necessity to remember possible needs to be clarified. Forgetting affects first and foremost the transmission of the past to the present. By affecting the transmission of the past, forgetting does not efface the past itself. That is, past events do not cease to be merely because we have forgotten them.

The effect of this is quite profound. While one the one hand, the conditions in which Palestinians found themselves afterwards prevented them from being able to clearly engage with and understand their own past. The depictions of displacement, violence, and uncertainty emphasize both that remembering what happened so long ago is not merely unnecessary but also impossible. Violence and death happen so often that it is easy to go on with daily conversations; it is "not as if nothing has happened but as if it happens often enough that it hardly merits a word."[37] Many of his interactions with the people living there reveal displaced lives and skepticism of anyone who would offer an alternative vision. In one particular scene, Sacco and his friend and guide Abed return to the place of a home they visited only the previous month. It had since been leveled and buried. While one of the elderly women who lived there suggests that she has found a new place to live, she nevertheless expresses a profound feeling of displacement and helplessness.[38]

That these levels intertwine in various ways through Sacco's imaginative remembering reveals several ways that memory can be dangerous. First, these memories arrest the traditional experience of time. Rather than conceive of time as linear, the dangerous memories that Sacco unearths disrupts that conception of time by calling attention to the ways that past remains present. This further suggests that the transmission of memory is not a straightforward transfer of cargo from one generation to the next. Rather, because some elements are forgotten, others transformed, and still others maintained, the transmission involves a creative engagement between different kinds of pasts. *Footnotes* brings different pasts into view—not just that of the forgotten events, but also their relationship to the current situation and with the predominant and official histories that we have received. In so doing, Sacco's work offers the opportunity to reposition ourselves and our relationship to both the past, in order to see the significance of it, and the present, which would allow us to work through the past for the sake of future actions.

Conclusion

What then are the implications for dangerous memories for graphic journalism and how does uncovering dangerous memories enable the broader reading public to come to terms with the difficult issues of remembering, forgetting, history and identity? It is clear that, on the one hand, Sacco's work begins the arduous task of critically analyzing the historical circumstances, their connection to the present, and the recognition of others' suffering. On the other, it is difficult to glean any specific or pragmatic suggestions for going forward. What, then, would be the usefulness of using graphic novels to depict dangerous memories?

For one, these disturbing and dangerous memories can help to establish a broader practices of memory of others' suffering in the broader public. Edward Said, the Palestinian theorist, closes his introduction of Sacco's *Palestine* with the reminder that most comic book stories are about good beating evil and the triumph of justice over injustice. Sacco's work, by contrast, is concerned with "history's losers."[39] His work allows readers to tarry a while with people whose "suffering and unjust fate have been scanted for far too long and with too litter humanitarian and political attention."[40] Recounting these stories prevents injustices from becoming banal, part of the ordinary part of one's life. By focusing on these dangerous memories, then, graphic novels can become a medium for opposing an unreflective account of the past.

At the same time, we might wonder the extent to which Sacco's account of the Palestinian experience supplants their ability to tell their own story. While it is clear that the graphic novel enables these stories to be told, they are, ultimately, told from the perspective that Sacco draws and inks. There thus remains a tension between the ability of Sacco's journalism on the one hand to enable the Palestinian story to be told as a Palestinian story—from their own perspective, and, on the other, the ways that the medium itself prevents them from doing so. *Footnotes in Gaza*, in other words, opens a space to raise questions about who speaks for the Palestinians and possibilities for speaking with them.

Just as important, in getting to know what happened, it is important to recognize that Sacco does not attempt to tell the Palestinians' stories for them. Rather, his approach opens up a space for Palestinians to narrate their own stories. Because oppression robs the ability to speak and narrate one's own perspective, Sacco's practices offer an opportunity for others to recount what happened and, just as important, it forces the readers to listen, read, and look at the effects of that dominant narrative that has been constructed about Israeli-Palestinian relations.

The potential effects of such reading are thus not only an opportunity to reflect on the suffering of others or allow others to narrative themselves. Reading becomes a way to broaden one's community by establishing and working through affective connections with others. In order to expand our understanding and become more sympathetic and empathetic, we need to find new ways to notice similarities and negotiate different interpretations of who "we" are. Joe Sacco's graphic journalism, and indeed graphic novels as a whole, offers such an opportunity.

Notes

1. "Special Report of the Director of the United Nations Relief and Works Agency for Palestine Refugees in the Near East." *Footnotes in Gaza*, 400.
2. I'll refer to Sacco's work as an instance of "graphic journalism" rather than as a "graphic novel."
3. *Footnotes in Gaza*, "Forward."
4. See Chomsky, *The Fateful Triangle*.
5. Sacco, *Footnotes*, ix.
6. Sacco, *Footnotes*, 112.
7. Sacco, *Footnotes*, 277.
8. Scott McCloud, in his popular and influential work *Understanding Comics*, offers the example of Magritte's famous image of a pipe with the phrase "Ceci n'est pas une pipe" ("This is not a pipe") written underneath it. It is, as McCloud points out, not only not a painting of a pipe, it is not a drawing of a painting. It is a printed copy of a drawing of a painting. Several, in fact, once all of them on the page are counted. McCloud, *Understanding Comics*, 24–25.
9. Mink, as quoted in David Carr's *Time, Narrative, and History*, 10
10. Ibid, 10
11. Douglas Wolk describes Sacco's as using "'cartoony' distortions and caricature." Others have noticed that his illustrations of persons also take cues from R. Crumb's style and Will Elder's artwork. Sacco, "The Myth Of Objective Journalism—Joe Sacco Interviewed," *The Quietus*.
12. Sacco, *Footnotes*, x.
13. Sacco, *Journalism*, xi.
14. Sacco, *Journalism*, xi.
15. Henri Bergson, *Matter and Memory*, 83.
16. Sue Campbell, *Our Faithfulness to the Past*, 14.
17. Ricoeur, *Memory, History, Forgetting*, 21.
18. Ricoeur, *The Course of Recognition*.
19. See Ricoeur, *The Course of Recognition*.
20. Sarah Ahmed, *The Cultural Politics of Emotion*.
21. Campbell, 44–49.
22. Sacco, *The Quietus* interview.
23. Eviatar Zerubavel, *Time Maps*, 3.
24. It draws from Walter Benjamin's notion of the "weak messianic power" of history. See "Theses on the Philosophy of History."
25. Though they might miss out on interesting side notes, such as this one.

26. Sacco, *Footnotes*, 9
27. Sacco, *Footnotes*, 9.
28. Sacco, *Footnotes*, 38.
29. Sacco, *Footnotes*, 70.
30. Sacco, *Footnotes*, 105–106.
31. Sacco, Footnotes, 252
32. Sacco, *Footnotes*, 255–256.
33. Sacco, *Footnotes*, 5.
34. See Martin Heidegger, *Being and Time*.
35. Or as William Faulkner put it, "The past is never dead. It's not even past."
36. Sacco, *Footnotes*, 98–99
37. Sacco, *Footnotes*, 297.
38. Sacco, *Footnotes*, 256.
39. Edward Said, "Introduction" to *Palestine*, v.
40. Said, v.

Further Reading

Books that address concerns about the social dimensions of memory have exploded in recent years. Nevertheless, there are a few ways to make some headway in this interesting and important topic.

Benjamin, Walter. "Theses on the Philosophy of History." In *Illuminations: Essays and Reflections*. Translated by Harry Zohn. Schocken: New York, 1968.

Campbell, Sue. *Our Faithfulness to the Past*. Cambridge University Press: Cambridge, 2013.

Nietzsche, Friedrich. *On the Use and Abuse of History*.

Ricoeur, Paul. *Memory, History, Forgetting*. Translated by Kathleen Blamey and David Pellauer. Chicago: University of Chicago Press: 2004

Sacco, Joe. *Footnotes in Gaza*. New York: Metropolitan Books, 2009.

Living in a Fictional World: Reading and Identification in *Lost Girls*

Alfonso Muñoz-Corcuera

Imagine yourself reading a pornographic novel. It depicts an orgy, and a woman is performing oral sex on the main male character of the scene. You may feel excited seeing it, and perhaps may even fantasize about being in his shoes. Then, one of the women in the background asks the male character to read aloud a porn story from a book he has. It seems like a good idea. But when he begins to tell the story, you feel disturbed. It is about a couple of siblings having sex with their parents. They are about eleven or twelve years old, and they are being introduced to those perversions by their own family. You hesitate about giving up on the novel. Indeed, the characters of the novel discuss its morality too. The main male character has the last word:

> MONSIEUR ROUGEUR: And then these children: how outrageous! How old can they be? Eleven? Twelve? It is quite monstrous ... except that they are fictions, as old as the page they appear upon, no less, no more. Fiction and fact: only madmen and magistrates cannot discriminate between them. Ah well. Let us read on. (Moore and Gebbie 2006, chapter 22, 4)

Here you have two options. You may think that depictions of sex with underage children are offensive and disgusting, even if they are *fictional* children. If this is the case, you will probably stop reading the book. On the other hand, you may feel that Monsieur Rougeur is right. It seems to be a good argument. You are reading fiction, and so there should be no reasons not to enjoy it. Besides, the book has been pretty interesting so far and you are not in the mood for philosophical discussions. If this is the case, you will leave morality aside and continue with your reading.

The scene described is taken from the third volume of Alan Moore and Melinda Gebbie's *Lost Girls*. And despite its highly dubious morality, I bring it here because it deals with another topic that is being discussed in contemporary aesthetics: identification with fictional characters. Many people outside academia would say that if you decided to continue reading *Lost Girls*, it was because you identified with the main male character of the scene. But that claim is controversial from a philosophical perspective: what is it supposed to mean? The etymological root of "identification" is of "making identical" (Gaut 2010, 254). Does that mean that you thought yourself to be identical with Monsieur Rougeur? Then, contrary to what the character claims in the quote above, it seems that you were not able to discriminate between fact and fiction.

Most philosophers find this conclusion unacceptable. Thus some hold that people cannot identify with fictional characters. When someone says that he identifies with a certain fictional character, he is just wrong, or, at best, using the term in a metaphorical sense (Carroll 2008, 162). Others are more friendly to the notion of "identification," and try to avoid the problem by defining the term in a different way. For example, Berys Gaut thinks that when people say that they identify with a certain fictional character, what they mean is that they are imagining themselves being in the character's situation. And because a given situation always has different aspects, identification happens with regard to different aspects too. To identify perceptually with a character is to imagine seeing what he sees; to identify affectively with him is to imagine feeling what he feels; to identify motivationally is to imagine wanting what he wants, and so on (Gaut 2010, 258).

For my part, I disagree with Monsieur Rougeur. Sometimes it is not easy to discriminate between fact and fiction. Thus, I think that it is possible to identify oneself with a fictional character even when we focus on the etymological root of the term. Sometimes when we identify with a fictional character, we think that we *are* the character. We think that we are identical with him, and thus we come to care about him in the same special way we only care about ourselves: egocentrically. Let's call this process "egocentric identification," to distinguish it from other uses of the term "identification."[1]

Obviously, I do not assert that the process of identification is mandatory. You may read *Lost Girls* and not identify yourself either with Monsieur Rougeur or any other character. Moreover, I do not hold that the process of egocentric identification is the only or even the main way through which we come to feel emotions with regard to fictional characters (See Carroll 1997, 200). We can also react emotionally when we sympathize or empathize with them (see Oatley 1994). I do not deny either that it is possible to identify oneself with a fictional character in a less radical way. In fact, when readers say that they identify with a fictional character, in most cases they probably are doing so in one of the particular senses of the term highlighted by Gaut. Even so, my point is that, at least in some cases, when readers identify with a fictional character, they are thinking that they are (identical with) that character.

There are at least three elements that explain why the process of egocentric identification happens in only some cases. First, the particular features of the fictional work have a role in the process. There are works that encourage the process of egocentric identification, but others seek that the reader take a certain emotional distance from the text. In this regard, Oatley and Gholamain think that egocentric identification only happens with children, or in genre literature, and never in great literature (Oatley and Gholamain 1997, 280). Second, the readers also have a main role, since it is they who must identify themselves with the character. In this sense, faced with a certain fictional character, some readers will be able to identify with him and others will not. Finally, the process of egocentric identification also depends to some extent on taking an interpretative stance. Even if the text is intended to encourage the process of egocentric identification, it is necessary that the reader collaborates, either actively (when the reader makes a conscious effort to feel that identification) or passively (when the reader does not put up resistance to the process). As such, egocentric identification can only happen when a reader faces a character with whom he or she can identify and collaborates so that the identification happens.

It could be that some readers are never able to identify egocentrically with a fictional character. It could also be that only a small number of fictional works allow readers to identify with their characters. This would explain why a good number of scholars argue that egocentric identification does not exist. It could be that they are incapable of identifying egocentrically with a character, or that they happen not to have read any work that has allowed them to. My position is consistent with these possibilities, though I do not believe them to be true. I think that the vast majority of readers are able to identify egocentrically with lots of fictional characters, and that the fact that many scholars do not do is because their own theories encourage them not to collaborate to make it happen. In any case, I will not try to defend this point. As I said earlier, for the moment my only intention is to defend that, at least in a small number of cases, a reader can identify egocentrically with a fictional character.

My argument has two parts. The first is theoretical, and it departs from narrative theories of personal identity to explain the concept of egocentric identification in depth, and to show how it is possible in general for someone to identify with a fictional character. The second part expands this theoretical basis and illustrates it through the analysis of the controversial work *Lost Girls*. This analysis will let me explore the importance of the three elements mentioned above for the process of identification: the features of the fictional work, the characteristics of the readers themselves, and the stance they take toward the text.

But before we move on, given the nature of the graphic novel I will analyze, it is necessary to say a few things about it. As some readers may know, *Lost Girls* is a provocative pornographic reinterpretation of the stories of three famous female characters from children's literature: Alice from *Alice's Adventures in Wonderland*; Dorothy from *The Wonderful Wizard of Oz*; and Wendy from *Peter Pan and Wendy*. As grown-ups, they meet at the Hotel Himmelgarten in Vienna just before the First World War broke out. There they spend a few months having lots of sex and telling each other their own stories of sexual awakening. However, their sexual awakening happened before they came of age, and thus the scene I quoted at the beginning of this article is not the only one depicting underage children having sex. In fact, most of the book does so—although in the vast majority of cases they are teenagers. Given that depictions of the underage having sex are highly controversial, and may even be banned in some countries,[2] it may be objected that it is not a good idea to take *Lost Girls* as a case study. Moreover, as my intention is to hold that one can identify oneself with a fictional character, it may be argued that most would not likely identify with Monsieur Rougeur, a character who enjoys child pornography, but would feel aversion to him.

In spite of this, I think that *Lost Girls* is a good case study. First and mainly, because I want to make the strongest case for my argument. If one wants to defend that one can identify egocentrically with a fictional character, the more modest claim would be to say that we can identify only with characters who are like ourselves, or with characters who we can admire. In contrast, Monsieur Rougeur is probably very different from most of the readers of this paper. Moreover, it is very unlikely that they will admire him, as he is not only attracted to fictional depictions of underage children, but claims to have had sex with children (Moore and Gebbie 2006, chapter 22, 5; chapter 23, 3). Sex with children is widely considered morally reprehensible across different cultures, and thus almost everybody will agree that they would not want to be like Monsieur Rougeur. Consequently, if I can show that one can identify with this sort of person, my claim that the vast majority of readers are able to identify egocentrically with lots of fictional characters will be better supported.

There are at least three more reasons why I think that *Lost Girls* is a good case study. First, as I show in my analysis below, *Lost Girls* explicitly encourages the process of identification in a profound way, as one of Moore and Gebbie's intentions with the book was to let people set their sexual imagination free (Di Liddo 2009, 155–171). Second, the book will also let me show the importance of the characteristics of the readers themselves. As I noted above, not everyone is able to identify with any character. In this regard, even if the book explicitly encourages the process of identification, most people will not find depictions of fictional children having sex exciting, and thus they will not identify with Monsieur Rougeur.[3] Finally, the case of *Lost Girls* also makes it clear that the stance the reader takes toward the text is equally or even more important for the process of egocentric identification, because even if the book encourages that process, and the reader finds depictions of fictional children having sex exciting, it may be possible that one finds the fact of feeling excited by these pornographic depictions morally reprehensible. If this is the case, the reader may be constantly reminding himself that he is not like Monsieur Rougeur, as he feels guilty about his own arousal. This will cause him not to be able to forget about himself and thus not to be able to experience his identity as merging with that of the character.

Having clarified this aspect, I will turn to the first point of my argument: explaining the concept of egocentric identification in depth and showing how it is possible in general for someone to identify with a fictional character.

Fiction and Possibility: The Process of Egocentric Identification

As I pointed out at the beginning of this article, the concept of "identification" is problematic, since it seems to be used with different meanings. I will use it to refer to a certain mental process that consists in thinking about oneself as being identical with another subject. That is, thinking about oneself in such a way that the other subject is not conceived as an "other" anymore, but as oneself. In the process of identification, as I understand it, the thinking subject experiences his identity as merging with the identity of the subject he is thinking about, so that he does not consider the existence of two different subjects, but only one.[4]

The paradigmatic cases of this type of mental process happen when we think about our own past and future. Recently, various philosophers working on the topic of personal identity have argued for establishing a distinction between two entities that we are: the self, which is the subject of our phenomenological experiences; and the person, an entity defined from our biological, psychological, and social properties (see, for example, Johnston 2010; Menary 2008; Schechtman 2007). Thus, according to some of these authors, such as Strawson or Stokes, a series of successive selves inhabit our body, each of these selves being different from each other, since each of our experiences is owned by a different self (Stokes 2014; Strawson 2009). Being so, the self that we currently are is different from the self who did or will experience our past or our future. However, when thinking about those other temporal moments, usually the self that we currently are identifies with the selves who did or will experience those other moments. This is because, unlike selves, what we are as persons persists over time, so that when we think about our past or our future, our current self experiences those temporal moments as belonging to himself. He feels that the subject he is thinking about is no one else but himself in another stage of his own life. In this way, numerically distinct selves phenomenologically experience themselves as being a single entity, the same person.

The fact that the process of egocentric identification usually happens only toward other stages of our own life as persons can lead us to think that it is only possible to identify egocentrically with oneself. That is, that the process of egocentric identification requires that the self feels the identification and the self that he is identifying with, are part of the life of the same person. Nevertheless, although the process of identification can be related to the problem of personal identity in a metaphysical sense, in principle it is not necessary (see Stokes 2013). For example, we can remember that someone did certain action in the past and think that we were that person. When this happens we are identifying with the self who experienced that temporal moment. However, it is not unusual that we make misattributions when we think about our past (see Schacter 2001). That is, it can happen that, though we remember a certain action in a seemingly accurate way, we are attributing it to the wrong person. In this way, if the action we are remembering was not performed by ourselves but by our brother, we are identifying with a person different from ourselves. Thus the process of identification is happening in the absence of metaphysical identity.

The process of identification has at least two components, one cognitive and another emotive. The cognitive component consists in thinking that our current self and some other different self both belong to the life of the same person. The emotive component consists in what philosophers of mind call "egocentric concern," a term that refers to the special type of concern that we only feel toward ourselves and that is different from the type of concern we can feel toward others. For example, think about the difference between the way we feel concerned if we are told that a person will die tomorrow, and being told that that person will be us. In the first case we can feel pity, but not the terror that usually goes with the idea of our own death (Perry 2002, 145).

Normally, both components of the process of egocentric identification happen at the same time. However, it is possible that they happen independently. For example, there are persons whose concern for their own past or future is nonexistent, since despite acknowledging that their past or future are their own, they subjectively feel that they were or will be experienced by someone else. Strawson calls these persons "episodics" (Strawson 2008). In this way, in episodic persons the cognitive component of the process of identification is present, but the emotive component is absent. In an analogous way, it can happen that someone feels egocentrically concerned for a person without thinking that that person is identical with him. This is what happens in some thought experiments used in the debate on personal identity. In these thought experiments, a hypothetical situation in which we would die is depicted. In spite of that, in that situation there would still be a living person for whom we feel egocentrically concerned (see Stokes 2013). An example of this would be if a person could split like an amoeba. Since identity is a one-one relationship, the person existing before the splitting cannot be (metaphysically) identical with his "descendants." As a consequence, in a situation like that, the cognitive component of the process of identification has to be absent. However, one could feel egocentrically concerned for those descendants, so the emotive component could be present.

The cognitive component of the process of identification is more or less trouble free. It consists just in thinking that the selves who experienced both temporal moments are part of the life of the same person.[5] In contrast, the emotive component is more problematic. Although philosophers have traditionally considered that egocentric concern is an essential but unanalyzable component of the process of identification, this claim is unsatisfactory. If the process of identification could happen only toward other stages of our own life, and thus it implied the existence of metaphysical identity, then it could be that egocentric concern is an emotion based in our innate ability to recognize ourselves and needs no further explanation. However, since we can identify and feel egocentrically concerned for subjects who are different from ourselves, it seems necessary to explain what guides our egocentric concern if it is not an innate ability to track our own metaphysical identity as persons.

One way to account for the way in which egocentric concern functions is that offered by narrative theories of personal identity. The advantage of this explanation is that it is not only illuminating, but it also lets us connect the problem with the topic at hand: identification with fictional characters.

One of the basic premises of narrative theories of personal identity is the thesis that persons understand themselves in narrative form. In doing so, they understand their own identity as the product of the narrative through which they understand themselves (see Dennett 1992; MacIntyre 2007; Ricoeur 1994; Schechtman 1996). Consequently, persons feel that every event in their lives is united to the rest of their lives through a narrative, which makes it easy to explain what guides and justifies egocentric concern: if a past event belongs to the narrative by which we understand ourselves, then we will identify with the self who experienced that event, independently of whether the narrative by which we understand ourselves is accurate; at the same time, if a future event is coherent with the narrative by which we currently understand ourselves (in the sense that we could tell a coherent narrative that united our past life with that future event), then we will also be able to feel egocentrically concerned for the self who will experience that event (see Slors and Jongepier 2014).[6]

These considerations by narrative identity theorists can be extended to understand how egocentric concern works in the kind of thought experiments used in the debate on personal identity. As I said above, the main methodological resource used by analytical philosophers to understand the relationship between egocentric concern and personal identity consists in proposing thought experiments. The settings of these experiments are usually science-fiction scenarios—teleportations, brain transplants, clonings, and so forth—that have an impact on personal identity. Would I survive if my cerebrum were transplanted into someone else's body? And if I did, which body would I survive in? In the one that was mine before the experiment or in that which my cerebrum would awake in? These experiments obviously require that we be able to think about ourselves not as existing in a real future—probably cerebrum transplants will never be biologically possible—but in a possible world. And independently of its value for research on the problem of personal identity, these experiments are the link with fiction. Since, just as thought experiments deal with possible worlds, it can be interpreted that literature and cinema do the same (see Doležel 1998; Lewis 1978; Ryan 2001).[7]

If we understand fiction this way, we can think that the process of identification can happen toward fictional characters in just the same way it can toward a possible subject in a thought experiment. In the case of thought experiments (for example, in the case of a cerebrum transplant), a person will identify with one of the survivors of the experiment if he is able to build an implicit narrative that unifies in a coherent way his own self-conception with an interpretation of the thought experiment in which he survives, thanks to the body of another of the survivors. This explains why different people give different answers to the same thought experiment (Stokes 2013, 208–212). In the case of a cerebrum transplant, a person must understand himself as being fundamentally his mental life so that he can think that he will survive in the body that will carry his cerebrum, and so to be able to identify with the person that will have his cerebrum after the experiment. In contrast, if a person conceives of himself as being an unbreakable union of mind and body, then he will be unable to build a coherent narrative that justifies his survival as any of the persons existing after the experiment, and so he will think that the experiment implies his own death. In the same way, faced with a fictional work, a reader will be able to identify with one of the characters if he is able to build an implicit narrative that unifies in a coherent way the narrative through which he understands himself and the narrative through which he understands the character.

Leaving the details for the next section, in which I will analyze *Lost Girls*, we can address a first objection to my comparison between fiction and counterfactual thinking in general, which seem to be two different kinds of thinking. For example, it is not the same to think that Napoleon could have won the Battle of Waterloo as it is to read a novel in which he does so. In the first case, we situate ourselves in the real world and thus look at that possible world from a standpoint in which Napoleon loses. In the second case, what happens is what Ryan calls the process of "re-centering" (Ryan 2001, 103–104). Here, the readers are not in the real world anymore, but mentally transport themselves to the fictional world in which Napoleon won the battle. Thus, they interpret his victory not as a mere possibility, but as a statement of fact within the fictional world. This example seems to show that counterfactual thinking lacks an essential feature of fiction, and that it would be wrong to assimilate counterfactual and fictional thinking. However, even if the process of re-centering is absent from some counterfactual thoughts, it is not in the case of thought experiments, because they also encourage the performer of the experiment to transport themselves to a possible world and to analyze from that standpoint. Being so, this objection does not invalidate my position.

A second objection may be leveled against the comparison between fiction and thought experiment in particular: thought experiments are built on the premise that we exist in the possible world of the experiment, while fictional worlds are built on the opposite premise that we do not exist in them. However, this is a claim about what is more usual in fictional worlds, not about what is logically necessary. Postmodern writers usually question the belief that we do not exist in fictional worlds. We can think about Paul Auster's novels, in which he frequently appears as one the characters. In *If on a Winter's Night a Traveler*, Italo Calvino, the author, directly addresses the reader as the main character of his own reading. Or even, if we think about popular literature, in gamebooks in the style of the *Choose Your Own Adventure* book series. In this sense, if a fictional work has the appropriate features, it can allow, or even encourage, the reader to think about himself as another inhabitant of the fictional world. As we will see, this is also the case with *Lost Girls*.

To sum up what we have said up to now, egocentric identification is a mental process that consists in thinking about oneself as being identical with another subject, so that this subject is no longer conceived as an other, but as oneself. This process has two components, one cognitive and one emotive. The cognitive component consists just in thinking that our current self and some other different self belong to the life of the same person. The emotive component consists in feeling concerned for that self in the special way we only feel concerned about ourselves; that is, it consists in feeling egocentric concern. This emotive component only happens when the narrative through which we understand ourselves includes the life of the self we are thinking about as a part of our own life as persons or when our own narrative can be extended so that it includes it through a coherent (implicit) narrative. Although the cognitive and emotive components of the process of identification can happen separately, only when they happen at the same time we can talk properly about egocentric identification.

The Case of *Lost Girls*

Once we have established the concept of egocentric identification and the way it can be applied generally to the case of identification with fictional characters, I would like to extend the model through the analysis of *Lost Girls*. The goal, as I said in the introduction, is to show how the reader can identify with Monsieur Rougeur in the scene quoted. To do so, I will analyze the role that three different elements play in the process of identification: the features of the fictional work, the characteristics of the readers themselves, and the stance they take toward the text.

It will be useful to start my analysis with a brief comment on Alan Moore and Melinda Gebbie's *Lost Girls*. In spite of what it may seem at first sight, *Lost Girls* is not just another piece of what is sometimes euphemistically called "one-handed reading." Besides being defiantly sexual, even the most cursory reading makes it clear that it is also a deeply serious work (Scott 2012, 214–217). In fact, some critics have complained about its "over-explicit philosophizing," which cause them to feel "more bored than titillated" (see, for example, Di Lido 2009, 136–137; Kidd 2007; Faber 2008). However, according to Moore, *Lost Girls* is an attempt to rehabilitate pornography from its position as "a wretched ghetto with which no respected artist would desire to be associated, and which therefore rapidly becomes the province of those with no literary or artistic leanings whatsoever" (Moore 2009, 18). And I think that this requires at least a bit of philosophizing.

Moore thinks that sexual imagination is central to our lives. But contemporary society, especially in English-speaking countries, ignores this fact. Western society is highly sexualized on its surface, but hypocritically repressive in its essence (Di Liddo 2009, 155). This has caused pornography to regress to its most rudimentary forms and its consumers to feel guilty for stimulating their imagination with those grotesque images (Moore 2009, 76–77). The main consequence of this, according to Moore, is shown in sexual crime rates, which are statistically higher in Great Britain and the United States than in countries such as Denmark or Spain, where pornography is experienced in a more natural way (Moore 2009, 73). Thus, Moore's project to bring pornography to the venerated place that he thinks it deserves in art is intended to help people enjoy it without feeling guilty. He believes this would have a beneficial effect in society, as (he argues) sexual crime rates, especially those against children, would decrease (Moore 2006). But the main benefit of accepting pornography would be seen on the individual level. Moore considers sexual imagination to be necessary to a healthy mental life. Consequently, he thinks that people who are repressed are less capable of talking, thinking, and acting freely (Di Liddo 2009, 156). They deny a central part of themselves and so they know little about their own minds. But if we could raise the standards of pornography—turn it into a respectable art form—and make it socially acceptable, then these people could enjoy it and embrace their whole being. So Moore understands this "good and artistic" pornography not just as a healthy entertainment, but as an excellent way to better understand an important element of who we are. It would allow us to discuss sexuality more comfortably and to find that sexual imagination is something common to all humans, something we can share (Moore 2009, 81).[8]

In this sense, it is not difficult to imagine that Moore and Gebbie want the readers of *Lost Girls* to engage with their pornographic fiction in a personal way. They want them to open their minds and set their sexual imagination free. And one way to achieve this is to encourage their readers to identify with some of their characters. But how is this project expressed in *Lost Girls*? How does the book encourages its readers to identify with some characters—for example, Monsieur Rougeur?

First, the book is explicitly advancing Moore's conception of pornography and fiction since the very beginning. In the first chapter, Alice and Monsieur Rougeur—the manager of Hotel Himmelgarten—discuss Alice's own pornographic stories and the nature of fiction:

> MONSIEUR ROUGEUR: Indeed, as a connoisseur of such literature, may I say that in your ladyship's hands, fiction becomes the very *mirror* of reality ... where memorable idealized characters reflect our *truest* selves.
> ALICE: Hmmm, I'm flattered, Monsieur Rougeur ... though I cannot endorse your view of fiction. I rather favour Plato's view ... the *ideal* is the thing; the world beyond fiction's mirror, *that* is the true world ... and we are but faintest of reflections grown pale beneath the glass. (Moore and Gebbie 2006, chapter 1, 6)

There are at least three important aspects that are worth mentioning with regard to this scene. First, the conversation deals with the relationship between reality and fiction, showing that, for both characters, the distinction is not that simple. Second, it advances the importance of fiction and pornography for knowing ourselves, a theme that was also addressed in Moore's essay on pornography quoted above. And third, the whole chapter is drawn so that we only see what is reflected in Alice's mirror. Since the characters are comparing fiction with a mirror, the chapter invites the reader to associate the mirror with the comic itself (Alaniz 2006, 315), and thus the drawing highlights the centrality of the conversation that Monsieur Rougeur and Alice have: the blurry distinction between reality and fiction and the importance of pornography for knowing ourselves are the main two subjects of *Lost Girls*.

These two subjects are tightly intertwined throughout the novel, thus making explicit the importance of identification with fictional characters. I will give just a few examples of how these two topics are present in *Lost Girls*. In chapter 10, Alice, Dorothy, and Wendy go to the ballet. They begin to have sex together in their seats, and when writing about it, Alice states that she is unable to distinguish between what happened on the stage and what happened to them in the audience. She even declares, "I scarcely knew which one of us I was, nor if I was the chosen girl stood there with beast-skinned witchmen skulking widdershins about" (Moore and Gebbie 2006, chapter 10, 6). In chapter 11, Wendy's husband writes a letter to his boss, and while we see him masturbating in the bathtub reading a pornographic book, the letter says that sometimes men need to be alone to "open up" and show their real selves (Moore and Gebbie 2006, chapter 11, 8). In chapter 22, just after the scene I quoted at the beginning of the article, in which Monsieur Rougeur reads a pornographic story from his book, he states that "pornographies are the enchanted parklands where the most secret and vulnerable of all our many selves can safely play" (Moore and Gebbie 2006, chapter 22, 8). And in the next chapter, while Alice sodomizes Monsieur Rougeur with a strap-on to make him tell his true story, he claims that he feels like he is in one of his book's stories (Moore and Gebbie 2006, chapter 23, 2).

This explicit approach to the topic of identification with fictional characters is intended to ease the cognitive component of the process of identification: it seeks to put the readers in the appropriate mood to be open to identifying with some characters in the book. But it is not the only resource that Moore and Gebbie use in this regard. If we focus on the scene that depicts Monsieur Rougeur reading that story about incest and pedophilia, there are two aspects that work in the sense of easing the emotive component of the process of identification. First, even if the story is one of the dirtiest in *Lost Girls*, it is not the only one which depicts underage sex. As we have already noted, the whole book is about three famous female characters of children's literature talking about their stories of sexual awakening, which of course began when they were underage. Alice's story even involves child abuse, because she was raped by her father's oldest friend (Moore and Gebbie 2006, chapter 9). In this sense, most of the previous scenes try to desensitize the reader to fictional underage pornography.[9] Moreover, the opinions expressed by the characters themselves also try to desensitize the reader. They experience sex freely, and none of them seem to regret their past.[10] When it comes to the story we are concerned with, Monsieur Rougeur is in charge of giving us his last reason not to feel guilty about enjoying purely fictional child pornography. It is just fiction:

> MONSIEUR ROUGEUR: You see, if this were real, it would be horrible. Children raped by their trusted parents. Horrible. But they are *fictions*. They are uncontaminated by effect and consequence. Why, they are almost *innocent*. (Moore and Gebbie 2006, chapter 22, 5)

The second aspect that I wanted to highlight with regard to this scene is the way it is drawn. When Monsieur Rougeur takes his book and starts reading the story, Gebbie splits into two the pages of the novel. In the upper part we see the pages of the book Monsieur Rougeur is reading. In the lower part, we see the hotel manager having sex and reasoning about why no one should feel guilty about enjoying a story of fictional underage sex. Here, as

Scott points out, the reader is explicitly asked to consider his own complicity in reading the same pages that Monsieur Rougeur is reading (Scott 2012, 217). Following Gaut, we could say that we are asked to imagine that we see what Monsieur Rougeur sees, and thus to identify perceptually with him. But not only that. We are also encouraged to imagine that we feel the same discomfiture, self-indulgence, and arousal that he feels; that we want to read on as he wants; that we believe like him that fictional child pornography is not something to feel guilty about; that we are reading the same book he is. In sum, we are encouraged to identify with him, at least, perceptually, affectively, motivationally, epistemically, and practically (Gaut 2010, 258). Even more, we are not merely asked to imagine that we are in Monsieur Rougeur's situation, as Gaut would claim. Because we, as readers, are probably going to actually share some of these features too. We are actually seeing what Monsieur Rougeur sees—a book containing an incestuous story—and we are actually doing what he is doing—reading that story. Thus, probably we are feeling the same discomfiture, self-indulgence, and (perhaps) arousal he is, we want to read on as he does, and we believe that it is not that bad to do so just as he believes. If not, we would probably stop reading.[11]

Gaut would say that this is going one step beyond in the process of identification: we would be feeling empathic identification with Monsieur Rougeur. But empathic identification also happens with regard to different aspects, and thus it is not the same as egocentric identification (Gaut 2010, 260–62). Empathic identification does not involve thinking about oneself as being identical with the character. It only involves imagining oneself possessing some of the character's features and actually feeling some of the feelings that the character feels. Gaut thinks so because, following Carroll, he believes that if we identified egocentrically with a character, then we would be actually merging our identity with his, which is metaphysically impossible: two persons cannot be made the same without ceasing to exist (Carroll 1990, 89; Gaut 2010, 254). However, as I explained above, the process of egocentric identification is not necessarily related to the problem of personal identity in a metaphysical sense. People can identify egocentrically with someone and thus experience themselves as being identical with that someone without actually merging their actual identities with his. But even if they were, we would not be talking about persons, but about selves. And it does not seem to be immediately obvious that we can talk about the identity of a phenomenological entity just in the same way we talk about the identity of physical entities. However, explaining this would lead us far away from the topic at hand.[12] Thus, I maintain my claim that one can identify egocentrically with a fictional character.

What I have explained until now is the role of the book in easing the process of egocentric identification. On the one hand, it encourages the cognitive component of the process by explicitly stating Moore's conception of fiction and pornography. On the other hand, it facilitates the emotive component by trying to desensitize the reader to fictional child porn, by asking him to identify with certain characters in different aspects and by trying to cause certain feelings in the reader that are identical to those felt by the characters. I turn now to the importance of the features of the reader for the process of egocentric identification.

As I said in the previous section, one can identify with a literary character if he can build an implicit narrative that unifies in a coherent way the narrative through which he understands himself and the narrative through which he understands the character. And here, I would only like to say something about the respective importance of these narratives.

In theory, all fictional characters can be placed on a continuum with regard to their determinacy. On the one hand, we have the most simple characters, such as those appearing as shadows in the background. We know nothing about them except that they exist. On the other hand we have the richly delineated characters of a nineteenth-century realistic novel. With regard to these characters, we could ask no question to which there were not a clear and definite answer.

In principle, it seems that the simpler the character, the more easily the identification process would happen. And with regard to the cognitive component of the process of identification, I agree with much of this conclusion. The simpler the character, the less the fictional work will demand from our imagination. If we think about a fictional work in which there is an extremely indeterminate character, we can identify with him just by thinking that we are in his place, without acquiring any new feature and without losing any of ours. We do not need to modify the narrative through which we understand ourselves at all.

However, if a simple character can ease the cognitive component of the process of identification, the emotive component works the other way round. We usually do not care about a character about whom we know nothing, and if we do care, it is to know something about him, not to be him. There is nothing about him that can catch our attention, nothing we can envy or desire. Nothing that can move us to unify the narrative through which we understand ourselves with the narrative through which we understand the character. For most of us, it is a specific feature of a certain character that attracts us and makes us feel concerned about him. It is his being red-haired, or orphaned, or afraid of pink unicorns. It is the similarity between our past lives, or between his current situation and our dreams (Cohen 2001, 252). In this sense, the more determinate the character, the more features it has that we can feel attracted to. As such, the determinacy of a fictional character can ease the emotional component of the identification process.

In the case of *Lost Girls*, Monsieur Rougeur is a secondary character, and thus we know less about him than we know about other characters who are more important. But we know some things about him that can ease the process of identification for some readers: we know his name, physical appearance, and job; we also know about his interest in pornography and his past in France. All this information can be of interest for different readers and thus they can ease the process of identification for some, though they may also make it harder for others. For example, someone sharing his name, or his physical appearance will likely be more attracted to the idea of thinking about himself as being identical to Monsieur Rougeur. In contrast, an activist against child pornography is likely to feel aversion to the character. However, it is difficult to weigh these different aspects from a theoretical point of view since each individual will have a different personal history that affects his own emotional response to the text.

In any case, the most important aspect of this part of the process of identification is not the narrative through which we understand the character, but that through which we understand ourselves. As I said above, when narrative identity theorists say that we understand ourselves through the narrative of our life, they are talking about an implicit narrative. We do not have in our minds the whole narrative of our lives ready to be published in a book. The narratives that narrative identity theorists talk about are better conceived of as the lens through which we experience ourselves (Schechtman 1996, 113). But in spite of that, they are thought of as being narratives because they share many features with explicit narratives. For example, explicit narratives make judgements about its components. They value both their morality and their importance with regard to the rest of the events within the narrative (Ricoeur 1994, 164). Thus, every narrative is presented as containing some central elements which are essential to the narrative, while others are presented as peripheral. And the same applies to the implicit narrative through which we understand ourselves. It contains some aspects which we consider essential to our being, while others are just things that contingently happened to us (Schechtman 1996, 81–85). Moreover, the aspects that we consider essential to our being change depending on many different factors. They change over time as we grow up, clearly. But they can also change depending on what we are thinking about in a given moment, for example (Oatley 1994, 55;

Strawson 2008, 191). Thus, sometimes we will experience ourselves through a very detailed narrative which considers almost our whole life as being essential to who we are, but sometimes we will also experience ourselves through a much more schematic narrative.

When it comes to the process of identification with fictional characters, if the narrative through which we understand ourselves is more schematic, it will be easier for the process of identification to happen. In this sense, *Lost Girls* presents an evident advantage: being a pornographic and graphic novel, it is meant to increase our sexual excitement. And one side-effect of sexual arousal is to reduce our consciousness of ourselves. As Dorothy says when recalling one of her past sexual experiences:

> DOROTHY: Thing about comin' is, after a couple o' times, I kinda let go an' slip away into this whole other person who'll do just anythin.' (Moore and Gebbie 2006, chapter 24, 3).

In this regard, we can note that certain features such as the gender or the race of the reader may have a role in easing or hindering the process of identification, but they are not decisive. In the case of Monsieur Rougeur, in principle it will be easier for men to identify with him, as the process will require less imaginative effort. However, this does not mean that women cannot identify with him. As we have just noted, we do not experience ourselves always in the same way, but the narrative through which we understand ourselves may vary from one moment to another, and it can contain more or less detail about one's life. In this sense, someone may experience oneself as not being essentially gendered at a given time. A woman who is experiencing herself in that way would find no problems in telling a coherent narrative that unifies the narrative through which she is understanding herself and the narrative through which she understands Monsieur Rougeur. Consequently, she could identify with him and experience herself as being identical to that fictional man. And the same goes for men: if they are able to experience themselves as not being essentially gendered, they would have no problems in identifying with a female character

The last element I want to say something about is the interpretative stance that the reader must take toward the text so that the process of identification happen. This may be the most important element in the process of identification. If the process is to happen, the reader must be open to the possibility and collaborate with the text. In some cases, the fictional work will cause the reader to feel wholly immersed in the fictional world, and if all the other elements that we have reviewed are present, then it will only be necessary that the reader not put up resistance to the process. But in other cases the immersion will not be as deep. Then, the collaboration of the reader must be more active. He must actively commit himself to interpret the text in this sense as a personal invitation: "You who approach these pages, imagine that they are talking about you." The case of *Lost Girls* is also interesting from this perspective. On the one hand, it tries to ease the cognitive and the emotive components of the process of identification. Specifically, being a *pornographic* novel, it attempts to make the reader feel wholly immersed in the fictional world and forget about himself. And one cannot overestimate the importance of the graphic component in this regard. However, on the other hand, because its content is highly controversial and considered immoral by many, it can push the reader away. If the content crosses the line of what the reader considers acceptable, it will make him feel conscious of himself again, thus preventing the process of identification to happen.

Notes

1. However, I will omit "egocentric" when it is not necessary.
2. Certainly *Lost Girls* has had some problems in this regard (see Di Liddo 2009, 135).
3. One could think that only pedophiles would find depictions of fictional underage children exciting, as non-pathological human beings do not feel excited by children. If this were the case, only pedophiles would be able to identify with Monsieur Rougeur, and my argument would be seriously compromised. However, one should not think that, when fantasizing, one can only feel excited about the same things one is excited about in real life. The results of a recent study of female undergraduates indicated that 62 percent of women fantasize about being raped (Bivona and Critelli 2009), but I doubt many of them want to be raped in real life. Unfortunately, I have found no studies with regard to the prevalence and frequency of sexual fantasies involving underage children in non-pathological adults. But if we include teenagers in the group of underage children, surely they are not very rare.
4. Note that my definition of the process of identification is somewhat vague: *thinking* about another subject as being identical with us could mean either *believing* that we are identical with that subject or *imagining* so. Obviously there is an important difference between both things. However, I hold that both claims are true, and my argument could apply to either interpretation. As I have no space to address this distinction here, the more skeptical readers can interpret "thinking" as meaning "imagining." The boldest ones can interpret it as meaning "believing." This section is a summary of my views on the topic, and thus anyone interested in exploring it further may read my "Sometimes I Am Fictional: Narrative and Identification" (Muñoz-Corcuera, forthcoming).
5. Though it could still be disputed whether that thought must be explicit or implicit.
6. It is important to note that the narratives that narrative-identity theorists are talking about are fundamentally implicit. That is, they are not a text that we produce in a verbal way

or that is codified somewhere in our brain. Narratives are the lens through which we experience ourselves. We talk about "narrative" understanding because the lens through which we experience ourselves is the same lens through which we experience literature (see for example Bruner 1986, 11–43).

7. For an analysis of how possible-worlds semantics can be applied to the interpretation of graphic novels, see McLaughlin 2005.

8. At this point it seems necessary to clarify something. It may be thought that Moore is encouraging people to make their sexual fantasies come true. And because *Lost Girls* contains a considerable amount of scenes depicting sex with underage participants, it may seem that Moore is promoting pedophilia. This is far from being true. Moore clearly distinguishes between sexual imagination and real sex acts. According to him, imagination—which is one of the most important topics in his works—must be considered as such, and it has the right to be completely free (Di Liddo 2009, 158). However, this does not mean that we must be free to make our sexual fantasies come true. Real sex acts involve real people who can be harmed, and thus we should keep some of our fantasies in the realm of imagination, where they belong. In this sense, even filmed and photographic pornography is questioned by Moore, as they involve real actors who might not have actually wanted to do that for a living (Moore 2006). With regard to *Lost Girls*, the importance of distinguishing between sexual imagination and real sex acts is shown in the scene where Wendy, fantasizing about being raped, is almost raped by the sexual counterpart of Captain Hook (Moore and Gebbie 2006, chapter 27).

9. We can doubt whether this is morally appropriate or not. However, as we have seen, Moore's idea is that imagination has the right to be completely free, and *Lost Girls* is intended to help the reader in that regard. Consequently, he would argue that one should not be sensitized to fictional child porn, as this would be to put constraints on our sexual imagination.

10. At least, not until the end of the novel. There we will learn that the cause of Wendy's frigidity lay in her past sexual history, because her fantasizing about being raped almost led her to being actually raped (Moore and Gebbie 2006, chapter 27); that Dorothy's travel to Europe was a way to forget and to hide that she had had sex with her father (Moore and Gebbie 2006, chapter 28); and that Alice's homosexuality was probably caused by her being abused when she was a child (Moore and Gebbie 2006, chapter 29). However, after sharing their life stories and enjoying sex freely as they had done throughout the novel, they feel better, and it seems that they are ready to get over their pasts (Moore and Gebbie 2006, chapter 30). See Alaniz (2006) for an analysis of this therapeutic effect of telling the stories of sexual awakening.

11. Obviously one can continue reading the book even if one does not agree with Monsieur Rougeur. My point here is that the book is asking the reader to identify with the character. And given the controversial theme of the book, if one does not agree with the character he will probably not be interested in reading it, although there may be exceptions.

12. If the reader is interested in this topic, I refer them to the analysis and critique of Strawson's theory of the self made by Stokes (2014).

Bibliography

Alaniz, José. "Speaking the 'Truth' of Sex: Moore & Gebbie's Lost Girls." *International Journal of Comic Art* 8.2 (2006): 307–318.

Bivona, Jenny, and Joseph Critelli. "The Nature of Women's Rape Fantasies: An Analysis of Prevalence, Frequency, and Contents." *Journal of Sex Research* 46.1 (2009): 33–45.

Bruner, Jerome S.. *Actual Minds, Possible Worlds*. Cambridge: Harvard University Press, 1986.

Carroll, Noël. *The Philosophy of Horror; or Paradoxes of the Heart*. New York: Routledge, 1990.

———. 1997. "Art, Narrative, and Emotion." In Mette Hjort and Sue Laver (eds.), *Emotion and the Arts*. Oxford: Oxford University Press. 190–211.

———. *The Philosophy of Motion Pictures*. Oxford: Blackwell, 2008.

Cohen, Jonathan. "Defining Identification: A Theoretical Look at the Identification of Audiences With Media Characters." *Mass Communication & Society* 4.3 (2001): 245–64.

Dennett, Daniel C. "The Self as a Center of Narrative Gravity." In Frank S. Kessel et al. (eds.), *Self and Consciousness: Multiple Perspectives*. Hillsdale, NJ: Erlbaum, 1992. 103–15.

Di Liddo, Annalisa. *Alan Moore: Comics as Performance, Fiction as Scalpel*. Jackson, MS: University Press of Mississippi, 2009.

Doležel, Lubomír. *Heterocosmica: Fiction and Possible Worlds*. Baltimore: Johns Hopkins University Press, 1998.

Faber, Michel. "Released at Last." *The Guardian*, January 5, 2008. Accessed June 9, 2016. https://www.theguardian.com/books/2008/jan/05/comics.

Gaut, Berys. *A Philosophy of Cinematic Art*. Cambridge: Cambridge University Press, 2010..

Johnston, Mark. *Surviving Death*. Princeton, NJ: Princeton University Press, 2010.

Kidd, Kenneth. "Down the Rabbit Hole." *ImageTexT* 3 (2007). Accessed June 9, 2016. http://www.english.ufl.edu//imagetext/archives/v3_3/lost_girls/kidd.shtml.

Lewis, David K. "Truth in Fiction." *American Philosophical Quarterly* 15.1 (1978): 37–46.

MacIntyre, Alasdair. *After Virtue: A Study in Moral Theory*. Third edition. Notre Dame, IN: University of Notre Dame Press, 2007.

McLaughlin, Jeff. "What If? DC's Crisis and Leibnizian Possible Worlds." In Jeff McLaughlin (ed.), *Comics as Philosophy*. Jackson, MS: University Press of Mississippi, 2005. 3–13.

Menary, Richard. "Embodied Narratives." *Journal of Consciousness Studies* 15.6 (2006): 63–84.

Moore, Alan. Interview with Noel Murray. *A.V. Club*, August 2, 2006. Accessed June 9, 2016. http://www.avclub.com/article/alan-moore-14006.

———. *25,000 Years of Erotic Freedom*. New York: Abrams.

Moore, Alan, and Melinda Gebbie. *Lost Girls*. Atlanta, GA: Top Shelf Productions, 2006.

Oatley, Keith. "A Taxonomy of the Emotions of Literary Response and a Theory of Identification in Fictional Narrative." *Poetics* 23 (1994): 53–74.

Oatley, Keith, and Mitra Gholamain. "Emotions and Identification: Connections between Readers and Fiction." In Mette Hjort and Sue Laver (eds.), *Emotion and the Arts*. Oxford: Oxford University Press, 1997. 263–81.

Perry, John. "The Importance of Being Identical." In John Perry (ed.), *Identity, Personal Identity and the Self*. Indianapolis, IN: Hackett, 2002.. 145–66.

Ricoeur, Paul. *Oneself as Another*. Chicago: University of Chicago Press, 1994.
Ryan, Marie-Laure. *Narrative as Virtual Reality: Immersion and Interactivity in Literature and Electronic Media*. Baltimore: Johns Hopkins University Press, 2001.
Schacter, Daniel L. *The Seven Sins of Memory: How the Mind Forgets and Remembers*. Boston: Houghton Mifflin, 2001.
Schechtman, Marya. *The Constitution of Selves*. Ithaca, NY: Cornell University Press, 1996.
——. "Stories, Lives and Basic Survival: A Refinement and Defense of the Narrative View." In Daniel D. Hutto (ed.), *Narrative and Understanding Persons*. Cambridge: Cambridge University Press, 2007. 155–78.
Scott, John Keith L. "Lost Boys, *Lost Girls*, Lost Innocence: J. M. Barrie and Alan Moore." In Alfonso Muñoz Corcuera and Elisa T. Di Biase (eds.), *Barrie, Hook, and Peter Pan: Studies in Contemporary Myth; Estudios sobre un mito contemporáneo*. Newcastle: Cambridge Scholars Publishing, 2012. 209–23.
Slors, Marc, and Fleur Jongepier. "Mineness without Minimal Selves." *Journal of Consciousness Studies* 21.7–8 (2014.): 193–219.
Stokes, Patrick. "Will It Be Me? Identity, Concern and Perspective." *Canadian Journal of Philosophy* 43.2 (2013): 206–26.
——. "Crossing the Bridge: The First-Person and Time." *Phenomenology and the Cognitive Sciences* 13.2 (2014): 295–312.
Strawson, Galen. "Against Narrativity." In *Real Materialism and Other Essays*. Oxford: Oxford University Press, 2008. 189–207.
——. *Selves: An Essay in Revisionary Metaphysics*. New York: Clarendon Press, 2009..

Further Reading

Promethea. Written by Alan Moore and drawn by J. H. Williams III (America's Best Comics, 1999–2005). One of the most relevant works of Alan Moore that shows the importance of imagination of this author.

Peter Pan. Written and drawn by Régis Loisel (Soaring Penguin Press, 2013). A dark and highly interesting prequel of J. M. Barrie's classic.

Dans mes yeux (*In My Eyes*). Written and drawn by Bastien Vivès (KSTЯ, 2009). Probably the best graphic novel to analyze the process of character identification. Unfortunately, it has not been translated into English yet.

The Surrogates. Written by Robert Venditti and drawn by Brett Weldele (Top Shelf Productions, 2006). A twist on the topic of virtual worlds. What if we could have an avatar in real life?

Violent Cases. Written by Neil Gaiman and drawn by Dave McKean (Escape Books, 1987).

Contributors

Eric Bain-Selbo is department head of philosophy and religion at Western Kentucky University and cofounder of the WKU Institute for Citizenship and Social Responsibility. He also is the executive director of the Society for Values in Higher Education. He has authored numerous articles and three books.

Jeremy Barris is professor of philosophy at Marshall University, in Huntington, West Virginia. As a philosopher, he is mainly interested in the various relations between reality, thinking, style of expression, humour, and justice. His publications include *The Crane's Walk*; *Plato, Pluralism, and the Inconstancy of Truth*; and *Sometimes Always True: Undogmatic Pluralism in Politics, Metaphysics, and Epistemology*.

Maria Botero is assistant professor in the Psychology and Philosophy Department at Sam Houston State University. Her research focuses on animal cognition, specifically on the relationship between cognition and modes of communicative interaction, and on the moral status of those, such as children and nonhuman primates, who do not possess or exhibit complex cognitive abilities in the same way as nondisabled adult humans.

Manuel "Mandel" Cabrera Jr. is assistant professor of philosophy at Underwood International College, Yonsei University. His principal research interests are in Spinoza's ethics and philosophy of religion, metaphysics, and philosophy and the arts.

David J. Leichter is assistant professor at Marian University, in Fond du Lac, Wisconsin. He earned his PhD from Marquette University, where he wrote his dissertation on phenomenology and collective memory.

David Mack is the Emmy-nominated, *New York Times* best-selling author and artist of *Kabuki*; writer of *Daredevil*; cover artist of Neil Gaiman's *American Gods* and Chuck Palahniuk's *Jessica Jones* and *Fight Club 2*; artist on Netflix's *Jessica Jones* opening titles and *Captain America: The Winter Soldier* film titles; and ambassador of arts and story for the US State Department.

Mack's work has garnered nominations for seven Eisner Awards, four International Eagle Awards, and both the Harvey and Kirby Awards in the category of Best New Talent, as well as many other national and international awards and nominations.

Jeff McLaughlin is associate professor of philosophy at Thompson Rivers University in Kamloops, BC, Canada. While he teaches mostly applied ethics courses, his interests are far ranging: from comic books to the Holocaust. His books include *Comics as Philosophy*, *Stan Lee: Conversations*, *An Introduction to Philosophy in Black and White and Color*, and *How to Think Critically: A Concise Guide*.

Ian MacRae is associate professor in English and the society, culture, and environment programs at Wilfrid Laurier University, Brantford. He has graduate degrees in environmental studies and comparative literature and worked for many years producing and writing documentary films for television—hence his longstanding interest in the politics of visual representation. He has published on Canadian literature and poetry in transnational contexts, as well as on indigenous cinema and visual anthropology.

Alfonso Muñoz-Corcuera is Postdoctoral Research Fellow at the National Autonomous University of Mexico (UNAM). He holds a PhD in philosophy and two MAs, one in philosophy and another one in literary studies. He received all three degrees from the Complutense University of Madrid, where he was a Research Fellow for four years.

Corry Shores is assistant professor at the Middle East Technical University in Ankara, Turkey. He focuses primarily on phenomenologies of arts, especially painting and cinema. He is interested in exploring a reader response/phenomenological approach to comics studies that makes use of such Deleuzian concepts as Body without Organs, incompatible sensations, variable present, and affirmative synthetic disjunction.

Jarkko Tuusvuori is a philosopher and independent scholar living in Helsinki, Finland. He is a founding member and an active co-worker of the philosophical community formed around the (world's only Finnish and Swedish speaking) philosophical magazine *niin & näin* (1994–), the n & n book series (2002–), and the web portal Filosofia.fi (2007–). Apart from his doctoral dissertation on Nietzsche (University of Helsinki, 2000), Tuusvuori has published several translations and original books, including a widely acclaimed monograph on human hands in 2013.

Index

abandonment, 18, 55–57, 73, 74, 84, 115, 154
abstraction, 30, 97, 98, 101
absurdity, 50, 105, 108, 138, 140, 143, 165
abuse, 98, 139, 143, 169, 201, 207
academia, 13, 190
acceptance, 9, 15, 22, 29, 54, 65, 73, 74, 76, 199, 206
access, 73, 78, 79, 81, 96, 177
adults, 14, 22, 25, 30, 65, 67, 70, 71, 74, 81, 83, 84, 86, 134, 135, 166, 167, 206
advantage, 28, 30, 89–91, 113, 162, 164
aesthetics, 18, 19, 22, 28, 43, 59, 85, 141, 190
agents, 30, 31, 64–76, 78–81, 83, 84, 140, 182
agreements, 12, 19, 24–27, 30, 31, 88, 89, 157
alcohol, 154
alliances, 156, 157, 159, 160, 162, 182
ambiguity, 8, 135, 145, 146, 153, 157, 174
ambivalence, 43, 50, 117, 137
America, 9, 18, 20, 21, 23, 24, 35, 44, 48, 49, 51, 56–58, 130, 138, 150, 151
anger, 5, 18, 96–99, 120
animals, 9, 14, 50, 57, 68, 69, 150–54, 156, 159–61, 164, 166
Anja, 152, 155–57, 168
anti-Semitism, 18, 19, 31
apocalypse, 54–58
arguments, 9, 13, 14, 65, 67, 69, 71, 73, 79, 80, 91, 95, 110, 133, 154, 155, 180, 189, 191–93, 206
Aristotle, 52, 54, 59, 126

arousal, 193, 202, 205
art and artists, 4–10, 12, 14, 17, 22, 28, 32, 41–44, 49, 50, 59, 71, 73, 74, 81, 83, 84, 130, 132, 135, 137, 138, 140, 142, 150, 166, 167, 179, 199
Asterix, 13, 105–8, 110–17, 119–21, 123, 124, 129
audience, 6, 8, 32, 51, 200
Auschwitz, 152, 157, 158, 162, 165
authenticity, 27, 49, 85, 161, 162
autobiographies, 130–32, 135, 138, 139, 146, 166
autonomy, 13, 65–81, 83, 137, 140

babysitters, 139, 142
Bain-Selbo, Eric, 13
Baker, Matt, 21, 67
Bakhtin, Mikhail, 105, 106, 108, 109, 111, 116–18, 121, 123
balloons, 5, 82
banality, 51, 131, 180, 186
Barris, Jeremy, 13
Barthes, Roland, 121, 124
Baudrillard, Jean, 122
Bechdel, Alison, 13, 130–33, 137, 140, 142, 144, 146, 147
Bechdel, Bruce, 133, 135, 137–46
becoming, 14, 43, 106, 116, 144, 150, 151, 154, 160–64, 186
becoming-animal, 156, 159–63, 166, 168
beliefs, 4, 25, 31, 66, 68–71, 79, 134, 178, 198, 199, 202, 206

benefits, 3, 7, 8, 35, 49, 79, 87, 90–92, 155, 158, 160, 199
Benziger, 27
Bergson, Henri, 177
bibles, 19, 21, 27, 29
Bilefsky, Dan, 67, 85
biographies, 14, 18, 20

Canada, 72, 130
capitalism, 19, 35, 122, 158
captions, 23, 49, 176, 182
caricatures, 24, 118, 153
caregivers, 14, 19, 35, 65, 68–71, 73, 76, 78–81
carnival, 105, 106, 108, 117–21, 123
Carroll, Noel, 190, 202
cartoons, 5, 9, 10, 14, 17, 21, 24, 45, 108, 126, 129, 130, 150, 151, 153, 161, 164, 166, 176, 178, 187
characters, 5, 7, 9, 14, 15, 17–19, 21, 23–25, 32, 35, 42, 44, 47, 49, 55–57, 62, 74, 75, 82, 95, 105, 111, 113, 114, 116, 118–20, 129, 150, 151, 153, 154, 158, 164, 189–93, 196–98, 200–205
children, 11, 13, 18, 35, 47–49, 56, 64, 65, 67–72, 74, 75, 77–84, 98, 99, 131, 135, 138, 152, 157, 159, 166, 181, 189, 191–93, 199, 201–4
childhood, 48, 56, 65, 82, 83, 100, 162
Christianity, 52–54
chronology, 47, 52, 58, 59
citizens, 53, 87, 88, 90–95, 97, 101, 102, 113, 114
civilians, 89, 92, 93, 163, 174, 181
cognition, 32, 67, 80, 83, 125, 175, 178, 194, 195, 198, 201, 203, 206
community, 18–20, 29, 31, 90, 121, 138, 157, 173, 180, 186
compact with God, 27–29
consciousness, 42, 47, 51, 53, 54, 67, 69, 78–81, 117, 136, 146, 191, 205, 206
consent, 29, 30, 66, 143
Contractarianism, 30
Contractualism, 12, 18–20, 22–26, 28–32, 34, 88, 155
contradictions, 26, 106, 109, 114, 116, 175

counterfactualism, 31, 197
covenants, 26–29, 35

Dachau, 165
daughters, 17, 18, 25, 30, 31, 136, 139, 141, 142, 144, 146
death, 17, 26, 27, 31, 32, 52, 56, 67, 72, 73, 75–77, 83, 99, 123, 130, 134, 135, 138–40, 143, 145, 146, 152, 185, 195, 197
dehumanization, 14, 153, 156, 165
Deleuze, Gilles, 158
Derrida, Jacques, 144
Descartes, Rene, 19
deterritorialization, 160, 161, 163
displacement, 181, 185
documentaries, 68, 146, 150, 166, 167, 169, 182
Drake, Arnold, 20, 21
Dworkin, Gerald, 66, 84, 85

Ecclesiastes, 52
ego, 92, 119, 190–96, 198, 202, 203
Egypt, 172, 181, 182
Eisner, Will, 11–13, 17–26, 28, 30, 32, 33, 43, 44, 59, 120, 167
emotions, 6, 71, 75, 87, 88, 91–94, 102, 103, 136, 179, 190, 194, 195, 198, 201, 203, 206
empathy, 8, 153, 186, 202
epistemology, 8, 131–38, 140, 141, 143–45
equality, 29, 30, 69, 90, 91, 93, 121, 122
eroticism, 133, 138–41, 143, 144, 146
Essex County, 9, 13, 64, 65, 71, 72, 81, 82, 84
ethics, 12, 18, 19, 24, 25, 30, 54, 55, 57–59, 143, 173
euthanasia, 66
exploits, 31, 44, 50, 133, 135, 146, 158
eyewitnesses, 166, 175, 176, 178, 181, 183

faith, 30, 35, 131, 132, 144, 176–80, 187, 188
fantasies, 50, 56, 57, 189, 206, 207
Fascism, 95, 96, 99
fathers, 14, 26, 47–49, 55–57, 64, 74, 75, 77, 78, 81, 82, 130–46, 151, 153, 154, 156, 201, 207

Index

Fawkes, Guy, 98
females, 97, 145, 160, 192, 201, 205, 206
filialness, 142, 144, 156, 157
Foucault, Michel, 121
Frankfurt, Harry, 69
freedom, 67, 70, 87–89, 96–99, 101, 121, 122, 136, 146, 147, 180
friends, 64, 68, 93, 105, 116, 141, 157, 183, 185, 201
Frimme, 18, 19, 25–32, 35
funerals, 30, 32, 77, 138

Gaza, 11, 14, 172–74, 176, 180, 182, 184, 186
Gebbie, Melinda, 14, 189, 190, 192, 193, 198–201, 205
gender, 132–34, 136, 137, 139, 143, 145, 147, 205
genres, 17, 20, 23–25, 28, 42, 133, 135, 166, 167, 191
Germany, 153, 158, 159
girls, 8, 10, 15, 190, 192, 193, 197–201, 204–6
God, 11, 12, 17–19, 21, 23–33, 53, 54
Goscinny, Rene, 105, 117, 118
government, 17, 21, 88, 89, 95, 97, 100–102, 157, 181, 182
Groensteen, Thierry, 22, 82
guerillas, 174, 181

happiness, 31, 35, 89, 101
harm, 89, 93, 98, 156, 207
Heidegger, Martin, 183
heroes and heroines, 45, 76, 113, 115, 139
heterogeneity, 145, 156–58, 160, 162, 168
heteronormativity, 137, 138, 143
heterosexuality, 137
history, 5, 14, 18, 21–23, 30, 32, 42–45, 47–51, 53–59, 73, 94, 99, 124, 132–35, 137, 139, 140, 146, 147, 151, 166, 167, 172, 173, 175, 180–86, 204, 207
Hobbes, Thomas, 28–30, 88, 89, 91, 102
hockey, 64, 72–74, 76–78
Holocaust, 9, 14, 150, 151, 153, 156, 162, 165–67
homosexuality, 95, 97, 132, 136, 139, 143, 145, 207

horror, 14, 42, 154, 165, 166
humanity, 35, 89, 92, 151
humility, 143, 146
humor, 9, 13, 24, 105–9, 111, 113–19, 124

Icarus, 141, 142
identification, 6, 15, 190–96, 198, 200–206
identities, 44, 92, 134–38, 143–45, 147, 158, 161–64, 172, 173, 178, 180, 186, 191, 193–96, 202, 204
ideology, 121–23, 158, 175, 180, 183
illusions, 50, 135, 138–40
imagery, 5–7, 19, 24, 43–50, 57–59, 65, 77, 78, 82, 83, 99, 118, 120, 121, 132, 135, 136, 138, 142, 152, 153, 175–77, 180, 182–84, 199
imagination, 8, 22, 32, 50, 56, 57, 64, 72, 75–78, 98, 108, 142, 143, 175, 189, 190, 193, 199, 202, 203, 206, 207
immigrants, 31, 151, 164, 165, 181
incest, 201, 202
inhumanity, 14, 151, 153
injustice, 87, 94, 95, 98, 121, 122, 172, 173, 184, 186
intentions, 5, 7–9, 18, 108, 150, 172, 191–93
intertexts, 28, 133, 135, 146
intimacies, 19, 68, 70, 97, 121, 139, 145
introspection, 41, 78, 79
Israel, 35, 172–75, 179, 181–83, 186; Israeli-Palestinian relations, 171, 178

James, Henry, 47, 139
Jaspers, Karl, 109
Jesus, 27, 29, 53, 54
Jews, 14, 18–20, 23, 26, 150–53, 156–59, 161–66, 181
Jimmy Corrigan, 13, 43, 44, 47–51, 55–59, 61, 64, 65, 72, 74–77, 85, 86, 140; and father William, 55, 57
Job, 35
journalism, 11, 173–77, 179, 183, 185–87
Joyce, James, 133, 139, 141, 144, 145
justice, 29, 65, 67, 90–94, 97–102, 122, 123, 176, 177, 184, 186

Kaczynski, Tom, 24
Kafka, Franz, 151, 158, 161, 162, 164–66
kairos, 51–59
Kant, Immanuel, 64, 67
killing, 66, 68, 82, 130, 161, 163, 172, 174, 177, 181, 183, 184
knowledge, 3, 4, 10, 29, 51, 52, 77, 78, 100, 103, 127, 132–35, 137, 140, 141, 143–46, 154, 155, 175, 176, 200

labyrinths, 139, 142, 147
Leichter, David J., 14, 172
Lemire, Jeff, 13, 64, 65, 71–79, 81–84
lesbians, 130, 139, 146, 147
Lester, 64, 65, 71–78, 81–83
Leviathan, 88, 89
liberals, 92–94
liberty, 29, 87, 89–91, 93, 95, 96, 98, 101, 102, 145
Locke, John, 29

Marx, Karl, 122
masturbation, 132, 145, 200
Mauldin, Bill, 24
Maus, 9, 11, 12, 14, 150–53, 155–59, 161–67
McCloud, Scott, 11, 28, 126
memories, 14, 20, 73, 75, 77, 78, 83, 131, 133–35, 137, 141–45, 153, 156, 172, 173, 175, 177–81, 183–86
metaphors, 14, 116, 151–53, 164, 165, 177, 180, 190
metaphysics, 13, 109–12, 117–19, 121–23, 125, 129, 194, 195, 202
Monsieur Rougeur, 189, 190, 192, 193, 198, 200–202, 204, 205
monsters, 138, 139, 142, 147
Moore, Alan, 14, 15, 87, 189, 190, 192, 193, 198–201, 203, 205
morality, 12, 17, 19, 20, 24, 29–31, 33, 65–67, 89, 90, 92, 101, 132, 143, 144, 156, 189, 190, 192, 193, 204
mothers, 49, 55, 58, 69, 72, 73, 75–78, 83, 86, 131, 132, 136, 139, 140, 144, 152, 155, 159

motivations, 19, 30, 69, 78, 92, 150, 153, 182, 184
movies, 6–8, 46, 51, 140, 145
Mullin, Amy, 65–71, 73–75, 78–80
Muñoz-Corcuera, Alfonso, 15, 189, 206
Munro, Alice, 136, 137
Muybridge, Eadweard, 50, 51, 57, 61
myth, 30, 42, 54, 140, 142

Nagel, Thomas, 4, 15, 80
narration, 23, 24, 29, 43, 82, 132, 135, 141, 179, 181, 182, 184, 186; non-linear, 47, 48, 134, 183
Nazis, 14, 94, 150–53, 156, 157, 159, 161, 162, 164, 166
Noah, 27, 29, 30
norms, 20, 30, 108, 121, 136, 137, 145, 146, 177, 178
nostalgia, 10, 20, 49, 72, 141
Nussbaum, Martha, 87, 88, 91–94, 97, 102

Obelix, 105, 114, 115, 117, 118, 120
obligations, 18, 29, 30, 184
Olympics, 11, 105–8, 110–14, 117, 119, 120
oppression, 87, 90, 95, 96, 99, 101, 102, 123, 127, 154, 156, 163, 164, 173, 180, 186
outsiders, 143, 157

Palestine, 172–74, 176, 181, 183, 185, 186
parents, 66, 70, 98, 100, 134, 137, 139, 145, 153, 189, 201
parliament, 29, 66, 98
paternalism, 67
patriotism, 93, 94
pedophilia, 143, 201, 207
phenomenology, 13, 14, 194, 202
philosophers, 3, 4, 9, 19, 43, 54, 81, 107, 109, 121, 134, 150, 154, 177, 183, 190, 193–96
phronêsis, 52
picto-fiction, 22
Plato, 109, 200
pleasure, 4, 70, 108, 129, 145
politics, 14, 90, 113, 123, 136, 137, 144, 163, 164, 172, 173, 182

pornography, 12, 15, 143, 146, 189, 192, 193, 199–206
portrayals, 20, 28, 32, 45, 46, 48–50, 54, 57, 81, 87, 92, 119, 135, 151–53, 157, 171
pragmatism, 5, 11, 186
principles, 30, 31, 69, 89–94, 99–101, 103, 108, 126, 194
prisons, 3, 100, 101, 152, 153, 158, 164
propaganda, 151–53, 157, 164
protagonists, 7, 15, 24, 27, 31, 56, 87, 95

quality, 4, 10, 25, 65, 71, 80, 81, 83, 89, 93, 140
quantity, 154, 158
queers, 13, 130, 133, 136–40, 142–46

Rawls, John, 65, 67, 89–93, 99–102
reconstruction, 20, 21, 59, 133–35, 175
religion, 12, 19, 24–26, 35, 53, 92, 93, 158
remembering, 72, 80, 98, 101, 135, 143, 153, 172, 173, 175, 177–80, 183, 185, 194
representation, 6, 13, 20, 63, 97, 126, 131, 132, 135, 138–40, 154, 173, 176–79, 212
repression, 138, 156, 199
resistance, 137, 151, 191, 206
responsibility, 65, 66, 102, 137, 152, 173, 179
rhetoric, 51, 52, 58, 114, 137
Ricoeur, Paul, 177, 196, 204
right and wrong, 12, 20, 29, 31, 89–91, 93, 113, 121, 163, 175, 184, 190, 197
Rosen, Alan, 165
Rousseau, Jean-Jacques, 29, 30, 88, 89, 91, 100, 102

Sacco, Joe, 11, 14, 167, 173–87
sacrifice, 53, 93, 96, 103
Schechtman, Marya, 194, 196, 204
self-conceptions, 17, 18, 30, 32, 41, 43, 44, 47, 58, 59, 65, 67–72, 77–79, 92, 134, 136, 138, 139, 141, 146, 151, 152, 154, 156, 159, 160, 162, 163, 196, 202
selfishness, 19, 100, 138, 153, 164
sequentiality, 11, 21, 25, 43, 44, 47, 50, 57, 59, 72, 73, 76, 82, 115, 116, 132, 140

sexuality, 17, 49, 55, 100, 132–34, 136–40, 143, 147, 189, 192, 193, 198–201, 205, 207
socialness, 13, 14, 18–20, 25, 29–31, 33, 47, 66, 87–92, 95, 96, 99–102, 109, 113, 121, 134–36, 138, 140, 146, 158, 178, 180, 194
society, 28, 29, 67, 79, 87, 89–95, 97–99, 102, 121–23, 134, 142, 145, 156, 163, 164, 178, 199
soldiers, 24, 152, 158, 176
Spiegelman, Art, 14, 45, 59, 150–55, 157–59, 161, 164–66
Spiegelman, Vladek; 151–53, 155–59, 161–63, 165
Spinoza, Baruch, 154, 155
spirituality, 17, 92, 139, 142, 144, 145
Steranko, Jim, 22
Strawson, Galen, 194, 195, 205
suffering, 31, 35, 64, 67, 94, 99, 113, 121, 165, 166, 173, 180, 181, 186
suicides, 130, 132, 134, 138, 140, 141, 143, 154, 155
superheroes, 21, 49, 50, 56, 57, 72, 73, 76–78, 166
survival and survivors, 14, 18, 102, 155, 162, 163, 166, 196, 197
Susan, Adam, 87, 95–99
symbolism, 132, 135, 142, 164
sympathy, 92, 98, 114, 153, 154, 168, 186, 190

Theaetetus, 109
theology, 12, 26, 35, 52–54, 180
Tillich, Paul, 54, 55
Tolkien, J. R. R., 42, 43
topsy-turvyness, 106, 108, 113, 114, 118
transformations, 14, 18, 28, 53, 124, 137, 161, 173
trauma, 153, 155, 162, 163, 173, 178
truth, 4, 9, 28, 77, 98, 100, 103, 106, 108, 112, 114, 117, 122, 125, 132, 133, 138, 139, 141, 143, 146, 175, 176

Uderzo, Albert, 118
Ulysses, 133, 139, 144, 145

unjustness, 28, 122, 123, 177, 186
utilitarianism, 89, 90, 95, 101

V, 97–99, 101, 102
V for Vendetta, 13, 87, 88, 91, 92, 94, 96, 102
Valerie, 97–101
victims, 120, 152, 153, 164, 165, 173, 180

Ware, Chris, 44, 47, 48, 50, 56, 58–60
Wittgenstein, Ludwig, 11, 107, 109
worlds, 8, 196–98
worldviews, 19, 96

Zen, 119
Zoopraxiscope, 48, 50, 57, 61

www.ingramcontent.com/pod-product-compliance
Lightning Source LLC
Chambersburg PA
CBHW030621230426
43661CB00053B/2100